Microsoft®

ACCESS 97
VISUAL BASIC®
Step by Step

Other titles in the *Step by Step* series:

*Microsoft Access 97 Step by Step

*Microsoft Excel 97 Step by Step

*Microsoft Excel 97 Step by Step, Advanced Topics

*Microsoft FrontPage 97 Step by Step

 Microsoft Internet Explorer 3.0 Step by Step

 Microsoft Office 97 Integration Step by Step

*Microsoft Outlook 97 Step by Step

*Microsoft PowerPoint 97 Step by Step

 Microsoft Team Manager 97 Step by Step

 Microsoft Windows 95 Step by Step

 Microsoft Windows NT Workstation version 4.0 Step by Step

*Microsoft Word 97 Step by Step

*Microsoft Word 97 Step by Step, Advanced Topics

Step by Step books are also available for the Microsoft
Office 95 programs.

 * These books are approved courseware for Certified Microsoft
Office User (CMOU) exams.

Microsoft®
ACCESS 97
VISUAL BASIC®

Step by Step

Microsoft Press

PUBLISHED BY
Microsoft Press
A Division of Microsoft Corporation
One Microsoft Way
Redmond, Washington 98052-6399

Library of Congress Cataloging-in-Publication Data
Callahan, Evan, 1966-
    Microsoft Access 97/Visual Basic step by step / Evan Callahan.
        p.   cm.
    Includes index.
    ISBN 1-57231-319-6
    1. Microsoft Access.   2. Microsoft Visual BASIC.   3. Database
management.   I. Title.
QA76.9.D3C333   1997
005.75'65--dc21   96-37208
                                                            CIP

Printed and bound in the United States of America.

10 11 12 13 14 15   WCWC   3 2 1 0

Distributed in Canada by Penguin Books Canada Limited.

A CIP catalogue record for this book is available from the British Library.

Microsoft Press books are available through booksellers and distributors worldwide. For further
information about international editions, contact your local Microsoft Corporation office. Or
contact Microsoft Press International directly at fax (206) 936-7329.

Microsoft, the Microsoft logo, Microsoft Press, the Microsoft Press logo, and Visual Basic are
registered trademarks and ActiveX and the Microsoft Internet Explorer logo are trademarks of
Microsoft Corporation.

Other product and company names mentioned herein may be the trademarks of their
respective owners.

Companies, names, and/or data used in screens and sample output are fictitious unless
otherwise noted.

For WASSER*Studio*   **For Microsoft Press**
Project Manager: Marcelle Amelia   **Acquisitions Editor:** Casey D. Doyle
Print Production Manager: Mary C. Gutierrez   **Project Editor:** Stuart J. Stuple
Desktop Publishing Lead: Kim Tapia
Desktop Publisher: Arlene Rubin
Copy Editor: Pm Weizenbaum
Technical Editor: James Simonson

Acknowledgments

Writing a book, like learning a new computer program, is an exciting and daunting experience. As I look back over the three years since I began the first edition of this book, the many hours I spend typing away on my 486 don't seem all that significant. Instead, I like to recall the many people I've had the good fortune to work with.

As an aspiring author, my first contact was Casey Doyle, who approached me about writing for Microsoft Press and helped me develop a vision for this book. Since then, I've enjoyed working with all the folks at Microsoft Press and WASSER, whose dedication to quality—and to a tight schedule—helped two sparkling editions appear on the bookstore shelves. Special thanks go to Pm Weizenbaum, whose judicious use of the editor's pen has added so much to the book. Additionally, I want to acknowledge the many talented and generous people I worked with on the Access team at Microsoft. Although there are too many to name here, I'm especially grateful to Margaret McGee, Bryce Holmes, and Frida Kumar for their important insights on my work.

I hope some day to write a book of more interest to my family and closest friends. For now, however, I'm happy to thank Margaret Delp, my parents Jim and Judy Callahan, and my sister Melissa Callahan for all their love and support. Any inspiration you find hidden in these pages comes from their influence in my life.

About the Author

Evan Callahan owns Callahan Software Solutions, a database consulting firm specializing in Microsoft Access. He worked for Microsoft Corporation from 1989 to 1995, where he created documentation, online Help, and sample applications for Microsoft Access and Visual Basic. He has delivered training in Microsoft Access and spoken at Microsoft TechEd and other conferences. He received a B.A. in philosophy and comparative literature from the University of Washington.

Evan was born and raised in Seattle, Washington. In his spare time, he enjoys hiking, cycling around the Pacific Northwest, and traveling to new places.

Table of Contents

Table of Contents

*Quick*Look Guide

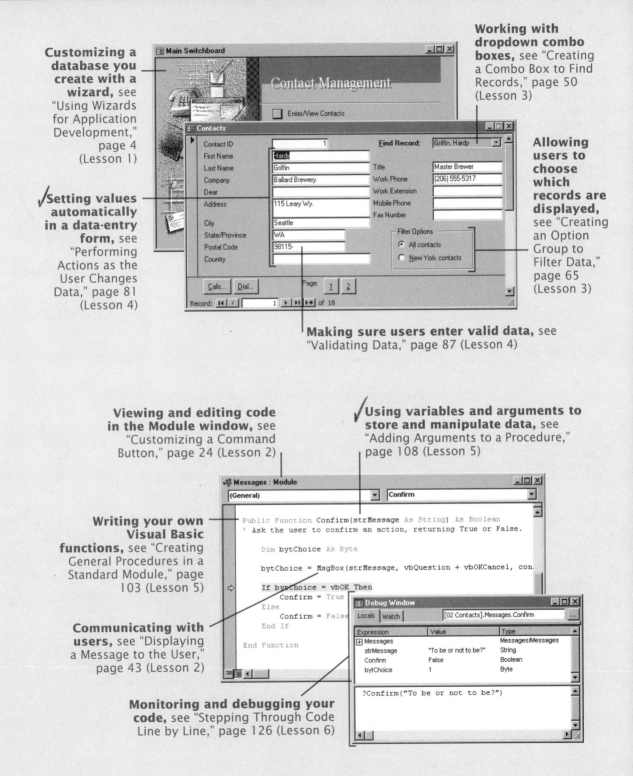

Customizing a database you create with a wizard, see "Using Wizards for Application Development," page 4 (Lesson 1)

Working with dropdown combo boxes, see "Creating a Combo Box to Find Records," page 50 (Lesson 3)

Setting values automatically in a data-entry form, see "Performing Actions as the User Changes Data," page 81 (Lesson 4)

Allowing users to choose which records are displayed, see "Creating an Option Group to Filter Data," page 65 (Lesson 3)

Making sure users enter valid data, see "Validating Data," page 87 (Lesson 4)

Viewing and editing code in the Module window, see "Customizing a Command Button," page 24 (Lesson 2)

Using variables and arguments to store and manipulate data, see "Adding Arguments to a Procedure," page 108 (Lesson 5)

Writing your own Visual Basic functions, see "Creating General Procedures in a Standard Module," page 103 (Lesson 5)

Communicating with users, see "Displaying a Message to the User," page 43 (Lesson 2)

Monitoring and debugging your code, see "Stepping Through Code Line by Line," page 126 (Lesson 6)

xi

Designing a dialog box form, see "Using Dialog Boxes in Your Applications," page 178 (Lesson 8)

Working with list boxes and other objects in code, see "Using a Multiple-Selection List Box," page 286 (Lesson 12)

Creating buttons that run Visual Basic code, see "Adding a Command Button to a Form," page 16 (Lesson 1)

Accessing databases directly in code, see "Working with Data Access Objects," page 288 (Lesson 12)

Responding to user actions in a form, see "Creating Event Procedures for Form Events," page 41 (Lesson 2)

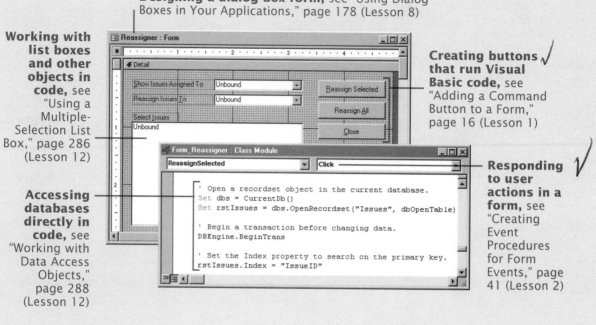

Preparing your custom application for delivery to users, see "Controlling How Your Application Starts," page 254 (Lesson 11)

Providing menus for your user interface, see "Creating a Custom Menu Bar," page 233 (Lesson 10)

Creating toolbar buttons that open forms and reports, see "Customizing Toolbars," page 243 (Lesson 10)

Helping users navigate in an application, see "Making Forms Work Together," page 210 (Lesson 9)

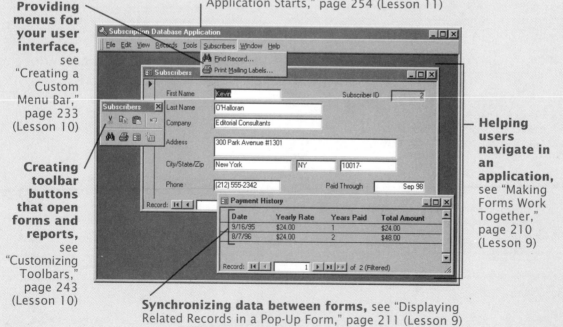

Synchronizing data between forms, see "Displaying Related Records in a Pop-Up Form," page 211 (Lesson 9)

Opening a report using Visual Basic code, see "Filtering Data in a Report," page 197 (Lesson 8)

Printing the results of calculations, see "Calculating Totals While a Report Is Printing," page 313 (Lesson 13)

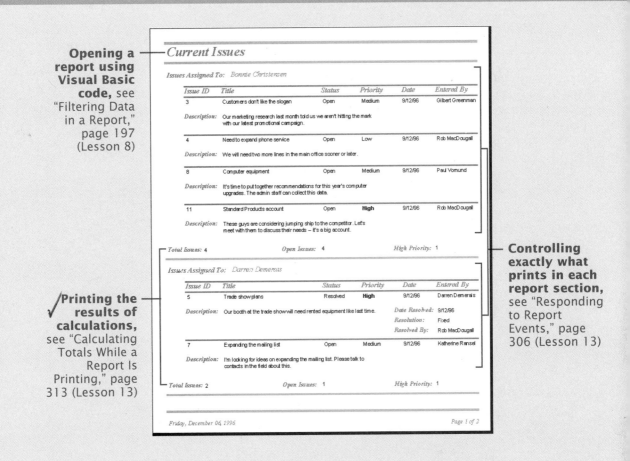

Controlling exactly what prints in each report section, see "Responding to Report Events," page 306 (Lesson 13)

Linking your application to the Internet, see "Using Hyperlinks," page 340 (Lesson 15)

Using the WebBrowser ActiveX control, see "Creating a Custom Web Browser," page 354 (Lesson 15)

Finding Your Best Starting Point

This book teaches you how to create database applications in Microsoft Access 97. If you're using Microsoft Access and are ready to move on to Visual Basic programming, this is the book for you.

Microsoft Access has taken the database world by storm with its ease of use for storing and retrieving information. As you'll see, it's also quite possibly the most productive tool available for creating database applications. Microsoft Access uses a powerful programming language, Visual Basic for Applications—the same language found in Microsoft Excel, Word, and Project. Using the programming techniques you'll learn in these lessons, you'll be able to take advantage of Microsoft Access in new ways, creating your own custom solutions in a short time. What's more, if you're working on databases for others to use, you'll learn to create a foolproof user interface to help them get their work done easily.

Microsoft Access 97/Visual Basic Step by Step walks you through tasks one at a time, keeping you on track with clear instructions and frequent pictures of what you should see on the screen. In each lesson, you'll solve a new puzzle and become familiar with another important area of Microsoft Access or Visual Basic.

IMPORTANT   This book is designed for use with Microsoft Access 97 (version 8.0) or Microsoft Office 97 Professional for the Windows 95 and Windows NT operating systems. To find out what software you're running, you can check the product package or you can start the software, click the Help menu, and click About Microsoft Access. If your software is not compatible with this book, a Step by Step book for your software is probably available. Many of the Step by Step titles are listed on the second page of this book. If the book you want isn't listed, please visit our World Wide Web site at http://www.microsoft.com/mspress/ or call 1-800-MSPRESS for more information.

Finding Your Best Starting Point in this Book

This book is designed for Microsoft Access users who are learning programming for the first time, and for programmers who are moving to Microsoft Access from another programming system, such as dBASE or Visual Basic. You'll get the most from this book if you're already familiar with the basic capabilities of Microsoft Access, such as designing and using forms. You can complete the steps in this book even if you're new to Microsoft Access, but to create your own databases, you'll also need to pick up basic skills not covered in this book.

The book is divided into four parts:

Part 1: Automating Database Tasks   starts you off with practical, straightforward solutions for customizing your Microsoft Access databases. It also introduces Visual Basic for Applications—the programming language in Microsoft Access—and teaches the basic concepts you'll need along the way. In this part, you'll use Microsoft Access wizards and simple programming code to create and customize a contact management database.

Part 2: Programming in Visual Basic   teaches you to use the programming tools built into Microsoft Access to write and debug Visual Basic code. In this part, you'll continue using the contact management database, creating additional features as you go.

Part 3: Creating a Custom Application   walks you through the process of creating a custom user interface for a database application. In this part, you'll work with a new database that manages subscriptions to a journal, preparing it to be delivered to users. Along the way, you'll create a dialog box, make forms and reports work together seamlessly, and add custom menus and toolbars.

Part 4: Working with Data and Objects   takes you further into the underlying structure of Microsoft Access. It will teach you how to take direct control of objects such as forms, reports, and databases—and how to manipulate objects in another application, such as Microsoft Word. In this part, you'll use advanced programming techniques to add features to an issue-tracking application.

Use the following table to find your best starting point in this book.

If you are	Follow these steps
New...	
to Microsoft Access	**1** Install the practice files as described in "Installing the Practice Files and Additional Microsoft Access Tools."
to Visual Basic programming	**2** Become acquainted with the basic features of Microsoft Access, referring to the online Help system and other documention as necessary.
	3 Learn skills for developing applications in Microsoft Access by working sequentially through Lessons 1 through 7 (however, if you're already experienced with Microsoft Access, you may want to skip Lesson 1). Then, you can work through Lessons 8 through 15 as you want to learn the additional techniques they cover.

If you are	Follow these steps
Switching...	
from Microsoft Visual Basic	**1** Install the practice files as described in "Installing the Practice Files and Additional Microsoft Access Tools."
from another Microsoft product that uses Visual Basic	**2** Learn about developing applications in Microsoft Access by working sequentially through Lessons 1, 3, and 4, skimming Lesson 2 along the way. Also, skim Lessons 5 through 7. Then, you can work through Lessons 8 through 15 as you want to learn the additional techniques they cover.

If you are	Follow these steps

Upgrading...

from Microsoft Access for Windows 95	**1** Learn about the new features in this version of the program that are covered in this book by reading through the following section, "New Application Development Features in Microsoft Access."
from a previous version of Microsoft Access	**2** Install the practice files as described in "Installing the Practice Files and Additional Microsoft Access Tools."
	3 Complete the lessons that cover the topics you need. Use the table of contents and the *Quick*Look Guide to locate information about general topics. You can use the index to find information about a specific topic or a feature from a previous version of Microsoft Access.

If you are	Follow these steps

Referencing...

this book after working through the lessons	**1** Use the index to locate information about specific topics, and use the table of contents and the *Quick*Look Guide to locate information about general topics.
	2 Read the Lesson Summary at the end of each lesson for a brief review of the major tasks in the lesson. The Lesson Summary topics are listed in the same order as they are presented in the lesson.

New Application Development Features in Microsoft Access

The following table lists the major new features in Microsoft Access 97 that are covered in this book. The table shows the lesson in which you can learn how to use each feature. You can also use the index to find specific information about a feature or a task you want to do.

To learn how to	See
Let Microsoft Access help you enter Visual Basic code as you type	Lesson 2
Debug your code more easily using new features such as Data Tips and the Locals pane of the Debug window	Lesson 6
Organize controls in a dialog box using the Tab control	Lesson 8
Create custom menu bars and toolbars that include commands and buttons to open database objects and run Visual Basic code	Lesson 10
Explore objects using the improved Object Browser	Lesson 12
Work directly with Microsoft Word objects using Automation code	Lesson 14
Work with the Internet using hyperlinks and the WebBrowser control	Lesson 15

Corrections, Comments, and Help

Every effort has been made to ensure the accuracy of this book and the contents of the practice files disc. Microsoft Press provides corrections and additional content for its books through the World Wide Web at

> http://www.microsoft.com/mspress/support/

If you have comments, questions, or ideas regarding this book or the practice files disc, please send them to us.

Send e-mail to

> mspinput@microsoft.com

Or send postal mail to

> Microsoft Press
>
> Attn: Step by Step Series Editor
>
> One Microsoft Way
>
> Redmond, WA 98052-6399

Please note that support for the Microsoft Access software product itself is not offered through the above addresses. For help using Microsoft Access, you can call Microsoft Technical Support at (800) 936-5700, or visit Microsoft Access Online Support on the World Wide Web at

> http://www.microsoft.com/MSAccessSupport/

Visit Our World Wide Web Site

We invite you to visit the Microsoft Press World Wide Web site. You can visit us at the following location:

http://www.microsoft.com/mspress/

You'll find descriptions for all of our books, information about ordering titles, notice of special features and events, additional content for Microsoft Press books, and much more.

You can also find out the latest in software developments and news from Microsoft Corporation by visiting the following World Wide Web site:

http://www.microsoft.com/

We look forward to your visit on the Web!

Installing the Practice Files and Additional Microsoft Access Tools

The disc inside the back cover of this book contains practice files that you'll use as you perform the exercises in the book. For example, when you're learning how to use Visual Basic code in Microsoft Access, you'll open one of the practice files—a database containing several tables, forms, and reports created for you—and then customize one of the existing forms it contains. By using the practice files, you won't waste time creating the samples used in the lessons—instead, you can concentrate on learning how to develop applications in Microsoft Access. With the files and the step-by-step instructions in the lessons, you'll also learn by doing, which is an easy and effective way to acquire and remember new skills.

IMPORTANT Before you break the seal on the practice disc package, be sure that this book matches your version of the software. This book is designed for use with Microsoft Access 97 (version 8.0) for the Windows 95 and Windows NT version 4.0 operating systems. To find out what software you're running, you can check the product package or you can start the software, and then on the Help menu click About Microsoft Access. If your program is not compatible with this book, a Step by Step book matching your software is probably available. Many of the Step by Step titles are listed on the second page of this book. If the book you want isn't listed, please visit our World Wide Web site at http://www.microsoft.com/mspress/ or call 1-800-MSPRESS for more information.

Install the practice files on your computer

Follow these steps to install the practice files on your computer's hard disk so that you can use them with the exercises in this book.

1 Remove the disc from the package inside the back cover of this book and insert it in your CD-ROM drive.

2 On the taskbar at the bottom of your screen, click the Start button, and then click Run.

Click Start...

...and then click Run.

The Run dialog box appears.

3 In the Open box, type **d:setup** (or, if your CD-ROM drive uses a drive letter other than "d," substitute the correct drive letter).

4 Click OK, and then follow the directions on the screen.

The setup program window appears with recommended options preselected for you. For best results in using the practice files with this book, accept these preselected settings.

5 When the files have been installed, remove the disc from your drive and replace it in the package inside the back cover of the book.

A folder called Access VBA Practice has been created on your hard disk, and the practice files have been put in that folder.

Microsoft
Press
Welcome

NOTE In addition to installing the practice files, the Setup program created a shortcut to the Microsoft Press World Wide Web site on your Desktop. If your computer is set up to connect to the Internet, you can double-click the shortcut to visit the Microsoft Press Web site. You can also connect to the Web site directly at http://www.microsoft.com/mspress/.

Installing All the Microsoft Access Tools You Need

To permit you to complete the steps in this book, the Microsoft Access installation on your computer must include the Advanced Wizards component, which includes tools for application developers. You'll also want to have all the available online Help and sample database files. Unfortunately, these components are not included by default when you run Setup to install Microsoft Access. If you selected the Typical or Minimal option in Setup, you don't have all the necessary tools. Before you begin the lessons, it's best to check your installation by running Setup again.

Fortunately, you don't have to reinstall Microsoft Access to check your installation or add the developer tools. When you run Setup, it will detect that Microsoft Access is already installed and allow you to add the necessary components.

Install Microsoft Access developer components

1   Start Microsoft Access 97 Setup (or Microsoft Office 97 Professional Setup).

2   When Setup asks what you want to do, click the Add/Remove button.

3   If you're using Microsoft Office Setup, select Microsoft Access in the Options list, and then click the Change Option button. (If you're using Microsoft Access Setup, you're already viewing Microsoft Access options, so you can skip this step and Step 5.)

4   Click the Select All button.

     This selects all Microsoft Access components, including Advanced Wizards, Programming Help, and the entire Sample Applications component. (You'll need all the Microsoft Access components for this book except two: Microsoft Briefcase Replication and Calendar Control. If you want, you can deselect these two components to save disk space.)

5   If you're using Microsoft Office Setup, click OK to return to the main list of components.

6   Click Continue.

     Setup installs all the necessary files.

Getting Help on Microsoft Access

Microsoft Access has a vast online Help system that you can use to learn new topics or get answers to your individual questions. And now that you've ensured that you have the Programming Help component installed on your computer, you'll find it especially valuable as you learn to create applications with Microsoft Access.

There isn't only reference information in Help—it also includes how-to information for nearly every task, graphical introductions to areas of Microsoft Access, and additional topics that help you find the information you need by answering questions. Additionally, there is a complete reference topic on every function, method, property, and other element you can use in Microsoft Access. And as you'll see, Help has several innovative ways for you to locate the topics you need.

What would you like to do?

- Create a list box or combo box that looks up values
- Create a field that looks up or lists values in tables
- DLookup Function
- FilterLookup Property
- About AutoLookup queries that enter data automatically
- DisplayControl Property

Looking up values

Search

| Tips | Options | Close |

Office Assistant The Office Assistant, a friendly animated "character" that sits on top of your work, lets you find Help topics by typing in a question or phrase *in your own words*—you don't have to guess the exact words that are in the online index. This capability makes the Office Assistant the most useful method for getting help if you have a question while you work. For example, if you wanted to know about displaying a list of values, you could simply type **looking up values**. The Office Assistant would interpret your text and display a range of topics.

To display the Office Assistant, click the Office Assistant button on the toolbar. Anytime you want to ask a question, just click the Office Assistant, type the text of your question, and then click Search. If you're working on Visual Basic code in the Module window, the Office Assistant automatically detects this and searches for programming topics instead of topics about Microsoft Access in general.

Contents   The Contents feature groups topics into logical order, which makes it a great place to browse Help, discover what's there, and begin your exploration of a new area in Microsoft Access. To browse the Contents list, click Contents and Index on the Help menu and then click the Contents tab.

Index   The Index feature works like a book index. You can look up any topic covered in Help and jump directly to that topic. To search the Index, click Contents and Index on the Help menu and then click the Index tab.

Find   While the online index includes the most important words in a topic, the Find feature lets you search the complete text of every single topic to find what you want. You may want to avoid this feature, however, since it requires Microsoft Access to set up a special index file the first time you use it—which takes time and disk space. To use the Find feature, click Contents and Index on the Help menu and then click the Find tab.

Keyword Help in the Module window   Anytime you're working on Visual Basic code in the Module window, the Help topic for any keyword on the screen is a single keystroke away. To display a Help topic, click to position the insertion point on the keyword you're interested in (such as a statement, function, or method) and press the F1 key.

Orders and Solutions Sample Applications   Earlier in this section, you instructed Setup to install the sample applications that Microsoft Access includes for developers. By looking at these applications, you can learn additional techniques, gather ideas for your own projects, and find useful Visual Basic code. The Orders application is a custom order-entry system. The Solutions database is a learning tool that shows you examples of many form, report, and Visual Basic strategies and includes instructions on how to create each sample object yourself.

You'll find these database files, called Orders and Solutions, in the Samples folder included with your Microsoft Access or Office installation (usually c:\Program Files\Microsoft Office\Office\Samples). When you open them, you'll see that each application has its own welcome screen and online Help file to guide you.

Using the Practice Files

Each lesson in this book explains when and how to use any practice files for that lesson. When it's time to use a practice file, the book will list instructions for how to open the file. Most of the files on the disc are Microsoft Access database files—they contain partially completed programming projects that you'll work on to learn programming techniques.

For those of you who like to know all the details, here's a list of the files included on the practice disc:

Lesson	Filename	Description
1	01Client	Text file containing names and addresses of imaginary clients, which you import into a Microsoft Access contact management application
2	02Contac	Database file for contact management application, similar to the one you create in Lesson 1 and use through Lesson 7
3	03Contac	Database file for contact management application
4	04Contac	Database file for contact management application
5	05Contac	Database file for contact management application
6	06Contac	Database file for contact management application
7	07Contac	Database file for contact management application
8	08Subscr	Database file for magazine subscription application, which you use in Lessons 8 through 11
9	09Subscr	Database file for magazine subscription application
10	10Subscr	Database file for magazine subscription application
11	11Splash	Bitmap file containing a picture you want Microsoft Access to display whenever users start the magazine subscription application
	11Subscr	Database file for magazine subscription application
12	12Issues	Database file for issue tracking application
13	13Issues	Database file for issue tracking application
14	14Issues	Database file for issue tracking application
	14Memo	Microsoft Word template file you use to create a memo containing data from the issue tracking application
15	15Issues	Database file for issue tracking application

Uninstalling the Practice Files

Use the following steps to delete the practice files added to your hard drive by the Step by Step program.

1 Click the Start button, point to Settings, and then click Control Panel.

2 Double-click the Add/Remove Programs icon.

3 Select Microsoft Access Step by Step from the list, and then click Add/Remove.

   A confirmation message appears.

4 Click Yes.

   The practice files are uninstalled.

5 Click OK to close the Add/Remove Programs Properties dialog box.

6 Close the Control Panel window.

Need Help with the Practice Files?

Every effort has been made to ensure the accuracy of this book and the contents of the CD-ROM. If you do run into a problem, Microsoft Press provides corrections for its books through the World Wide Web at

   http://www.microsoft.com/mspress/support/

We also invite you to visit our main Web page at

   http://www.microsoft.com/mspress/

You'll find descriptions for all of our books, information about ordering titles, notices of special features and events, additional content for Microsoft Press books, and much more.

Conventions and Features in this Book

When you use this book, you can save time by understanding, before you start the lessons, how the instructions, keys to press, and so on are shown in the book. Please take a moment to read the following list, which also points out other helpful features of the book.

Conventions

- Hands-on exercises for you to follow are given in numbered lists of steps (1, 2, and so on). An arrowhead bullet (➤) indicates an exercise that has only one step.
- Text that you are to type appears in **boldface**.
- New terms and the titles of books appear in *italic*.
- Names of keyboard keys for you to press appear in SMALL CAPITAL LETTERS. A plus sign (+) between two key names means that you must press those keys at the same time. For example, "Press ALT+TAB" means that you hold down the ALT key while you press TAB.
- Program code (on a separate line or lines) appears in monospace type:

```
Me.AllowEdits = False
```

The following icons identify the different types of supplementary material:

	Notes labeled	Alert you to
	Note	Additional information for a step.
	Tip	Suggested additional methods for a step or helpful hints.
	Important	Essential information that you should check before continuing with the lesson.

Other Features of This Book

Database Window button

- You can perform many operations in Microsoft Access by clicking a button on the toolbar or a tool in the toolbox. When the instructions in this book tell you to click a toolbar button, a picture of the button is shown in the left margin next to the instructions. The Database Window button in the margin next to this paragraph is an example.

- Screen capture illustrations show sample user interfaces and the results of your completed steps, and frequently include text that calls out the part of the illustration you should notice.

- Sidebars—short sections printed on a shaded background—introduce special programming techniques, background information, or features related to the information being discussed.

- You can get a quick reminder of how to perform the tasks you learned by reading the Lesson Summary at the end of a lesson.

- You can quickly determine what online Help topics are available for additional information by referring to the Help topics listed at the end of each lesson. The Help system provides a complete online reference to Microsoft Access.

- At the end of each lesson, you'll also find a list of references to a manual called *Building Applications with Microsoft Access 97*. A printed version of this book is included with Microsoft Access 97 and with Microsoft Office 97, Developer's Edition. If you have Microsoft Office 97 Professional on CD-ROM, you don't have the printed version of this book, but your Microsoft Office disc includes an HTML version of the book, which you can view using a Web browser such as Microsoft Internet Explorer. Alternatively, you can find the book on the World Wide Web at

  http://www.microsoft.com/AccessDev/BApp97/BApp97.htm

Part 1

Automating Database Tasks

Get Started Quickly with Wizards

Estimated time
30 min.

In this lesson you will learn how to:

■ Create a database with the Database Wizard.

■ Add an additional object to a wizard-created database.

■ Create a command button with a wizard.

Ever try to write a letter or a report, but you just can't get the first word down on the page? A blank page is a big obstacle to progress. This is why we often seek help from others, and why brainstorming is such a good technique— ideas good or bad help you come up with other ideas, and next thing you know, you have a good start.

Like working from a blank page, creating a database application from scratch is a difficult task. In fact, before you can do any customization or program- ming, you have to get most of your database in place and working! Fortu- nately, Microsoft Access includes several *wizards* that can help you get started quickly. Wizards ask you questions about databases or objects you want to create, and then create them for you. For example, the Database Wizard can create all the basic elements of a database application—tables, forms, reports, and other objects. After the wizard does its work, you can start using the application right away, or modify the user interface it creates, add new objects, even delete some of the objects it creates and replace them with your own.

In this lesson, you'll create an entire database application from scratch using the Database Wizard, and customize the application in various ways. Then, as you progress through Part 1, you'll learn how to use Visual Basic for Applications—as well as a number of other Microsoft Access wizards—to further customize the way the database works.

Start the lesson

➤ Start Microsoft Access 97. Click the Start button on the taskbar, point to Programs, and then click Microsoft Access.

Using Wizards for Application Development

It seems like wizards are popping up all over the place these days—usually to help end users perform difficult tasks without needing to know all the ins and outs of the software. But there are several wizards included in Microsoft Access that help make your job as an application developer much easier as well. In this book, you'll try out the following wizards:

- Database Wizard
- Import Text Wizard
- Command Button Wizard
- Combo Box Wizard
- Option Group Wizard
- Database Splitter Wizard

These wizards will not only help you get work done faster, they'll also help you learn more about application development as you work. Even so, it's important to remember that anything you accomplish with a wizard you could do on your own in Microsoft Access. In fact, the wizards themselves are written in the Visual Basic programming language and use ordinary Microsoft Access forms for their interface, just like the applications you'll create.

 IMPORTANT To complete the steps in these lessons, all Microsoft Access wizards and online Help must be installed. If you didn't install these components, or if you chose the Typical option when you installed Microsoft Access, run Setup again, choosing the Custom option and selecting all wizards and online Help components. For more information, see "Installing the Practice Files and Additional Microsoft Access Tools" in this book.

As you learn to program Microsoft Access using Visual Basic, you'll go much further than wizards can take you. But there's no sense turning down the help wizards have to offer.

Creating a Database Using the Database Wizard

The Database Wizard can create several common types of databases for business and personal use, including the following:

- Asset tracking
- Contact management
- Donations
- Event management
- Expenses
- Inventory control
- Ledger
- Membership
- Order entry
- Resource scheduling
- Service call management
- Students and classes
- Time and billing
- Various personal and home databases, including ones that store information about your address book, household inventory, and music, book, and video collections

---

NOTE Even if the Database Wizard doesn't have just the database you need, the databases it creates may provide you with ideas for your own applications. Additionally, all the techniques you'll use to modify the wizard-created database apply equally to tables and forms you create on your own. In fact, in Part 3, you'll bypass the Database Wizard entirely to create the elements of a user interface from scratch.

Create the Contacts database

New Database button

1   In the opening Microsoft Access dialog box, click Database Wizard and then click OK. Or, if you've already closed the opening dialog box, click the New Database button.

    Microsoft Access displays the New dialog box.

2   Click the Databases tab.

Microsoft Access displays icons for each type of database the Database Wizard can create for you.

A few of the databases the Database Wizard can create

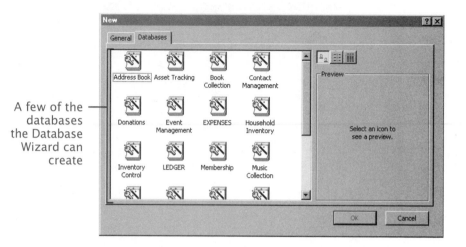

3 Double-click the Contact Management icon.

Microsoft Access asks you to provide a file name and location for the new database file.

4 Move to the folder where you installed the practice files (probably c:\Access VBA Practice).

5 In the File Name box, type **01Contac**, and then click Create.

The Database Wizard starts up and lists the types of information that the Contact Management database will include.

6 Click Next.

The Database Wizard asks if you want to include any optional fields in your database. You won't need any optional fields, so you needn't make any changes.

7 Click Next.

The Database Wizard asks what style you want it to use when creating forms for the application.

8 Click Standard, and then click Finish.

The Database Wizard gets busy creating the Contacts database, which may take a minute or two. It then opens the Main Switchboard form, which shows up each time the database opens and guides users through the database. A *switchboard* form provides buttons and text that open other forms and reports in an application—a sort of control center for users.

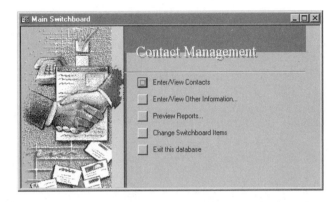

What Is a Database Application?

The Contacts database you've created is more than an ordinary Microsoft Access database: with its Switchboard form and the other forms and reports it contains, the Contacts database is an *application*. This term refers to the fact that the database has its own custom-built user interface, designed especially to help users of the database navigate through its forms and reports and get work done with the database. Database applications range from those as simple as the Contacts database, which has a very specific job in life, to complete business solutions that contain many objects and large amounts of Visual Basic code.

Developing custom applications is the central purpose of programming Microsoft Access with Visual Basic—and the central topic of this book. Throughout the book, you'll learn to tailor Microsoft Access databases to solve specific user problems and make information easier to get in and out of the computer. Because its simple interface leaves plenty of room for customization, the Contacts database is a great place to start.

View the Contacts form

The first item on the Switchboard form allows users to open the Contacts form, the main form in the application, where they can view and enter contact information in the database.

1   On the Switchboard form, click Enter/View Contacts.

The Contacts form opens, ready to accept new records. In addition to text boxes and other controls for all the information stored in the

Contacts table, the form includes a footer with command buttons that users can click to perform common actions.

2 Close the Contacts form. (Click the Close button—the one with the "X"—in the upper right corner of the form window.)

What Else Did the Wizard Create?

The Database Wizard creates all the bare essentials of a database application, along with a few goodies to help users navigate in the application. Here's a list of everything the Contacts database includes:

- Tables that store information about contacts, contact types, and phone calls. The wizard automatically sets table properties and creates relationships between the tables.

- Forms for entering contact information and phone call information.

- Reports that summarize information about contacts and phone calls.

- The Switchboard form and the Switchboard Items table, which make up the application switchboard that you see when you open the Contacts database.

NOTE The Switchboard form the wizard creates is a special form that you shouldn't try to change directly. It contains Visual Basic code that, along with the Switchboard Items table, displays the text you see on the form and makes the buttons work. Although you can't easily modify the way the Switchboard form works, you can add or remove buttons, as you'll see later in the lesson. Alternatively, you could replace the Switchboard form with your own custom startup form, a technique you'll learn in Lesson 11.

View the objects in the Contacts database

A quick look at the Database window shows all the objects the Database Wizard created for the application. This should help you see that there's nothing magical about the database the wizard creates—it's just a few objects pulled together with a nice cover sheet.

Database Window button

1 Click the Database Window button.

2 Click each of the Tables, Forms, and Reports tabs to view the four tables, seven forms, and two reports the wizard created.

For many Microsoft Access users, the tables, forms, and reports created by the Database Wizard are fine just the way they are. But as a custom database developer, you'll want to customize these objects and add new objects. Now that the Database Wizard has done its work, you can choose to keep all or part of the wizard-created database, adding or modifying objects to meet the needs of your users.

3 Minimize the Database window.

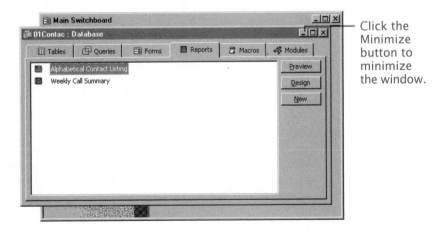

Click the Minimize button to minimize the window.

Entering Information into the Database

The first thing you need to do after creating a database is get some data into it. The Contact Management application lets you keep a list of the *types* of contacts you have, so that you can categorize each contact you enter in the database. Before going any further, it makes sense to enter this preliminary information.

Enter contact types

You can use the Switchboard form to open a form for entering contact types.

1   On the Switchboard form, click Enter/View Other Information.

2   Click Enter/View Contact Types.

    The Contact Types form opens, ready for a new record.

3   Type **Client**.

4   Click the New Record button.

— New Record button

    Microsoft Access saves the record and moves to a new record.

5   Type **Contractor**.

6   Click the New Record button, and then type **Personal**.

7   Close the Contact Types form (click the Close button in the upper right corner of the Form window).

8   Click Return To Main Switchboard.

    This returns you to the initial switchboard menu.

Now when you enter contacts, you'll be able to select one of these three types for each contact record.

Using Existing Data with a New Database

As you've seen, the Contacts form is empty—it doesn't display any records. But suppose you already have some contact information that you've been storing in another program, and you don't want to retype it into your Microsoft Access application. One of the sample files included on your disk is 01Client, a comma-delimited text file containing names, addresses, and phone numbers you can add to the Contacts table. This file could easily have been exported from another spreadsheet or database system in order to move it into Microsoft Access.

Before you import data into an existing table, you should make sure it's in a format that Microsoft Access can accept. For example, you can import an Excel worksheet, a dBASE file, or a text file. Additionally, the data in the file you want to import must be compatible with the structure of the table you're adding it to. If it isn't, you may need to edit the file before importing it, to get it ready for Microsoft Access. For example, the 01Client text file already has the correct field names for the Contacts table in the first row of the file, so Microsoft Access can determine which fields to store data in.

 TIP If you don't have any existing data to import when you first create an application, you may want the Database Wizard to include a few sample records in each of the application's tables. Just select the Include Sample Data check box when creating an application. You can delete sample records from tables when you're ready to enter real data.

Import data into the Contacts table

1   On the File menu, point to Get External Data and then click Import.

    Microsoft Access displays the Import dialog box, where you can select from a variety of data formats to import.

2   In the Files Of Type box, select Text Files.

    The Import dialog box shows the 01Client text file, which is provided with the practice files you installed.

3   Select 01Client, and then click Import.

    Microsoft Access starts the Import Text Wizard, which helps you select options for importing delimited or fixed-width text files. The wizard automatically detects that the 01Client text file is in Delimited format.

Import Text Wizard   [×]

The wizard has decided that your data is in a 'Delimited' format. If it isn't, choose the format that more correctly describes your data.

Choose the format that best describes your data:

◉ Delimited - Characters such as comma or tab separate each field
○ Fixed Width - Fields are aligned in columns with spaces between each field

Sample data from file: C:\ACCESS VBA PRACTICE\01CLIENT.TXT.

1	"FirstName","LastName","CompanyName","Title","Addres
2	"Hardy","Griffin","Ballard Brewery","Master Brewer",
3	"Kevin","O'Halloran","Editorial Consultants","Editor
4	"Kara","Stepanian","Big Bad Books","Publisher","480
5	"David","Hunting","Software Solutions","Consultant",
6	"Bonnie","Christensen","Dance Academy",,"4220 Main S
7	"Maura","O'Keefe","Helping Hand","Director","31 E. H
8	"Kevin","Geloff","Ballard Academy","Principal","2312

[Advanced...]   [Cancel]   [< Back] [Next >] [Finish]

— The wizard shows you the fields in the text file as Microsoft Access will import them.

4 Click Next.

5 Select the First Row Contains Field Names option, and then click Next.

6 Select the In An Existing Table option, select the Contacts table from the drop-down list, and then click Finish.

Select the Contacts table here.

Microsoft Access appends records from the text file to the existing Contacts table, and then displays a message indicating that it's finished successfully.

7 Click OK.

View new records in the Contacts form

Now, when users open the Contacts form, they'll see the client records you've added, and they'll be all set to start logging calls or adding additional contacts. You can also check to see that the contact types you added to the database are available on the form.

1 On the Switchboard form, click Enter/View Contacts.

The form displays the first record you imported into the Contacts table. Because the text file includes only a subset of the fields in the table, many of the text boxes are blank.

2 Click the Page 2 button in the form footer.

3 Click the drop-down arrow next to the Contact Type box, and then click Client.

As you can see, the three types of contacts you added are available in the list.

4 Close the Contacts form.

Adding an Object to Your Application

Although the Database Wizard creates several useful forms and reports for the Contacts database, you're sure to need additional ones in your application. Suppose users need to print an up-to-date phone list for current contacts, organized by the city they're located in. You can create this form easily by using the Report Wizard.

Create a contact list report organized by city

1 Click the Database Window button.

Database Window button

2 Click the Tables tab.

3 Click the Contacts table to select it.

New Object
button

4 Click the arrow next to the New Object button on the toolbar (which displays the button face for the last button you selected here), and then click Report.

AutoForm
AutoReport
Table
Query
Form
Report
Macro
Module
Class Module

5 Click Report Wizard in the list, and then click OK.

6 In the Available Fields box, double-click the City field, followed by the LastName, FirstName, CompanyName, Title, and WorkPhone fields.

The Report Wizard adds the fields to the Selected Fields list.

Report Wizard

Which fields do you want on your report?
You can choose from more than one table or query.

Tables/Queries:
Table: Contacts

Available Fields:
ContactID
FirstName
LastName
Dear
Address
StateOrProvince
PostalCode
Region

Selected Fields:
City

Double-click a field to add it to the report.

Cancel   < Back   Next >   Finish

7 Click Next.

The wizard asks what fields you want to use for grouping data in the report.

8 Double-click the City field in the list, and then click Next.

The wizard asks what fields you want to sort in the report.

9 Select the LastName field from the first sorting box, select the FirstName field from the second sorting box, and then click Next.

The wizard asks how you want to lay out your report.

10 In the layout box, select Outline 1, and then click Next.

11 Choose a style for your report (or accept the default style), and then click Next.

The wizard asks what title you'd like for the report.

12 Type **Contacts By City** and then click Finish.

The Report Wizard creates the Contacts By City report and displays it in Print Preview.

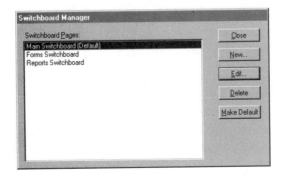

13 Close the report.

14 Minimize the Database window.

Add the new report to the Switchboard form

After you create new objects, you can add them to the Switchboard form that the Database Wizard created.

1 On the Switchboard form, click Change Switchboard Items.

Microsoft Access starts the Switchboard Manager, which helps you modify the items available on the Switchboard form.

2 Select Reports Switchboard, and then click Edit.

3 Click New.

4 In the Text box, type **Preview the Contacts By City Report**.

5 In the Command box, select Open Report.

6 In the Report box select Contacts By City, and then click OK.

7 Click Preview The Contacts By City Report, and then click Move Up.

8 Click Close.

9 Click Close again.

The Switchboard Manager updates the Switchboard Items table so that your new item appears in the Switchboard form.

Try the new Switchboard button

1 On the Switchboard form, click Preview Reports.

2 Click Preview The Contacts By City Report.

The reports page of the Switchboard form now shows your new option.

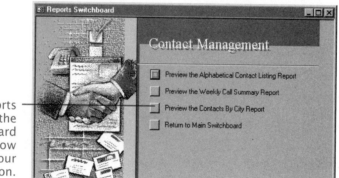

The button opens your report.

3 Close the report window.

4 On the Switchboard form, click Return To Main Switchboard.

Adding a Command Button to a Form

You've seen how the buttons on the Switchboard form help users open the forms and reports they need to use. In this way, buttons can help users navigate, tying objects together into a powerful application.

Once users get to the forms in your application, you want to put common tasks at their fingertips, so your forms are easy to use. One way to do this is by creating command buttons to automate tasks on your application forms. As you may have noticed, the Database Wizard already created some useful command buttons on the Contacts form.

Open the Contacts form and try a command button

1   On the Switchboard form, click Enter/View Contacts.

These command buttons open other forms or perform common actions.

2   Click the Calls button.

The Calls form appears. When you click the button, it runs a few lines of Visual Basic code programmed by the Database Wizard. Next, you'll add your own button to the Contacts form, which will work in much the same way.

3   Close the Calls form.

Create a command button to move to a new record

When you open the Contacts form, it displays the first existing contact record. If you want to enter a new contact, you can move to the new record at the end of the recordset by clicking the New Record button at the bottom of the form window. Or, you can use the Insert Record menu command with the same effect.

But suppose you want to make this command more accessible to other users, so they won't have to find it on the menu or know about the navigation buttons—after all, new users won't be as familiar with Microsoft Access as you are. To bring this command to the forefront, you'll go into the form's Design view and place another button in the form footer that performs this action whenever you click it. The Command Button Wizard makes the button work automatically by writing Visual Basic code for you.

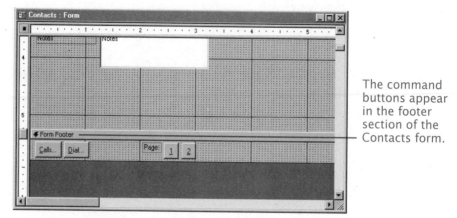

Design View button

1 Click the Design View button on the toolbar. (If the property Sheet is in the way, close it.)

2 Scroll down in the form to display the Form Footer section.

The command buttons appear in the footer section of the Contacts form.

Toolbox button

3 If the toolbox isn't displayed, click the Toolbox button on the toolbar.

4 In the toolbox, make sure the Control Wizards tool is selected, and then click the Command Button tool.

Control Wizards tool (selected)

Command Button tool

5 In the form footer, click just to the right of the Page 2 button.

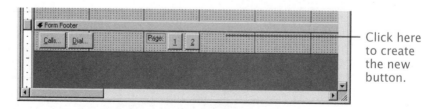

Click here to create the new button.

The Command Button Wizard starts, asking what actions you want the new button to perform.

6   In the Categories list, select Record Operations.

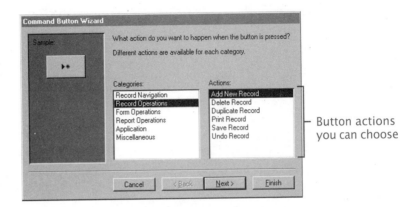

Button actions
you can choose

7   In the Actions list, select Add New Record, and then click Next.

The wizard asks whether you want a picture or text on your button.

8   Select the Text option, and then click Next.

When you create your own buttons, you may want to use the pictures
that the wizard provides for them—there's an extensive library of icons
available to choose from. The wizard even shows you a preview of the
picture for the button you've chosen. In this case, however, the existing
buttons on the Contacts form have text on them, so for the sake of consistency it makes sense to go with text on the Add Record button.

9   Type **AddRecord** as the button name, and then click Finish.

> **NOTE**   Although the button's caption (Add Record) includes a
> space, you don't want to include a space in the button's name.
> Throughout this book, you'll give objects names without
> spaces, because this makes them easier to refer to in Visual
> Basic code.

The wizard finishes creating the button and places it on your form.
Behind the scenes, it also writes several lines of Visual Basic code and
attaches them to the button for you.

19

Try the new command button

Let's make sure the Add Record button does what you intended.

Form View button

1 Click the Form View button on the toolbar.
2 Click the Add Record button.

Microsoft Access moves to the new record in the Contacts table, displaying a fresh form for you to enter data into.

How Does the Button Work?

If you create a button without using the Command Button Wizard, the button won't *do* anything when you click it. What did the wizard do to make the button perform as you asked?

Here's how it works: whenever you perform any action in a form—click a button or change a field's value, for example—an *event* occurs. Every event is a chance for your application to perform some action, such as running a macro or a Visual Basic procedure. When the Command Button Wizard created the button, it attached an *event procedure* to the button's Click event. This way, every time the button is clicked, the Visual Basic code in the event procedure runs, causing Microsoft Access to perform the desired action—in this case, moving to the new record.

Creating Other Command Buttons

You can see how easy it is to customize your forms by adding command buttons. And, as you saw when using the Command Button Wizard, adding a record is just one type of operation you can create a button for—the Command Button Wizard can create buttons for all kinds of other tasks as well. Here are some other common operations you can create buttons for:

- Navigating between records
- Finding and filtering data
- Opening forms and reports
- Printing and other miscellaneous tasks

Using the Command Button Wizard is like "programming without programming"—even after programming with Microsoft Access becomes second nature, you still may want to rely on the Command Button Wizard to give you a head start.

Close the Contacts form

1 Close the form window.

2 When Microsoft Access asks if you want to save changes to the Contacts form, click Yes.

 NOTE When you save the form, Microsoft Access saves not only the new button, but also the Visual Basic code that the wizard created for it. Because a form's module is stored along with the form, you don't have to save the Visual Basic code separately.

Close the application and exit Microsoft Access

1 On the Switchboard form, click Exit This Database.

2 On the File menu, click Exit.

Moving from Macros to Visual Basic

In the lessons to come, you'll learn to perform many database tasks using Visual Basic code. Some of these tasks can also be accomplished with Microsoft Access macros. However, macros are much less flexible and powerful than Visual Basic—and because there are Visual Basic equivalents for just about every macro action, you can do nearly all the same things in Visual Basic that you can in macros. Because of Visual Basic's power and flexibility, the Database Wizard and the Command Button Wizard create Visual Basic event procedures, not macros.

If you have existing macros in your databases, it will soon be time to convert them to Visual Basic—this way, you'll have a consistent strategy for customization in your applications. Microsoft Access makes the move to Visual Basic easy by including commands that replace your macros with Visual Basic procedures. To convert an individual macro, select the macro in the Database window, click Save As/Export on the File menu, and then click Save As Visual Basic Module. To convert all the macros used with a form, open the form in Design view, click Macros on the Tools menu, and then click Convert Form's Macros To Visual Basic. Microsoft Access not only creates procedures for all the macros, it attaches them to the same events, so that your application works just as before.

Lesson Summary

To	Do this	Button
Create a database using the Database Wizard	Click the New Database button and double-click the type of database you want.	
Import data into an existing database	On the File menu, point to Get External Data, and then click Import.	
Modify the Switchboard form in a database created by the Database Wizard	Click the Change Switchboard Items button on the Switchboard form.	
Create a command button on a form	In Form Design view, click the Command Button tool and click on the form where you want to place the button.	

For online information about	On the Help menu, click Contents and Index, click the Index tab, and then
Creating database applications	Search for "databases, creating"
Getting started with Visual Basic	Search for "Visual Basic"
Creating command buttons	Search for "command buttons"

For more information on	In *Building Applications with Microsoft Access 97*, see
Creating database applications	Chapter 1, "Creating an Application"
Getting started with Visual Basic	Chapter 2, "Introducing Visual Basic"
Creating command buttons	Chapter 3, "Using Forms to Collect, Filter, and Display Information"

Preview of the Next Lesson

In this lesson, you learned that wizards can create useful objects for you, complete with Visual Basic code. In the next lesson, you'll learn to view and make changes to the Visual Basic code the wizard creates, and to write your own simple event procedures to perform tasks that the wizards don't do.

Customize an Application with Visual Basic

Estimated time
40 min.

In this lesson you will learn how to:

- View and understand the Visual Basic code created by the Command Button Wizard.
- Edit Visual Basic code in the Module window.
- Set form and control properties using Visual Basic.
- Display a message box.

When you take the city bus around town, trip planning is of the utmost importance. Where does the bus stop? How close does it get you to your destination? Like it or not, the bus follows a predetermined route. But wouldn't it be nice if you had complete control of the bus route? You could just sit near the bus driver and say, "Take a left at the next light, then head that way for half a mile or so—I'll get off at the second building on the right."

We all love to be in control of our situation—a characteristic especially true of computer users and programmers. If there's one type of complaint you'll hear from computer users, it's along the lines of: "This machine doesn't let me do what I want it to," or "I sure wish I could make the software work a different way." Working with Microsoft Access is no exception. Sure, you can get lots of work done without too much extra work, and you can even customize the way your application looks and behaves. But if you want it to work a specific way, or if you're developing an application for others who have specific needs, it's time to get into Visual Basic. It's more work to customize an application, but there are unlimited possibilities when you make the effort to program your own solutions in Visual Basic.

In this lesson, you'll start taking control—telling the application how to work, rather than following the rules built into Microsoft Access.

Start the lesson

 Start Microsoft Access and open the 02Contac database in the practice files folder.

Customizing a Command Button

In the first lesson, you created a button using the Command Button Wizard, and the button worked just as planned—it moved to the new record in the Contacts form. But what if you create a button with a wizard, and it doesn't work quite right? Or what if the wizard doesn't offer a button that does what you want? You've probably guessed by now: the answer lies in the Visual Basic code that makes the button work.

In this section, you'll open the Visual Basic event procedure for the Add Record button. After exploring the Visual Basic code in the procedure, you'll write your first line of code, making a small improvement to the code the wizard created.

Open the Contacts form

On the Main Switchboard form, click Enter/View Contacts.

The Contacts form displays the first record in the recordset.

Contacts		
First Name	Hardy	Contact ID	1
Last Name	Griffin	Title	Master Brewer
Company	Ballard Brewery	Work Phone	(206) 555-5317
Dear		Work Extension	
Address	115 Leary Wy.	Mobile Phone	
		Fax Number	
City	Seattle		
State/Province	WA		
Postal Code	98115-		
Country			

Calls... Dial... Page: 1 2 Add Record

Record: 1 of 18

Here is the new button you created with the Command Button Wizard.

Next, you'll take a look at the event procedure that makes the Add Record button work.

Viewing the Visual Basic Code Behind a Command Button

Visual Basic code, such as the code that the Command Button wizard creates, is stored in *modules*. Each form and report in a database has its own attached *form module* or *report module* for storing Visual Basic code—for example, the code that the wizard created for your button is stored in the form module for the Contacts form. Most Visual Basic code you'll write will belong to an individual form or report; however, if you write code that applies to more than one form or report, you can store it in one or more *standard modules*, which are separate objects in the Database window.

Visual Basic code comes in units called *procedures*, each performing a single task—for example, the code that responds to the clicking of the Add Record button is one procedure. A module can contain many procedures, one for each event you want to respond to or task you want to perform.

The following diagram illustrates the relationships among all these objects, and shows where your Visual Basic procedures can live:

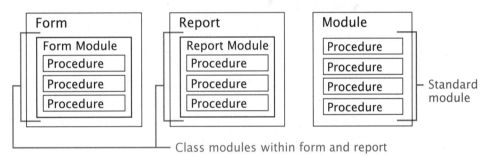

NOTE   When you view form or report modules or read about them in the Microsoft Access documentation, you may see them referred to as *class modules*. You needn't concern yourself with the meaning of this phrase (it's borrowed from object-oriented computer science); just remember that form and report modules are in the larger category of class modules, while standard modules are not. You'll see the term in the title bar of the Module window every time you open a form or report module, as you'll do for the first time in the following steps.

Open the button's Click event procedure

Let's take a look at a procedure—for starters, you can view the event procedure that the Command Button Wizard created for the Add Record button. Because the button belongs to the Contacts form, the wizard stored the procedure in the form module for that form, which you can get to from the form's Design view.

*Design View
button*

1 Click the Design View button.

2 Scroll down in the form to display the form footer.

3 With the right mouse button, click the Add Record button.

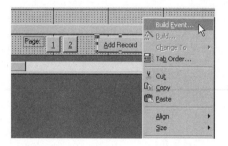

4 Click Build Event.

The Build Event command tells Microsoft Access to open the Visual Basic module for the current form and display the default event procedure for the selected object. For a command button, the default event procedure is the Click event procedure, so the module window shows the AddRecord_Click procedure.

Form module
for the
Contacts form

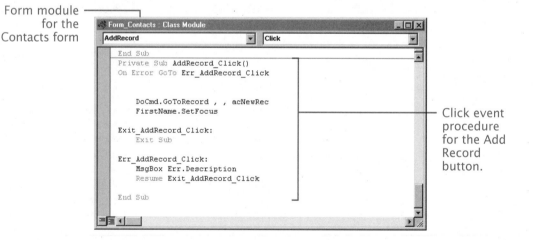

Click event
procedure
for the Add
Record
button.

When you first open the Module window, it includes all procedures in the module: if you scroll up and down in the Module window, you'll see several other Visual Basic procedures that the Database wizard created for the Contacts form. To simplify the display, you can switch from Full Module view to Procedure view so the Module window displays only one procedure at a time.

5 Click the Procedure View button (at the bottom left corner of the Module window).

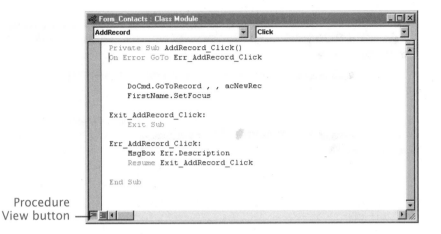

Procedure View button

```
Form_Contacts : Class Module
AddRecord                          Click

    Private Sub AddRecord_Click()
    On Error GoTo Err_AddRecord_Click


        DoCmd.GoToRecord , , acNewRec
        FirstName.SetFocus

    Exit_AddRecord_Click:
        Exit Sub

    Err_AddRecord_Click:
        MsgBox Err.Description
        Resume Exit_AddRecord_Click

    End Sub
```

Now the window displays only one event procedure, the
AddRecord_Click procedure.

The Visual Basic code in this procedure runs automatically each time you
click the Add Record button. The main attraction in the procedure is the following line of Visual Basic code, which tells Microsoft Access to move to the
new record:

```
DoCmd.GoToRecord , , acNewRec
```

How does this code work? Let's take apart this line piece by piece to understand
how it works. Along the way, you'll learn a few important terms.

■ Each word that Microsoft Access recognizes as part of the visual Basic language is called a *keyword*. There's a keyword for every statement, function,
   method, object, and property you use in Microsoft Access.

■ The first keyword in the line is DoCmd (read as "DO-command"), which
   you'll be seeing quite a bit when programming Microsoft Access. DoCmd
   is an *object*—it shares this honorable position with other objects you're
   already familiar with, such as forms, reports, and controls. You use the
   DoCmd object to perform common actions in the Microsoft Access interface, such as opening a form, printing a report, or choosing a menu
   command.

■ The second keyword is GoToRecord, which is a *method* of the DoCmd
   object. Each object that Microsoft Access recognizes has its own set of
   methods that you use with that object. The methods of the DoCmd object
   are all the actions it allows you to perform—in fact, if you've created macros in Microsoft Access, you'll recognize the things you can do with the
   DoCmd object as the macro actions available in the Macro window. The
   GoToRecord method, as its name suggests, tells Microsoft Access to move
   to a specified record in the current recordset.

- To perform a method on an object, such as the DoCmd object, you type the object immediately followed by its method, separating the keywords with a period.

- What follows the GoToRecord method are its *arguments*, which provide any information that's necessary to carry out the method. The arguments for the GoToRecord method, for example, allow you to specify such critical options as which record you want to go to. You specify arguments by typing a space after the method, then typing the argument values separated by commas. If you don't need to specify one or more of the argument values, you can leave them out by simply typing a comma for each—for example, the line above skips the first two arguments, supplying only the third argument.

- Some methods, such as GoToRecord, have specially-defined *constant* values that you can enter as arguments. The argument acNewRec is a constant that tells the GoToRecord method to move to the new record at the end of the recordset (other options include moving to the next record or the first record in the recordset). The constant acNewRec actually stands for the number 5—but the constant name is much easier to remember and makes your code easier to understand.

To sum up, this line of code uses the GoToRecord method of the DoCmd object to move to the specified record—in this case, to the new record.

What Else Did the Wizard Create?

Although the DoCmd line we dissected and discussed is what really does the job in the AddRecord_Click procedure, you may be wondering about the rest of the code the Command Button Wizard created. Here's the complete procedure:

```
Private Sub AddRecord_Click()
On Error GoTo Err_AddRecord_Click

    DoCmd.GoToRecord , , acNewRec

Exit_AddRecord_Click:
    Exit Sub
Err_AddRecord_Click:
    MsgBox Err.Description
    Resume Exit_AddRecord_Click
End Sub
```

The Private Sub and End Sub lines designate the beginning and end of the procedure. You'll see similar lines at the beginning and end of every event procedure—but because Microsoft Access adds them to event procedures automatically, you won't usually have to think about them.

What Else Did the Wizard Create?, *continued*

> The remaining lines in the procedure—other than the DoCmd line—pro-
> vide *error handling* for the procedure. The Command Button Wizard in-
> cludes these error handling lines so that in case an error occurs, your
> application won't come to a halt. In Lesson 7, you'll learn how to add
> your own error handling code to procedures; for now, rest assured that the
> wizard took care of it for you.

Modifying a Command Button Created Using the Wizard

The Command Button Wizard is a great tool for customizing your applications,
but it isn't perfect. Although it creates buttons for a variety of tasks, it can't anticipate everything you'll want your buttons to do. Fortunately, if the wizard
doesn't get it quite right, you can modify the buttons it creates to suit your
application's needs. That's just what you'll do with the Add Record button in
this section.

There's nothing really *wrong* with the Add Record button—when you click it,
you jump to the new record in the recordset—but it could use some polishing.
To get it just right, you'll first change a property and then add a line of Visual
Basic code to the button's event procedure.

Add an accelerator key for the command button

The Add Record button is missing a handy feature that the other buttons on the
Contacts form already possess. The other buttons have *accelerator keys*—underlined characters that let you "press" the buttons using the keyboard. Because
many users like to have the option of using the keyboard instead of the mouse,
it's always wise to make your applications work as well with the keyboard as
with the mouse. For the Add Record button, you'll make the "A" into an accelerator key.

To provide an accelerator key for a button, all you have to do is edit the Caption property of the button—which determines the actual text shown on the
button—to include the ampersand (&) symbol. This symbol in a button's caption tells Microsoft Access that the next character in the caption is the accelerator key for the button.

1   On the Window menu, click Contacts : Form.

    The Contacts form, still in Design view, comes to the front. Note that you
    don't have to close the form module in the Module window to continue
    working on the form itself.

2 With the right mouse button, click the Add Record button, and then click Properties on the shortcut menu.

Microsoft Access displays the property sheet for the Add Record button.

3 Click the All tab in the property sheet.

4 In the Caption property box, click the left edge of the Add Record text (before the "A"), and then type &.

Adding the ampersand (&) symbol tells the wizard to make the "A" in Add Record the accelerator key for the button. This way, the user can press ALT+A to achieve the same effect as clicking the Add Record button. The button won't actually show the ampersand, but the "A" will appear underlined on the button.

5 Close the property sheet.

Use the accelerator key to press the command button

1 Click the Form View button on the toolbar.

2 Press ALT+A.

Microsoft Access moves to the new record in the Contacts table just as if you'd clicked the button using the mouse.

Form View button

Add a line to your event procedure to change the focus

The Add Record button needs one other modification. Notice that after you press the button, the *focus* is still on the Add Record button—there's no current field or insertion point for typing data. In order to begin entering data, the user must first click the First Name field on the form. Ideally, you'd like the focus to move automatically to the first field in the record. To make it do this, you'll write a single line of Visual Basic code.

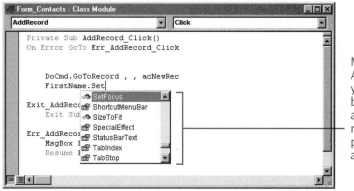

After you click the Add Record button... ...you want the focus to be on the first field so the user can begin entering data.

1 On the Window menu, click Form_Contacts : Class Module.

   The form's module comes back to the front, still displaying the AddRecord_Click event procedure.

2 Click the blank line underneath the DoCmd line in the event procedure, press TAB, and then type **FirstName**.

   FirstName is the name of a control object on your form. (Be sure not to insert a space into the name FirstName—the underlying control name doesn't contain a space.) Next, you'll specify a method that you want to use with the FirstName object: the SetFocus method. As you saw earlier in the lesson, you separate a method from its object with a period.

3 Type a period, and then type **Set**.

   When you type a period after an object name, Microsoft Access assumes that you want to follow the period with a method or property of that object. To help you enter a valid method or property, it displays a list underneath the line you're typing. As you continue typing, the list automatically scrolls down to display entries that begin with the characters you type.

Microsoft Access helps you enter code by displaying an object's methods and properties in a list.

Typing Set was enough to move to the SetFocus method in the list. Although you could continue typing code or double-click any method or property in the list, pressing SPACEBAR is the easiest way to enter the selected item in the list.

4 Press SPACEBAR, and then press ENTER.

Now the line of Visual Basic code is complete:

```
FirstName.SetFocus
```

This line tells Microsoft Access to set the focus to the specified form or control object—in this case, the FirstName control.

Here's the procedure with the new line of code:

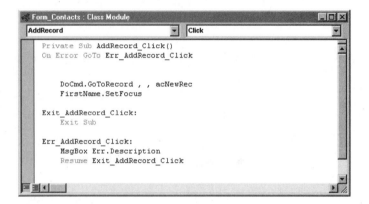

Test the command button

1 Close the Module window.

2 Click the Add Record button.

Microsoft Access moves to the new record in the Contacts table. This time, however, you'll notice that the insertion point is flashing in the FirstName field, ready for the user to enter data.

As you continue to polish your application, you'll want to use the SetFocus method whenever you can anticipate what users will want to do next. Moving to a form or control with SetFocus is a great way to save extra clicks—which makes your application easier to use.

Save your changes to the Add Record button

Now that you've finished modifying the button, save your changes.

Save
button

➤ Click the Save button on the toolbar.

Microsoft Access saves your changes to the form and its form module.

Editing a Form's Module While in Form View

You may have noticed that you were able to make your addition to the Click event procedure while the Contacts form was in Form view—in a sense, you changed the underlying design of the form without switching to Design view. This is a unique feature of Visual Basic as compared to many programming languages: you can edit a code module "on the fly" while the code in the module is potentially being used by the form. You'll soon discover how useful this can be, because you won't usually have to restart a complex application in order to make minor changes.

As you'll learn in later lessons, you can even edit code in a Visual Basic procedure while it's running. In cases where you make a significant change, Microsoft Access may need to reset your code and start over. For now, however, you can appreciate the fact that you don't have to constantly switch between Form and Design views to examine and edit code.

Making a Form Read-Only by Default

If you type in any of the fields in the Contacts form, you begin editing the recordset. This is one of the great advantages of Microsoft Access over many other database systems: data is almost always available for both viewing and updating. However, business users are commonly worried about "messing up" the information in a database—their data is important, and they don't want it to be too easy to make changes to data.

In this section, you'll modify the Contacts form to provide a solution to this common data-entry request. The idea is to make the default mode for a form *read-only*, so users can't make changes unless they specifically ask to. This way, users can open the form and look at contact information without worrying about accidentally making a change.

The first step is easy: to make a form read-only, you simply set the AllowEdits property for the form to No. But you also need a way for users to tell you when they *do* want to make changes. What you want is an additional two buttons on your form: one for indicating that they want to edit data, one for saving the record they've edited. For one of these buttons, you won't use the Command

Button Wizard at all—instead, you'll create the button on your own, and then write a custom Visual Basic event procedure to make the button work.

You'll make the form read-only by default...

...and then provide buttons that users can click to begin and finish editing a record.

Make existing records in the Contacts form read-only

Design View button

1   Click the Design View button on the toolbar.

2   Double-click the form selection box at the upper left corner of the form window (at the intersection of the rulers).

Double-click here to select the form and display its properties.

Microsoft Access displays the form's properties in the property sheet.

3   Click the AllowEdits property, and then set the property to No.

The AllowEdits property controls whether you can change existing records in the form.

34

That's all it takes to solve the problem of accidentally editing data; now when you open the form to an existing record, you won't be able to change data. Note that we're leaving the other two "Allow" properties—AllowDeletions and AllowAdditions—set to Yes, so users can still delete or add records. Accidental deletions shouldn't be a problem, because Microsoft Access warns users automatically before deleting records.

4   Close the property sheet.

5   Click the Form View button on the toolbar.

Form View button

6   Try to type a few letters in the First Name field.

Nothing happens, because the record is read-only—so the existing data is safe.

Creating a Command Button Without a Wizard

Now that the form is read-only, you need a command button that sets the AllowEdits property back to Yes. But the Command Button Wizard doesn't offer a button that changes the value of a property. It's time to up the ante and push beyond where the wizard goes!

First, you'll create the button and set its properties. Then, you'll use the Build Event command to create your own event procedure for the button's Click event.

Create the Edit Record command button

You want to place the Edit Record button in the form footer along with the existing buttons.

Design View button

1   Click the Design View button on the toolbar.

2   Scroll down in the form to display the form footer.

3   If the toolbox isn't displayed, click the Toolbox button on the toolbar.

Toolbox button

4   In the toolbox, click the Control Wizards tool to deselect it, and then click the Command Button tool.

Deselecting the Control Wizard tool tells Microsoft Access that you don't want to use a wizard to create this control—you'll set its properties on your own.

Control Wizards tool

5   In the form footer, click just to the right of the Add Record button.

Command button tool

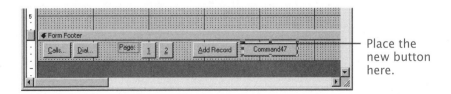

Place the new button here.

Without the Control Wizards tool selected, the button appears immediately, but with a default name (such as Command47) and no associated event procedure.

Properties button

6 Click the Properties button on the toolbar.

7 In the Name property box, type **EditRecord**.

8 Press ENTER, and then in the Caption property box type **&Edit Record**.

Command Button: EditRecord	
Format	Data	Event	Other	**All**
Name	EditRecord
Caption	&Edit Record
Picture	(none)
Picture Type	Embedded
Transparent	No
Default	No
Cancel	No
Auto Repeat	No
Status Bar Text	
Hyperlink Address . . .	
Hyperlink SubAddress	
Visible	Yes
Display When	Always

The ampersand (&) character in the button's caption tells Microsoft Access to make the "E" in Edit Record the accelerator key for the command button.

> **NOTE** Be sure to include a space in the button's caption, but *not* in the underlying control name. None of the fields or controls on the Contacts form contain spaces in their names, because spaces make fields and controls more difficult to work with (every time you type the name, you have to enclose it in brackets).

9 Close the property sheet.

Create the button's Click event procedure

As it stands, the new button won't *do* anything when you click it. You need to write a Visual Basic event procedure to make it work.

1 With the right mouse button, click the Edit Record button, and then click Build Event on the shortcut menu.

Microsoft Access displays the Choose Builder dialog box. (If you wanted to create an expression or a macro rather than Visual Basic code, you could choose Expression Builder or Macro Builder.)

2 Select Code Builder, and then click OK.

Microsoft Access opens the form module for the Contacts form and creates an event procedure for the button's Click event.

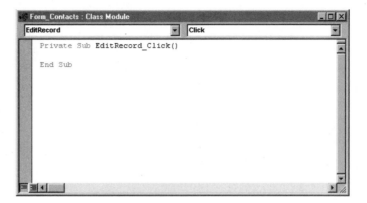

The procedure that Microsoft Access creates is called EditRecord_Click. The name of an event procedure has two parts, separated by an under-score character: the name of an object, and the name of the event that the procedure responds to. You can think of the name EditRecord_Click as meaning "the code that runs when you click the EditRecord control."

3 Press ENTER, press TAB, and then type the following line of Visual Basic code:

```
Me.AllowEdits = True
```

NOTE As you enter this line, you'll notice that Microsoft Access again helps you out by displaying a list of options under the code you're typing—first when you type the period, and again when you type the equal sign. In this case, just continue typing the entire command.

The equal sign (=) in Visual Basic code means "assign the value of the expression on the right to the thing identified on the left." The thing on the left here is the expression *Me.AllowEdits* which refers to the AllowEdits property of the form—to refer to a property of the current form in the form's module, you use the Me keyword, followed by a period, followed by the property name. This code tells Microsoft Access to assign True to the expression on the left. It's as if the form is telling Microsoft Access, "Set my AllowEdits property to True."

Setting a property to True in Visual Basic code is the same as setting the property to Yes in the form's property sheet. (To set a property to No in code, you assign it the value False.)

4 Press ENTER, and then type the following line so that the focus will move back to the first control on the form—just as in the Add Record event procedure:

```
FirstName.SetFocus
```

Your event procedure should look like this:

```
Form_Contacts : Class Module                    _ □ ✕
EditRecord                    ▼   Click                         ▼
    Private Sub EditRecord_Click()

        Me.AllowEdits = True
        FirstName.SetFocus

    End Sub
```

Try the Edit Record button

1 On the Window menu, click Contacts : Form.

The form window, still in Design view, comes to the front.

2 Click the Form View button.

3 Click the Dear field, and try to type in it.

You can't type anything—the record is still read-only.

*Form View
button*

4 Click the Edit Record button you just created.

Although it happened so fast you couldn't have seen it, Microsoft Access ran your event procedure when you clicked the button. The AllowEdits property should now be set to Yes. Also, you'll notice that the focus is on the First Name field as you specified using the SetFocus method in the event procedure. But you want to edit the Dear field to add this contact's nickname to the record.

5 Click the Dear field, and then type **Red**.

You can now edit data, which means that the button's event procedure successfully changed the AllowEdits property to True.

NOTE If you typed anything incorrectly when creating your event procedure, clicking the button will most likely cause an error message to appear. If this happens, don't worry—Microsoft Access brings up the Module window so you can check the code you entered against the one shown above. After making corrections to the procedure, click the Continue button on the toolbar.

Add comments to your event procedure

When you first take a look at any given Visual Basic procedure—even if you wrote it yourself—it's really tough to figure out what the procedure does and why it's there. To help make your applications easier to understand, it's extremely important to include *comments* embedded in your code. Comments are like notes to yourself, helping to explain what you were thinking of when you wrote the code.

To add a comment to the code in the Module window, simply precede the text of your comment with an apostrophe (').

1   On the Window menu, click Form_Contacts : Class Module.

    This brings the event procedure back up.

2   Click the blank line underneath the Sub statement in the procedure, and then type the following line:

    ` ' Make the Contacts form editable.`

    Now when you look at this event procedure later on, you won't need to figure out what it does or why you wrote it. You'll notice that Microsoft Access displays the comment text in green.

3   Press ENTER.

4   Click the far right side of the line that includes the SetFocus method, press TAB twice, and then type the following text:

    ` ' Move to the FirstName field.`

    As you can see, a comment can either begin on a new line or explain the line of code to the left. A comment on a line by itself often gives information about several lines of code or a whole procedure, while a comment to the right of a line of code generally explains what that one line does.

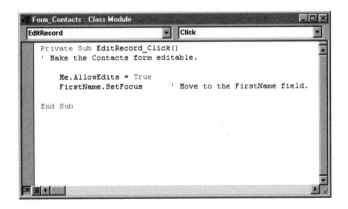

5   Close the Module window.

Create a command button to save the current record

With the two buttons you've created, users can either add new records or edit existing ones. But there's one more button you need to add.

When entering or editing data about a contact, you can save data by either moving to a new record or closing the form. Or, you can use the Save Record command (on the File menu) to explicitly save the current record. But you want to make this command more accessible to users, so they won't have to find it on the menu. Because the Command Button Wizard creates such a button, you may as well use it.

Design View button

Control Wizards tool

Command Button tool

1 Click the Design View button on the toolbar.

2 Scroll down in the form to display the form footer.

3 In the toolbox, click the Control Wizards tool to select it, and then click the Command Button tool.

4 In the form footer, click just to the right of the Edit Record button.

Form Footer							
Calls...	Dial...	Page:	1	2	Add Record	Edit Record	

Click here to create the new button.

The Command Button Wizard starts, asking what actions you want the new button to perform.

5 In the Categories list, select Record Operations.

6 In the Actions list, select Save Record, and then click Next.

The wizard asks whether you want a picture or text on your button.

7 Select the Text option.

8 In the Text box, click the left edge of the Save Record text, and then type &.

Adding the ampersand (&) symbol tells the wizard to make the "S" in Save Record the accelerator key for the button.

9 Click Next.

10 Type **SaveRecord** as the button name, and then click Finish.

The wizard finishes creating the button and its event procedure and places it on your form.

11 If necessary, resize and align the buttons in the footer so that they're uniform. (When you create buttons by different methods, it's easy for them to end up with different shapes or sizes.)

> **TIP** When you make final adjustments to controls on a form
> or report, you may find it difficult to line them up just right and
> make them all the same size. To align or size a group of con-
> trols easily, select the controls and then choose one of several
> Size or Align commands from the Format menu.

12 Click the Save button on the toolbar.

Save button

Microsoft Access saves both the form and its module.

Creating Event Procedures for Form Events

Up to this point, you've worked only with procedures for the Click event—
code that runs when you click a button. But there are many other events you
can respond to. In this section, you'll work with event procedures for two
form events.

When a user clicks the Edit Record button you created, your code makes the
form editable. When the user moves to another record or saves the current
record, you need to return the form to its read-only state, so that records
won't be vulnerable to accidental changes until the Edit Record button is
clicked again.

Much of the trick in programming with Microsoft Access is figuring out which
event to attach code to. You could have added code to the Save Record button
that would set the form's AllowEdits property back to False. But there are other
ways the user could save an edited record—using a menu command, for example—and your application needs to anticipate all these possibilities. Additionally, the user could move to another record without saving the record at all,
in which case you also want to return the AllowEdits property to False.

The two cases you need to catch are:

■ Whenever the user moves to another existing record

■ Whenever the user saves the current record using any method

For the first case, you'll add a line of code to the event procedure for the form's
Current event, which occurs whenever Microsoft Access displays an existing
record in a form procedure. (The Database Wizard already created this event
procedure.) For the second case, you'll create your own event procedure for the
form's *AfterUpdate* event, which occurs whenever a record is saved in a form.
Between the two, you'll be sure to return the form to its read-only state at the
appropriate times.

41

Edit the procedure for the form's Current event

Earlier in this lesson you used the Build Event command on the shortcut menu to create or open the Click event procedure for a button. But the Build Event command always opens the *default event* for the object you choose. Because the Current event isn't the default event for a form, you'll have to use a more general method to open the event procedure—you'll create the procedure by setting an event property in the property sheet.

1   Double-click the form selection box at the upper left corner of the form window (at the intersection of the rulers).

    Microsoft Access displays the form's properties in the property sheet.

2   Click the Event tab in the property sheet.

3   Click the OnCurrent property, and then click the Build button to the right of the property box.

— Build button

4   Select Code Builder, and then click OK.

    Microsoft Access creates the Form_Current event procedure and displays it in the Module window.

5   Press ENTER, and then type the following line of Visual Basic code:

```
Me.AllowEdits = False    ' Return the form to its read-only state.
```

By setting the form's AllowEdits property to False, this line of code returns the form to its read-only state each time you move to an existing record in the form.

6   Press ENTER.

Copy the procedure to the form's AfterUpdate event

You need the same code to run when the AfterUpdate event occurs, but the AfterUpdate event doesn't yet have any event procedure. Rather than retype the Form_Current code in the Module window, you can just copy the code from one procedure to another.

1   In the Module window, select the line of code you added (click to the left of the line of code—but to the right of the gray margin—so that the whole line is highlighted).

2   On the Edit menu, click Copy.

3   On the Window menu, click Contacts : Form.

4   Click the AfterUpdate property, and then click the Build button to the right of the property box.

5   Select Code Builder, and then click OK.

Microsoft Access creates the Form_ AfterUpdate event procedure and displays it in the Module window.

6   Press ENTER.

7   On the Edit menu, click Paste.

Displaying a Message to the User

It's important to communicate with users of your application. One way to do this is by using a message box. Using the MsgBox statement, you can give some feedback in response to events in your application.

The same users who worry about accidentally changing data are equally concerned that their changes get registered when they finish editing a record. For these users, you can display a message in response to the AfterUpdate event, confirming that the record was saved.

Add code that displays a message box

1   Press TAB, type **MsgBox**, and then press SPACEBAR.

A box appears underneath the line you're typing, displaying the names of the arguments available with MsgBox. This is another way that

43

Microsoft Access helps you as you enter code in the Module window—just when you need to know the syntax for a Visual Basic statement or function, there it is.

Syntax information for the MsgBox statement

2 Type "**Record Saved.**" and then press ENTER.

This completes the MsgBox line, passing as an argument the message that you want to display to the user. Because it's a string argument, you enclose the message in quotation marks. (In Visual Basic, any text data or combination of text and numbers is referred to as a *string*.)

Here's the complete code for the AfterUpdate event procedure.

3 Close the Module window.

4 Close the property sheet.

> **TIP** If the syntax that pops up for a function or statement doesn't provide enough information, you can always turn to online Help. To display a Help topic with complete information about any Visual Basic keyword in the Module window, just click the keyword and then press the F1 key.

Save your changes to the Contacts form

Now that you've finished adding all the buttons to the form and editing their event procedures, save your changes to the form.

*Save
button*

➤ Click the Save button on the toolbar.

Microsoft Access saves your changes to the form and its form module.

Try the buttons with your changes

Let's make sure the Edit Record and Save Record buttons work together as you intended. Suppose you found out the mobile phone number of the first contact, and want to enter it in the Contacts form.

*Form View
button*

1 Click the Form View button on the toolbar.

2 Click the Edit Record button.

3 Click the Mobile Phone field, and then type **206 555 2365**.

When you change data in a record and haven't yet saved the new information, the record selector (at the left side of the form) displays a pencil icon.

The pencil icon indicates that your changes haven't been saved.

First Name	Hardy
Last Name	Griffin
Company	Ballard Brewery
Dear	
Address	115 Leary Wy.
City	Seattle
State/Province	WA
Postal Code	98115-
Country	

Contact ID	1
Title	Master Brewer
Work Phone	(206) 555-5317
Work Extension	
Mobile Phone	(206) 555-2365
Fax Number	

Contacts

Calls... | Dial... | Page: 1 2 | Add Record | Edit Record | Save Record

Record: 1 of 18

4 Click the Save Record button.

Microsoft Access saves the record in the Contacts table and changes the pencil back to the current record indicator. Having saved the record, it fires the form's AfterUpdate event, which in turn runs your event procedure and displays your message.

5 Click OK.

6 Click the First Name field, and then try to type a few letters.

Because the form's AfterUpdate event procedure set the AllowEdits property back to False, you can't edit data any longer. Everything's working as planned!

7 Close the Contacts form.

Close the application and exit Microsoft Access

1 On the Switchboard form, click Exit This Database.

2 On the File menu, click Exit.

Lesson Summary

To	Do this
Open or create the default event procedure for a control	In Design view, with the right mouse button click the control, and then click Build Event.
Open or create any event procedure for a control	In the property sheet for the control, click the event property for the event, and then click the Build button.
Add an accelerator key for a command button	In the button's Caption property setting, precede the accelerator key with an ampersand (&).
Use a method of an object in code	Type the name of the object followed immediately by a period (.) and the name of the method.
Set a property in code	Type the name of the property followed by the equal sign (=) and then the value you want to assign to the property.
Add a comment to a procedure	Type an apostrophe followed by your comment text.

To	Do this
Let Microsoft Access enter a Visual Basic keyword for you	When a list of property names, method names, or values appears under the line you're typing, double-click the item you want. Or, type enough letters to move to the item you want, and then press SPACEBAR.

For online information about	On the Help menu, click Contents and Index, click the Index tab, and then
Editing code in modules	Search for "modules"
Setting form and control properties	Search for "setting properties"
Using methods in Visual Basic	Search for "methods"
Assigning values in Visual Basic	Search for "setting control values"

For more information on	In *Building Applications with Microsoft Access 97*, see
Editing code in modules	Chapter 2, "Introducing Visual Basic"
Setting form and control properties	Chapter 3, "Using Forms to Collect, Filter, and Display Information"
Using methods in Visual Basic	Chapter 5, "Working with Objects and Collections"
Assigning values in Visual Basic	Chapter 3, "Using Forms to Collect, Filter, and Display Information"

Preview of the Next Lesson

Now that you've learned to create and edit simple event procedures, you're ready to discover other ways to customize forms using Visual Basic. In the next lesson, you'll explore ways to help users find and filter data. You'll start with simple code like the code you saw in this lesson, but you'll also write some longer procedures—and learn new elements of Visual Basic along the way.

Find and Filter Records in a Form

Estimated time
45 min.

In this lesson you will learn how to:

- Create a combo box that moves to a specific record in a form.
- Filter data to show a subset of records.
- Use the Debug window to view and change properties.
- Respond to filtering events.
- Create an option group.

In the 19th century, scientists discovered the laws of thermodynamics, which govern all physical systems in nature. The second law, they said, is that every system tends toward entropy: everything is becoming more and more disorderly. Sound familiar? These scientists didn't intend the law to apply directly to our daily lives, but nonetheless, the premise seems to hold true. The more information we have, the more difficult it is to find what we want—and the more important it is that we locate the details we need quickly.

"Where did I put that phone number? I know it's in here somewhere...." How many times have you filed some important information away, only to spend precious time looking for it later? And while this routine is especially commonplace in the world of the "paper" office, it isn't altogether solved when you put information in your computer—you can still spend plenty of time wading through files and records trying to find what you need.

The key to a useful database is being able to find information quickly. As an application developer, you need to consider what information users will need, and help them get to it as quickly as possible. In the first two lessons, we concentrated on getting data into the database; in this lesson, we'll work on getting it back out.

Start the lesson

Start Microsoft Access and open the 03Contac database in the practice files folder.

Creating a Combo Box to Find Records

Perhaps the most common task you'll perform in any database application is to look up an existing record. In the Contacts database, when you need someone's phone number or address, you want to jump to the person's record quickly. The standard way users can find a specific record in a form is by using the Find command. To locate a record by last name, for example, first click the Last Name field, then click the Find button, and then type the name you're looking for and click OK. Not only does this method require several actions for a common task, it assumes that you know the exact last name and can spell it correctly.

There are better methods you can provide for finding records in your applications. One way is to create a combo box on the form where users can select a contact name from a list. This type of combo box requires setting quite a few properties, as well as writing a macro or event procedure that moves to the record. Fortunately, the Combo Box Wizard can do most of this for you—you need only put on the final touches to make it work just right.

You'll create a combo box where users can select a contact's name from a list.

Open the Contacts form and switch to Design view

1 On the Main Switchboard form, click Enter/View Contacts.

2 Click the Design View button on the toolbar.

Design View button

Create a combo box that finds records

To create the Find Record combo box, you'll use the Combo Box Wizard.

*Control
Wizards tool*

*Combo
Box tool*

1 In the toolbox, make sure the Control Wizards tool is selected, and then click the Combo Box tool.

2 Click the top of the form above the left side of the Title field.

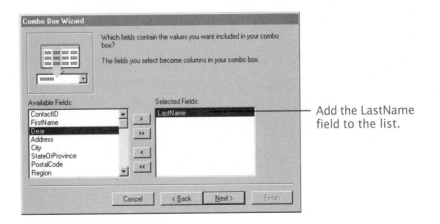

Click here to create the combo box.

The Combo Box Wizard starts, asking how you want the combo box to get the values it will display in the list.

3 Select the third option, Find A Record On My Form Based On The Value I Selected In My Combo Box, and then click Next.

The wizard asks which fields you want to include in the combo box.

4 Double-click the LastName field to add it to the Selected Fields list.

Add the LastName field to the list.

5 Click Next.

The wizard displays the list of last names.

51

6   Drag the right side of the field selector in the LastName column to make it about half again as wide, and then click Next.

The wizard asks what label you want for your combo box.

7   Type **&Find Record:** and then click Finish.

The wizard creates the combo box and places it on your form. Behind the scenes, the wizard has set properties and added a Visual Basic event procedure so that the combo box can find records in the form.

Change the appearance of the combo box

Before you try out the combo box, you'll want to modify its appearance just a bit. For starters, the size of the label control isn't big enough to fit the text. Additionally, because this is a special control on the form—it's a helpful tool, but users don't have to enter any data in it—you'll want it to stand out in appearance.

Bold button

1   Click the label to the left of the control, and then click the Bold button on the toolbar.

2   Move the mouse pointer to the right edge of the label until you see the sizing cursor, and then double-click.

The label changes to the correct size for the text.

3   Click the combo box itself, and then drag the right edge of the combo box to make it the same width as the controls below it.

Fill/Back Color button

4   On the toolbar, click the arrow next to the Fill/Back Color button, and then click the light gray box.

Try out the combo box

Now the Find Record combo box is ready to use.

Form View button

1   Click the Form View button on the toolbar.

2   Click the arrow next to the Find Record combo box.

Microsoft Access displays the list of contacts' last names in the list.

[Screenshot of the Contacts form showing fields: Contact ID 1, First Name Hardy, Last Name Griffin, Company Ballard Brewery, Dear (blank), Address 115 Leary Wy., City Seattle, State/Province WA, with a Find Record combo box listing Griffin, O'Halloran, Stepanian, Hunting, Christensen, O'Keefe, Geloff, MacDougall, and fields Title, Work Phone, Work Extension, Mobile Phone, Fax Number]

3   Click O'Keefe.

Microsoft Access moves to the record for Maura O'Keefe in the Contacts form.

Modify the combo box list

The Find Record combo box works as planned, but the list it displays isn't quite right. First of all, the list isn't alphabetized. Secondly, the list includes only last names. Ideally, you'd like it to display "last name comma first name"—such as Geloff, Kevin—so you can more easily find the record you want.

*Design
View button*

1   Click the Design View button on the toolbar.

2   With the right mouse button, click the Find Record combo box, and then click Properties on the shortcut menu.

Microsoft Access displays the property sheet for the combo box.

3   Click the All tab in the property sheet.

4   Click the RowSource property, and then click the Build button to the right of the property box.

[Screenshot of the Combo Box: Combo47 property sheet, All tab selected, showing: Name Combo47, Control Source (blank), Format (blank), Decimal Places Auto, Input Mask (blank), Row Source Type Table/Query, Row Source SELECT DISTINCTROW [Con..., Column Count 2, Column Heads No, Column Widths 0";1.4896", Bound Column 1, List Rows 8, List Width 1.4896"]

Click the Build
button to display
the Query Builder.

Microsoft Access displays the Query Builder window. In the window is the query that provides values for the combo box drop-down list.

You want to modify this query so it displays last names combined with first names.

5 In the Query By Example (QBE) grid in the lower part of the window, click the box displaying the LastName field, and change the text to the following expression: **LastName & ", " & FirstName** (inside the quotes, be sure to include a space after the comma).

This expression combines three string values with the ampersand (&) operator. When you want to put more than one string of text together in expressions or in Visual Basic code, you separate them with an ampersand. This is known as *concatenating* the strings. In this case, the expression concatenates each contact's last name and first name, separated by a comma and a space.

Note that when you click outside the expression, Microsoft Access automatically adds a label *(Expr1:)* for the expression and encloses the field names in brackets. If you want to see the whole expression, you can make the column wider by dragging the right edge of its column selector to the right.

6 Click the Sort box underneath the expression you just entered, click the drop-down arrow, and then click Ascending.

```
SQL Statement : Query Builder
  Contacts
  *
  ContactID
  FirstName
  LastName
  Dear

  Field:    ContactID        Expr1: [LastName] & ", " & [FirstName]
  Table:    Contacts
  Sort:                      Ascending
  Show:        ☑                    ☑                         ☐
  Criteria:
  or:
```

7 Close the Query Builder window, clicking Yes when Microsoft Access asks if you want to save changes to the query.

Try out the new list

Now the Find Record combo box should display complete names in alphabetical order.

Form View button

1 Click the Form View button on the toolbar.

2 Click the arrow next to the Find Record combo box.

Sure enough, Microsoft Access displays the list of names in order, last names followed by first names.

3 Click Geloff, Kevin (you may need to scroll up in the list).

Add code to keep the combo box synchronized

There's one last idiosyncrasy with the Find Record combo box: although it finds records well enough, it doesn't always display the name of the current contact. If you change records with some other method than using the combo box, the combo box doesn't stay synchronized—it continues to show the name you last selected there. Because this could be misleading, you'll add a line of code to the form's module to fix the problem.

1 Click the Next Record button at the bottom of the form window.

As you can see, while the form changes to the next record, the Find Record combo box doesn't update to display the current name—it still shows Geloff, Kevin.

When you move among records, the Find Record combo box doesn't stay synchronized.

Contacts	
Contact ID	8
First Name	Rob
Last Name	MacDougall
Company	
Dear	
Address	4550 W. Jefferson Blvd.
City	Los Angeles
State/Province	CA
Postal Code	90016-
Country	

Find Record: Geloff, Kevin

Title
Work Phone   (213) 555-8221
Work Extension
Mobile Phone
Fax Number

Calls...   Dial...   Page: 1   2

Record: 8 of 18

This happens because this combo box, unlike all other controls on the form, is an *unbound* control. Unbound controls can be very useful in an application, because users can change them without changing any data, and the application can respond accordingly. The flip side, however, is that if you want an unbound control to display data, you have to set its value in code yourself.

Design View button

2 Click the Design View button on the toolbar.

The Find Record combo box should still be selected, its properties shown in the property sheet. Note the name of the combo box in the title bar of the property sheet—something like Combo47—which is a default name given to the control when the wizard creates it. You'll need to know this name for the code you'll write.

3 Click the form selection box at the upper left corner of the form window (you may need to move or close the toolbox).

4 Click the Event tab in the property sheet.

5 Click the OnCurrent property, and then click the Build button to the right of the property box.

Form	
Format	Data	Event	Other	All
On Current	
Before Insert	
After Insert	
Before Update	
After Update	
On Delete	
Before Del Confirm . .	
After Del Confirm . . .	
On Open	
On Load	
On Resize	
On Unload	
On Close	

Click the Build button to display the Code Builder.

56

6   Select Code Builder, and then click OK.

Microsoft Access opens the form module for the Contacts form and automatically inserts the Form_Current event procedure. The module opens in Full Module view, so other procedures are displayed in the window before and after the Form_Current procedure.

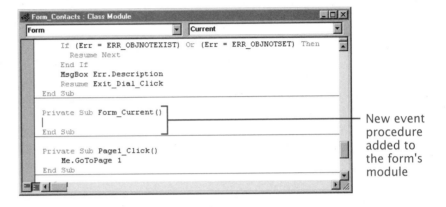

New event
procedure
added to
the form's
module

7   Press TAB, and then add the following line of Visual Basic code to the procedure (substituting the actual number of the combo box on your own form):

```
Combo47 = ContactID    ' Update the Find Record combo box.
```

This code sets the value of the combo box control to the value of the ContactID control. This way, each time you move to a new contact, the combo box will change along with the rest of the form. As when you set a property, all you do to set the value of a control is type the control name followed by the equal sign and the value you want to set it to.

8   On the Window menu, click Contacts : Form.

9   Click the Form View button on the toolbar.

*Form
View button*

10   Click the arrow next to the Find Record combo box, and then click Geloff, Kevin.

11   Click the Next Record button at the bottom of the form window.

While the form changes to the record for Rob MacDougall, the Form_Current event procedure runs, and your code synchronizes the Find Record combo box: it displays MacDougall, Rob.

57

Save your changes to the Contacts form

It took a bit of work, but now the Contacts form has a highly visible, easy-to-use tool for jumping to a contact's record. Now save your changes to the form.

Save button

Click the Save button on the toolbar.

Microsoft Access saves all changes to the form and its form module.

Filtering Data

The combo box you created jumps to an individual record in the recordset. However, all the rest of the records are still available—you can move to other records by clicking the record navigation buttons at the bottom of the form window. But when you're trying to locate certain contacts, you may not want all the records to be available. For example, suppose your company is located in New York City, and you want to place calls to local customers. To browse through contacts located in New York City, excluding all contacts in other cities, you use a *filter*.

Apply Filter button

You can think of a filter as a funnel for data that lets through the specific records you ask for, but keeps all the rest out of view. In fact, the filter icon in Microsoft Access is a funnel—you can see it on the Apply Filter button on the toolbar.

There are three Microsoft Access filtering commands available to the user:

Filter By Selection limits data to records that have the currently selected value. For example, if you're viewing a contact in New York, you can click the City field and then the Filter By Selection button, and contacts from all other cities will be filtered out of the recordset.

Filter By Form displays a blank version of the current form, where you can select from existing field values and then apply the filter to view records that match the selected criteria. For example, you can click the Filter By Form button, select New York in the list of City values, and then click the Apply Filter button to show only contacts in New York. Using Filter By Form, you can specify criteria for more than one field at a time.

Advanced Filter/Sort displays a query window, where you can drag fields to the QBE grid and specify criteria for sorting. This type of filter is the most flexible, but requires an understanding of the Microsoft Access query window.

Unless you disable them, these standard filtering commands are available to users. Even if your application doesn't do any filtering of its own, users can choose these commands to browse through a subset of data in a table or form.

Filter records in the Contacts form using Filter By Form

Suppose you want to view contacts in New York City.

**Filter By
Form button**

1 Click the Filter By Form button on the toolbar.

The form changes to display the Filter By Form view, where users can specify criteria for the records they want to see.

2 Click the City field, and then click the down-arrow next to the text box.

Microsoft Access displays all the cities where contacts are located.

3 Click New York.

**Apply Filter
button**

4 Click the Apply Filter button.

The form displays only contacts in New York City. Note that the text at the bottom of the form window indicates that the recordset in the form is filtered.

Only contacts
in New York
City are
shown.

Responding to Filtering Events

Although the filtering interface in Microsoft Access is very flexible, there's always room for improvement. If you want to control or customize filtering in your application, you can write Visual Basic event procedures that respond to one of two filtering events. The first of these events is the Filter event, which is triggered whenever a user chooses the Filter By Form or Advanced Filter/Sort command. You can respond to the Filter event to customize these commands.

The other filtering event is the ApplyFilter event, which occurs when the user finishes specifying a filter and clicks the Apply Filter button, or when the user clicks the Filter By Selection button, which applies a filter immediately. This event also occurs when the user removes a filter—basically, whenever the set of records displayed is about to be changed. You can respond to the ApplyFilter event to change filtering behavior when the user chooses these buttons or commands.

To start, you'll provide a simple customization of the Filter By Form command by responding to the Filter event with an event procedure.

Display a message when the user filters

For beginning users, the Filter By Form interface can be confusing—when a user clicks this button, the form changes slightly in appearance and goes blank, and a user might not know what to do next. It would be helpful to display a simple message, providing the user with a hint explaining what to do.

1 On the Window menu, click Form_Contacts : Class Module.

Microsoft Access brings the Contacts form's module back to the front, still showing the Form_Current event procedure. Because you're already viewing an event procedure for the form, the easiest way to create the procedure is by using the Module window's Procedure box, which lists all the procedures and events for a given object and allows you to switch between procedures.

2 In the Procedure box at the top of the Module window, select Filter from the list of events.

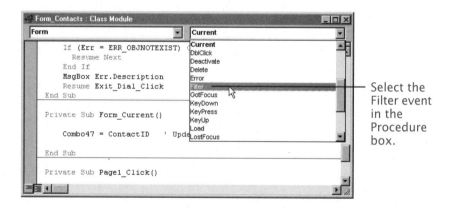

Select the Filter event in the Procedure box.

Microsoft Access creates the Form_Filter procedure for you—you don't have to go back to the property sheet. Behind the scenes, Microsoft Access also automatically attaches the procedure to the control's Filter event. It does this by setting the control's OnFilter property (the one that corresponds to the Filter event) to [Event Procedure].

3 Enter the following Visual Basic code for the procedure:

```
' Display instructions for Filter by Form.

    MsgBox "Select field values and click Apply Filter button."
```

This code displays the message whenever the user chooses a filtering command.

Using the If...Then Statement to Check a Condition

There's just one problem with the Filter event procedure: there's more than one filtering command that can trigger the Filter event. Because your message is applicable only if the user chose the Filter By Form command, you want your code to check and make sure this was the command. Fortunately, it's easy to find out which command the user chose—Microsoft Access provides this information using the FilterType argument of the event procedure.

Check whether the user chose Filter By Form

To perform steps in code only when a condition is met, you use the Visual Basic If...Then statement. In this case, the condition you want to check is whether the FilterType argument of the event procedure is equal to the constant value acFilterByForm. If it is, that's when you want to display your message.

> Add lines of code before and after the existing line in the procedure, so that it reads as follows (you'll also want to add a tab before each line to indent it properly):

```
If FilterType = acFilterByForm Then
    MsgBox "Select field values and click Apply Filter button."
End If
```

The code between the If...Then and End If statements gets run only if the condition is true—in this case, if the FilterType argument is equal to the value of the constant acFilterByForm. In plain English, you can read these three lines of code as saying, "If the filter type the user chose is Filter By Form, then please display this message; otherwise, please do nothing." (Of course, you should always say please.)

Try the event procedure

Now that it's fixed, let's make sure the event procedure works as planned.

Filter By
Form button

1 On the Window menu, click Contacts.

2 Click the Filter By Form button on the toolbar.

   The Filter event occurs, triggering your event procedure. Because you chose the Filter By Form button, the condition in the If...Then statement is true, and the MsgBox statement runs and displays your message.

3 Click OK.

   After your procedure finishes, the form appears in Filter By Form view.

4 Click the Close button on the toolbar.

Using conditional code as you've done here makes your application "smart"—it provides logic to your procedures, and is the first step toward powerful Visual

Basic programming. This simple use of the If...Then statement performs just one action. But that's only the beginning of what you can do using conditional statements in Visual Basic. Soon, you'll use the If...Then statement to perform several lines of code depending on the value of a condition.

Understanding Filtering Properties

Whenever the user filters data using any of the standard filtering commands, Microsoft Access sets two form properties that reflect the filtering status of the form: the Filter property and the FilterOn property. The Filter property describes the criteria for the current filter—for example, the criterion for contacts in New York can be expressed as:

```
City = "New York"
```

The FilterOn property setting determines whether the filter is currently applied. When there's no filter, the FilterOn property is set to False; when the user applies a filter, it gets set to True.

In Visual Basic code, you can use the Filter and FilterOn properties to determine what the current filter is and whether it's in effect. More importantly, you can set these properties to affect the current filter on a form—actually changing the records that are displayed. This allows you to provide a custom filtering interface, setting the filtering status behind the scenes whenever you want. In this section, you'll see how these properties work on the Contacts form, and then provide a custom method for changing the filter on the form.

Using the Debug Window to View and Set Properties

In programming lingo, a "bug" is an error or mistake in programming code. Microsoft Access has several tools that help you find bugs or problems. The most important of these tools is the Debug window. In later lessons, you'll learn many techniques for *debugging* Visual Basic code with the Debug window and other tools. But there are also simple uses for the Debug window—one of which you'll try out in this section as you learn more about filtering data.

The bottom half of the Debug window, called the *Immediate pane*, is the most basic debugging tool in Microsoft Access. Usually, you place Visual Basic code in a module, and the code runs later on—for example, in response to an event. But in the Immediate pane, when you type Visual Basic code, it runs right away: as soon as you press ENTER.

Try out the Debug window

Because it's so convenient, the Debug window is a great place to try things out. It's also a good place to find out the current value of a property or expression. If you want to know the value of any Visual Basic expression, you can display it in the Immediate pane of the Debug window by typing a question mark (?) followed by the expression.

1 On the Window menu, click Form_Contacts : Class Module.

Debug Window button

2 Click the Debug Window button on the toolbar.

Microsoft Access displays the Debug window. You can overlook the top half of the Debug window for now—you'll learn to use it in Lesson 6 to help diagnose problems in your code. The Immediate pane is ready for you to enter Visual Basic commands.

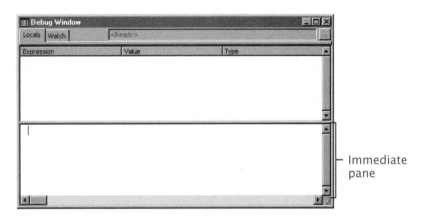

Immediate pane

3 Type **Beep**, press ENTER, and listen closely.

Your computer beeps—Beep is a Visual Basic statement, and when you type it in the Debug window, it runs immediately.

4 Type **?1+1** and press ENTER.

Typing this statement asks Microsoft Access a question: "What is the value of 1+1?" Microsoft Access displays the answer directly underneath your statement in the Debug window—it's 2. Bet you didn't know that Microsoft Access was such a fancy calculator!

Use the Debug window to set filtering properties

Making your computer beep (or add) is hardly a powerful use of the Debug window. Now that we've established what it does, let's put the Debug window to work. First, you'll use the Debug window to find out the value of the filtering properties for the Contacts form. Then, you'll actually change the value of these properties from the Debug window—in just the same way you've set properties in your event procedures.

1 Type **?Forms!Contacts.Filter**.

This statement asks Microsoft Access to tell you the value of the expression to the right of the question mark—an expression that refers to the

63

Filter property of the Contacts form. This expression is like an address to someone's house, describing to Microsoft Access exactly what property you're talking about. Here's how the expression works: the keyword *Forms* refers to the collection of forms in the current database; you follow it with an exclamation point and the name of a form, such as Contacts. Then, to indicate a property of the form, you follow the form reference with a period and the name of the property.

In short, this statement asks the question, "What is the value of the Filter property for the Contacts form?"

2 Press ENTER.

Microsoft Access displays the value of the expression—the filter you applied earlier to see only contacts in New York.

Value of the Filter property on the Contacts form

3 Type **?Forms!Contacts.FilterOn** and press ENTER.

The window displays the value of the FilterOn property for the Contacts form. Because the filter is currently applied on the Contacts form, the value of the FilterOn property is True.

4 Type **Forms!Contacts.FilterOn = False** and press ENTER.

This statement sets the FilterOn property of the Contacts form to False, effectively removing the filter from the form—just as if the user had clicked the Remove Filter button.

5 Close the Debug window.

6 On the Window menu, click Contacts.

As you can see, the form now displays all contact records—you successfully removed the filter using the Debug window.

All contacts are available.

By viewing and setting the Filter and FilterOn properties in code, you can monitor or change the filter of any form. Now that you've seen how these properties work in the Debug window, it's time to use them to customize the Contacts form.

Creating an Option Group to Filter Data

Suppose the filter you've set—to view contacts in New York—is very common in your application. You should make it easy for users to filter records, even if they don't know how to use Filter By Form. A good way to do this is by adding an *option group* to the form: a group of buttons from which users can choose the records they want to see.

In this section, you'll add an option group to the Contacts form with two options for viewing records: all contacts, or just New York contacts. Whenever the user clicks a different option in the group, an event procedure that you

65

write will respond by changing filtering properties to affect which records are displayed in the form.

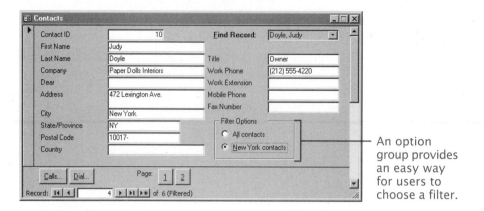

An option group provides an easy way for users to choose a filter.

Create the option group

An option group has many parts—but you can create them all at once using the Option Group Wizard. The wizard lets you specify all the options in the group, and it takes care of the details.

Design View button

1 Click the Design View button on the toolbar.

2 Close the property sheet.

3 If the toolbox isn't displayed, click the Toolbox button on the toolbar.

Toolbox button

4 In the toolbox, click the Option Group tool.

5 Scroll down a bit in the form window, and click the open space below the Fax Number field.

Option Group tool

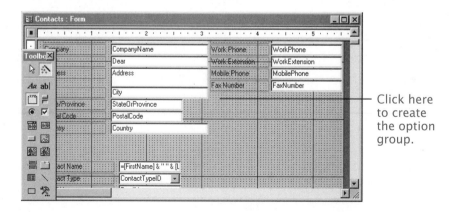

Click here to create the option group.

The Option Group Wizard starts, asking what option buttons you want in the option group.

6 Type **A&ll contacts** and then press TAB.

7 Type **&New York contacts** and then click Next.

The wizard asks if you want a default button to be selected automatically when you open the form, suggesting the All Contacts button.

8 Click Next.

The wizard shows you the values that each of the options will have. The All Contacts option corresponds to the number 1, the New York Contacts option to the number 2.

9 Click Next.

The wizard asks whether you want to use the value later or store the value in a field; that is, whether you want your option group to be an unbound or a bound control. You want the default option—Save The Value For Later Use—making the option group an unbound control.

10 Click Next.

The wizard asks about the style you want for your option group and buttons. Change it if you want to be fancy—the wizard shows you an example of what your choice will look like—or just accept the default style.

11 Click Next.

The wizard asks what label you want for the option group.

12 Type **Filter Options** and then click Finish.

The wizard creates the option group and its two buttons, and then places it on your form.

Contacts : Form	_ □ ×

Unfortunately, the wizard doesn't give the option group a very sensible name (it's something like Frame49). Because you want to refer to the option group in Visual Basic code, you should rename it in the property sheet.

Properties button

13 Click the Properties button on the toolbar, and then click the Other tab in the property sheet.

14 In the Name property box, type **FilterOptions**.

Add an event procedure to run the option group

The option group you've created is an unbound control, like the Find Record combo box you created earlier. To make it work, you need to write an event procedure that sets the filter properties for the Contacts form. Each time you click an option in an option group, its AfterUpdate event occurs, so you can respond accordingly. In the event procedure, you'll perform a different action depending on which option button the user clicks.

1 Click the Event tab in the property sheet.

2 Click the AfterUpdate property box, and then click the Build button to the right of the property box.

3 Select Code Builder, and then click OK.

Microsoft Access opens the Module window and creates the AfterUpdate event procedure for the option group.

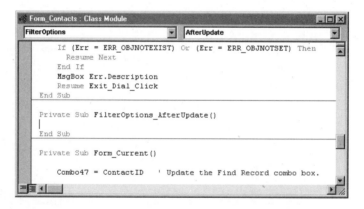

4 Enter the following code for the procedure (except the Sub and End Sub lines, which are already there):

```
Private Sub FilterOptions_AfterUpdate()
' Apply or remove the filter for the option the user chose.

    If FilterOptions = 2 Then
        Me.Filter = "City = 'New York'"
        Me.FilterOn = True      ' Apply the filter.
    Else
        Me.FilterOn = False     ' Remove the filter.
    End If
End Sub
```

Let's walk through this code line by line:

■ As you've seen, the If...Then structure lets you perform an action only if a certain condition is true. But before, you added only one line of code between the If...Then and End If statements. This code uses If...Then in a powerful new way—if the condition is true, Microsoft Access runs all the indented lines under the If...Then statement. This is known as a *block* of code, which is indented to show that it all belongs within the same If...Then...End If structure.

The condition here tests whether the value of the option group is 2, the number of the New York Contacts option. If the user clicks the second option in the group, the condition is true, and Microsoft Access will run the code in the block.

■ The first statement in this block of code sets the Filter property for the form. The Filter property accepts a string setting, which means you surround the setting in quotation marks. This setting says that you only want the form to show records for which the City field is equal to the value 'New York'—which you surround with single quotation marks, because it's also a string value.

■ The second statement in the block sets the form's FilterOn property to True, applying the filter. When Microsoft Access runs this statement, it will requery the records in the form, displaying only those that meet the filter criteria.

■ The If...Then structure in this procedure uses another new feature: the Else keyword, which allows you to add a line or block of code that runs if the condition is false. You can think of this If...Then statement as saying, "If the option group value is 2, do this block of code; otherwise do this other block of code."

■ The other block in this case is a single line that sets the FilterOn property to False. This way, if the user clicks the All Contacts option, your event procedure will remove the filter.

■ The End If statement marks the end of the Else code block. Any lines after this one would run regardless of whether the condition is true. Every If...Then statement must have a corresponding End If statement.

Try the option group

It's time to test the code by clicking values in the option group.

1 On the Window menu, click Contacts : Form.

2 Close the property sheet.

3 Click the Form View button on the toolbar.

The option group shows its default value—the All Contacts option—and all records are available in the form.

Form View button

4 Click the New York Contacts button in the option group.

The AfterUpdate event occurs for the option group, and your event procedure runs. Because the option you selected is option number 2, your code sets the Filter property to show only New York contacts and applies the filter.

The code in your event procedure applies the filter to show only contacts in New York.

5 Click the All Contacts button in the option group.

This time, your event procedure removes the filter.

Add an event procedure to act when the user filters

The option group works great, but there's still one problem with this strategy— it doesn't take into account the fact that other standard filtering commands are still available. What if the user changes the filter in another way? Will the option group update automatically?

As you customize your applications, it's important to anticipate conflicts like this. Let's take a look at this problem, and add another event procedure to solve it.

1 Click the City field.

For this contact, the value of the City field is Seattle.

*Filter By
Selection
button*

2 Click the Filter By Selection button on the toolbar.

The form now displays only contacts in Seattle. But the option group still shows All Records—which is no longer true! To avoid misleading users, you should update the option group control whenever users filter data.

The easiest way to indicate that the user's filter is in effect is for the option group to show neither option in the group as selected. To do this, you want to set the value of the option group control to Null any time the user applies a filter. (*Null* is a special value in Microsoft Access that means "no value at all.")

If the user removes the filter, on the other hand, you might as well set the option group value to 1 (the All Contacts option), because removing the filter is the same as clicking the All Contacts option.

3 On the Window menu, click Form_Contacts : Class Module.

4 In the Object box at the top of the Module window, select Form from the list of objects.

5 In the Proc box, select ApplyFilter from the list of events.

Select the Form object... 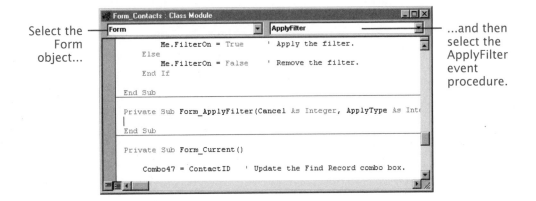 ...and then select the ApplyFilter event procedure.

6 Enter the following code for the procedure:

```
Private Sub Form_ApplyFilter(Cancel As Integer, ApplyType As Integer)
' Set the option group value to match the user's filtering action.

    If ApplyType = acShowAllRecords Then
        FilterOptions = 1        ' Set the All Contacts option.
    ElseIf Filter <> "City = 'New York'" Then
        FilterOptions = Null     ' Don't set any option value.
    End If

End Sub
```

Here's what this code does:

- The If...Then statement checks to see whether the ApplyType argument to the event procedure is equal to the constant value acShowAllRecords. This ApplyType value would indicate that the user removed the filter to show all contact records.

- If the condition is true—the user did remove the filter—the line of code after the If...Then statement sets the FilterOptions control value to 1, automatically selecting the All Contacts button in the option group.

- If the condition is false, it probably means that the user selected a filtering command other than your option group, so you'll want to set the option group control to Null. However, the ApplyFilter event might have been triggered when your own option group code set the filter for New York contacts—in which case you don't want to change the option group setting at all. To determine which of these is the case, the ElseIf line checks to make sure the Filter property is *not equal* (<>) to the string for New York contacts.

- Assuming this second condition is true—the user applied a filter to see a set of records other than New York contacts—the line of code after the ElseIf statement sets the value of the FilterOptions control to Null, causing the control to show neither option as selected.

7 On the Window menu, click Contacts.

8 Select the New York Contacts option.

   The form displays only those records for which the city is New York.

Remove Filter button

9 Click the Remove Filter button on the toolbar.

   When you remove the filter, the ApplyFilter event procedure runs, automatically returning the option group to the All Records option.

Filter By Selection button

10 Click the City field, and then click the Filter By Selection button on the toolbar.

   The form now displays only contacts in Seattle, just as you requested. Even better, because of your event procedure, the option group now appears without either option selected, indicating that you have applied your own filter.

As you can see, filtering is a powerful feature—but you'll need to consider carefully how the various filtering commands interact. Fortunately, between the Filter and ApplyFilter events and the Filter and FilterOn properties, Microsoft Access provides all the tools you need to control filtering in your Visual Basic code.

Close the application and exit Microsoft Access

1 Close the Contacts form, clicking Yes when Microsoft Access asks if you want to save changes.

2 On the Switchboard form, click Exit This Database.

3 On the File menu, click Exit.

Lesson Summary

To	Do this
Create a combo box to find records	Choose the Find A Record On My Form... option in the Combo Box Wizard.
Concatenate (combine) string values in an expression	Separate each string value with the ampersand (&) character.
Set a control's value in code	Type the control reference followed by the equal sign (=), then the value you want to assign to the control.
Run a block of code conditionally	Surround the block of code with the If...Then and End If statements, specifying a true or false condition to determine whether the code runs. To include a block that runs if the condition is false, add the Else statement.
Run a Visual Basic command immediately	Type the command in the Debug window and press ENTER.
View the value of an expression, property, or control	In the Debug window, type a question mark (?) followed by the expression, and then press ENTER.
Perform actions when a user chooses the Filter By Form or Advanced Filter/Sort command	Write an event procedure for the form's Filter event.
Perform actions when the user chooses to apply or remove a form's filter	Write an event procedure for the form's ApplyFilter event.
Change the filter of a form	Set the form's Filter property. To apply or remove the filter, set the FilterOn property.

For online information about	On the Help menu, click Contents and Index, click the Index tab, and then
Creating and using combo boxes	Search for "combo boxes"
Finding and filtering records in a form	Search for "finding data"
Referring to forms and controls in an expression	Search for "expressions"
Using the Debug window	Search for "Debug window"

73

For more information on	In *Building Applications with Microsoft Access 97*, see
Creating and using combo boxes	Chapter 3, "Using Forms to Collect, Filter, and Display Information"
Finding and filtering records in a form	Chapter 3, "Using Forms to Collect, Filter, and Display Information"
Referring to forms and controls in an expression	Chapter 5, "Working with Objects and Collections"
Using the Debug window	Chapter 8, "Handling Run-Time Errors"

Preview of the Next Lesson

In the next lesson, you'll explore the common events that occur on a form during data entry, and create event procedures to respond to many of those events. Along the way, you'll make some final enhancements to the Contacts form, and learn new ways that your application can interact with the user.

Respond to Data Entry Events

Estimated time
40 min.

In this lesson you will learn how to:

- Set the value of a control in code.
- Respond to users' actions as they move around in a form.
- Make sure that the data a user enters is valid.
- Ask a question and perform different actions based on a user's choice.

Data entry can be time-consuming and monotonous, especially with a database system that's poorly designed. But data entry is also an art—when you get on a roll, you can surprise yourself with how quickly you enter information. The key to a successful data entry system lies in anticipating what information gets entered; providing shortcuts; and avoiding unnecessary clicking, typing, and moving around. With an efficient data entry form, there's time to concentrate on getting the information right, rather than just getting the job done.

As a database developer, one of your primary concerns is to facilitate this job of getting information into the database—after all, a database is not worth much more than the data you can put into and get out of it. Your goal is to make the job of data entry personnel as easy and fast as possible. At the same time, you want to ensure that the data they enter is complete and accurate. It's a big challenge. In this lesson, you'll learn how to enhance a data entry form by anticipating the way users will enter data and writing Visual Basic code to respond to events.

Start the lesson

 Start Microsoft Access and open the 04Contac database in the practice files folder.

Understanding Form and Control Events

Events are happening on your forms and controls all the time. Every time you press a key, use the mouse, or change data, an event occurs. Click the mouse—event! Change a field—event! And each event gives you a chance to make something happen in your application by attaching code to the event procedure.

Open the Contacts form

 On the Main Switchboard form, click Enter/View Contacts.

Every time you click the mouse, press a key, or change data, events are occurring behind the scenes.

From the point of view of your application, the events on a form occur randomly. You have no way of knowing *why*, for example, the user enters a certain control, or what the user will do next—you have to take each event as it comes. In some ways, events are like little fires popping up here and there, and your application is the fire department, running in to put them out. And like the fire department, your application must be prepared for anything.

The trick to programming events is figuring out which events to respond to and how. After you set up the responses, your application works automatically. Here's a list of the most common things users do on a data entry form, along with the events that you can respond to.

User actions	Associated event procedures
Opening and closing the form	Open, Close, Load, Unload
Moving to and from the form	Activate, Deactivate
Moving from control to control	Enter, Exit, GotFocus, LostFocus
Moving from record to record	Current
Pressing keys	KeyDown, KeyUp, KeyPress
Clicking the mouse	Click, DoubleClick, MouseDown, MouseUp
Changing data and saving records	BeforeUpdate, AfterUpdate
Adding records	BeforeInsert, AfterInsert
Deleting records	Delete, BeforeDelConfirm, AfterDelConfirm
Filtering records	Filter, ApplyFilter

These are only the most common events you might want to respond to in code—there are still others. In this lesson, you'll write Visual Basic code to respond to just a few of these events.

Performing Actions as the User Moves in a Form

Microsoft Access provides some cues to the user moving through a form: the title bar changes color when a form is active, the blinking insertion point indicates the current field, and the record indicator shows the current record, just to name a few. But you may want to customize this behavior or add additional cues for the user. You do this by responding to certain events. For example, when the user switches to a form, the Activate event occurs. To change something about the form or the Microsoft Access interface when a form becomes the active window, you write an event procedure for the Activate event. To return the interface to its previous state when the user moves to another form, you write code for the Deactivate event to reverse the effect.

You can also respond as the user moves within a form. As you saw in Lessons 2 and 3, each time the user moves from one record to another, the Current event occurs. In addition, several events occur each time the user moves between controls on a form. When the user moves from one control to another, the Exit and LostFocus events occur for the control the user leaves, and the Enter and GotFocus events occur for the control the user moves to.

Suppose you want to change the color of a control whenever it is the active control on a form. You can do this by creating event procedures for the control's Enter and Exit events.

> **NOTE** The Enter and Exit events occur when the user moves into or out of a control, but not when the user switches between windows in Microsoft Access. If you only care which control is current on the form, you can use Enter and Exit; if you also want to run the same code each time a control gets the focus from another window, use GotFocus and LostFocus as well.

Change the background color of a combo box

In Lesson 3, you created the Find Record combo box and set its background color to light gray to show that entering data in the control isn't required. But you'll want to make this control appear white again whenever it's the active control—after all, it seems a bit strange to select data from a control that's gray, as if it were disabled. To do this, you'll write a simple procedure for the control's Enter event.

You'll change the background of this control to white.

Design View button

1 Click the Design View button.

2 With the right mouse button, click the Find Record combo box, and then click Properties on the shortcut menu.

3 Click the Event tab in the property sheet.

4 Click the OnEnter property, and then click the Build button next to the property box.

— Click the
Build button.

5 Select Code Builder, and then click OK.

Microsoft Access opens the form module for the Contacts form and creates the event procedure for the combo box.

Remember, the name of the combo box is actually a default name—something like Combo47—that the Combo Box Wizard assigned when you created the control. You can see the actual name by looking at the event procedure's name (in the Sub statement at the top of the window).

6 Press TAB and type the following line of Visual Basic code for the procedure (substituting the actual number of your combo box for "47"):

```
Combo47.BackColor = 16777215    ' Change background to white.
```

This code sets the BackColor property to color 16777215, the code for the color white. As when you set a property of a form, you set a control property by typing the property name followed by the equal sign and the value you want to set it to. With a control property, however, you also have to let Microsoft Access know which control you have in mind. To do this, you type the control name and a period before the property name.

Add a procedure to change the color back

The combo box will now change to white when you enter it—but you want to leave it the way you found it. To change the color back to gray when you leave, you'll write another procedure for the control's Exit event.

1 In the Procedure box at the top of the Module window, select Exit from the list of events.

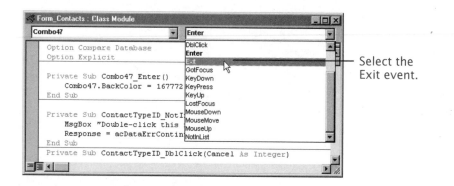

Select the Exit event.

Microsoft Access creates the Exit event procedure for you—and also sets the control's OnExit property to [Event Procedure] so the procedure will run when you exit the control.

2 Press TAB and type the following Visual Basic code for the procedure (again substituting the number of your combo box):

```
Combo47.BackColor = 12632256    ' Change background to gray.
```

This code sets the BackColor property of the combo box to the code for gray.

80

> **TIP** Want to use other colors? You can find out the code for another color easily by setting a color using the palette in Form Design view, and then looking in the property sheet to see the corresponding code for the color you chose.

Try out the new event procedures

1 On the Window menu, click Contacts : Form.

2 Click the Form View button.

Form View button

3 Click the drop-down arrow next to the Find Record combo box.

The Enter event for the combo box occurs, and your code changes the control's background to white.

4 Click the First Name field again.

Back to an inconspicuous gray!

Performing Actions as the User Changes Data

Each time you change the value of a control, several events occur. Most of the events have to do with pressing keys and changing the focus, but two events deal specifically with changes to data: BeforeUpdate and AfterUpdate. BeforeUpdate occurs when the user tries to move out of a changed control or save a changed record; AfterUpdate occurs when the change is successfully completed.

In this section, you'll respond to the AfterUpdate event to perform an action after the user changes a control. Later in the lesson, you'll respond to the BeforeUpdate event to perform an action when the user tries to save a record.

Setting the Value of a Control "Auto-magically"

When entering data, there's nothing better than having the database enter information for you wherever it can. One way you can do this is to set the DefaultValue property for fields in your tables, so that when you add a new record, Microsoft Access fills in the field's value automatically. But this strategy doesn't work well if you want to fill in a field "on the fly" in response to an entry in another field. In this case, you can use an event procedure to respond to the user updating the one field, and provide Visual Basic code that updates the other field.

For example, the Contacts form has a Dear field that stores an informal name or nickname to be used in the salutation of a letter. For a person named Thomas, you might want to set this value to Tom, so that a letter you send out can use the familiar name in its greeting. Thing is, you'll want to address most people by their first name—so during data entry, you'd like the Dear field to get filled in automatically with the value the user enters in the First Name field. Then, if necessary, you can always change the Dear field to something else.

You want to fill in this field automatically.

Add an event procedure to set the Dear control's value

The event that occurs when the user moves out of a field after changing its value is the AfterUpdate event. You'll place code in the AfterUpdate event procedure for this event to copy the FirstName value to the Dear field.

Design View button

1 Click the Design View button.

2 Click the FirstName control.

The property sheet shows event properties for the FirstName control.

3 Click the AfterUpdate property, and then click the Build button.

Click the Build button.

4 Select Code Builder, and then click OK.

Microsoft Access opens the form module for the Contacts form and creates the FirstName_AfterUpdate event procedure.

```
Form_Contacts : Class Module                                    _ □ X
FirstName                          ▼    AfterUpdate                    ▼
        Else
            Me.FilterOn = False      ' Remove the filter.
        End If

    End Sub


    Private Sub FirstName_AfterUpdate()
    |
    End Sub

    Private Sub Form_ApplyFilter(Cancel As Integer, ApplyType As I
    ' Set the option group value to match user's filtering action.
```

5 Type the following Visual Basic code for the procedure:

```
' Copy the FirstName value to the Dear control.

    Dear = FirstName
```

This line of code sets the value of the Dear control to the same value as the FirstName control.

Try out the event procedure

1 On the Window menu, click Contacts : Form.

2 Click the Form View button.

Form View button

3 Click the New Record button on the toolbar.

4 In the First Name field, type **John**, and then press TAB.

When you move out of the field, the AfterUpdate event occurs. Your code runs, setting the value of the Dear field. At this point, you could continue entering the record, either skipping the Dear field or manually changing its value if necessary. Instead, now that you know it works, undo the new record without saving it.

New Record button

5 Press ESC.

Add code to check whether the Dear field is blank

There's a minor glitch with our plan for the Dear field. Imagine this scenario: you enter a record for a Thomas Blanque, the first name Thomas gets copied to the Dear field, but you then change the Dear field to Tom. Then you realize you misspelled Thomas, so you go back and spell it correctly. Can you guess what happens? Your event procedure copies over the Dear field containing Tom—

which really isn't what you want. Instead, you want the Contacts form to be smarter: you want it to copy the first name to the Dear field only when the Dear field is blank.

1 On the Window menu, click Form_Contacts : Class Module.

2 Add two lines of code before and after the existing line in the procedure, so that it reads as follows (you'll also want to add a tab before the word Dear to indent the line):

```
If IsNull(Dear) Then
    Dear = FirstName
End If
```

The IsNull function in Microsoft Access returns True if the item in parentheses is null (contains no value), False if it contains a value— so in this line, the code after the Then keyword gets run only if the Dear control is blank.

3 On the Window menu, click Contacts.

4 In the First Name field, type **Tomas**, and then press TAB.

Your event procedure runs. Because the Dear field is null, it copies the first name value to the Dear field just as it did before.

5 In the Last Name field, type **Blanque**.

6 Press TAB twice, and then in the Dear field, type **Tom**.

7 In the First Name field, click between the "T" and the "o" and type the **h** in Thomas.

8 Press TAB.

Your event procedure runs. This time, however, it doesn't copy the first name value to the Dear field because you've already filled it in—which means the expression *IsNull(Dear)* is false.

Responding to Keyboard Events

One way to provide shortcuts for users of your application is by giving them special keys that perform common actions. Keyboard shortcuts aren't as visible as command buttons—but you can have only so many command buttons on a form. In this section, you'll write an event procedure that responds to keyboard events and sets the value of several controls on the Contacts form.

Every time you press a key on a form, three events occur: KeyDown, KeyPress, and KeyUp. You use KeyPress to respond to normal characters—such as letters and numbers—as the user types them. You use the KeyDown and KeyUp events to handle the exact keys that are being pressed on the keyboard, including combinations that use special keys like SHIFT, ALT, and CTRL.

Add a KeyDown event procedure to set control values

Most of your contacts are in New York City, so you want a quick way to enter values for New York City in a contact's record. To do this, you'll create a KeyDown procedure for the City field that detects when a user presses the CTRL key and the number 1 key at the same time.

Design View button

1 Click the Design View button.

2 Click the City field to select it.

The property sheet should display the Event properties for the City field.

3 Click the OnKeyDown property, and then click the Build button.

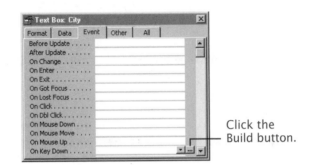

Click the Build button.

4 Select Code Builder, and then click OK.

Microsoft Access opens the form module for the Contacts form and creates the City_KeyDown event procedure.

5 Enter the following Visual Basic code for the procedure (the Sub and End Sub lines are already present):

```
Private Sub City_KeyDown(KeyCode As Integer, Shift As Integer)
' If key is CTRL+1, enter values for New York.

    If KeyCode = 49 And Shift = 2 Then     ' CTRL+1 was pressed.
        City = "New York"
        StateOrProvince = "NY"
        Country = "USA"
    End If
End Sub
```

The code in this procedure runs whenever a key or combination of keys is pressed. Using the KeyCode and Shift arguments, which contain num-bers representing the key that was pressed and the status of the SHIFT and CTRL keys at the time it was pressed, the procedure determines whether the key combination was in fact the number 1 key along with the CTRL key. (The KeyCode value for the number 1 key is 49, and the Shift code of 2 indicates that the CTRL key was pressed.) If the key combination is CTRL+1, the three statements in the block assign values for New York City to the three controls on the Contacts form.

Form View button

6 On the Window menu, click Contacts : Form.

7 Click the Form View button on the toolbar.

8 Click the New Record button on the toolbar.

9 Click in the City field, and then press CTRL+1.

Your event procedure runs, filling in the three fields.

New Record button

10 Press ESC.

Apply the keyboard handler anywhere on the form

As it stands, your keyboard shortcut works only if the focus is on the City field. If you want it to apply anywhere on the form, you'll have to modify the code to respond to the KeyDown event for the form instead of just for the City control. There's also another step you'll need to know about. Normally, keyboard events all occur for the control that has the focus, but they don't occur for the form. If you want all key events to be available to the form's event procedures, you can set the KeyPreview property for the form.

Design View button

1 Click the Design View button.

2 Click the form selection box (it's in the upper left corner of the window, at the intersection of the rulers).

The property sheet displays form properties.

3 Set the KeyPreview property to Yes.

Now all key events, regardless of which control they belong to, will fire the form's keyboard-handling procedures first, followed by those for the control that has the focus.

4 On the Window menu, click Form_Contacts : Class Module.

The Module window returns to the front, still displaying the previous event procedure.

5 In the procedure header (the Sub statement), select the word City, type **Form**, and then click on another line of code in the procedure to register the change.

Change the name from City_KeyDown to Form_KeyDown.

```
Form_Contacts : Class Module                                    _ □ ×

Form                              ▼   KeyDown                     ▼

  Option Explicit

  Private Sub Form_KeyDown(KeyCode As Integer, Shift As Integer)
  ' If key is CTRL+1, enter values for New York.

      If KeyCode = 49 And Shift = 2 Then     ' CTRL+1 was pressed.
          City = "New York"
          StateOrProvince = "NY"
          Country = "USA"
      End If

  End Sub
```

Now the same code responds to the *form's* KeyDown event, so it will apply from anywhere on the form.

6 On the Window menu, click Contacts : Form.

7 Click the Form View button on the toolbar.

Form View button

8 Click the New Record button on the toolbar.

9 Press CTRL+1.

Your event procedure runs, filling in the three fields.

New Record button

10 Press ESC.

11 Click the Save button on the toolbar.

Microsoft Access saves your changes to the form.

Save button

The Contacts form is coming along very nicely—with code to set control values automatically, it's getting easier to use all the time. But we're not finished yet!

Validating Data

When entering data, it's easy to make mistakes or leave out important information. Errors or omissions in your data make your database less valuable and harder to use. One advantage of a database system is that it can check the data you enter, sometimes even refusing to save data that doesn't follow the rules. This process is referred to as *validation*, because it involves checking data to make sure it is valid.

There are several ways Microsoft Access checks data, most of which don't involve any programming. For a complex data-entry form, you'll typically use one or more of the following validation features:

Data types   This is the most simple form of validation, used in every database. Quite simply, Microsoft Access doesn't allow you to store data in a field if the data is inappropriate for the field's data type. For example, Microsoft Access makes sure a Date field always stores only a date.

InputMask property   This property helps users enter data in fields that have formatting characters, such as the hyphens and parentheses in ZIP codes or phone numbers. Microsoft Access allows only values that fit the input mask. The phone number and postal code fields in the Contacts database have input masks (they were created automatically by the Database Wizard).

Required property   By setting this property for fields in a table, you can make sure they aren't left blank. If a user tries to blank a required field or save a record without entering a value for a required field, Microsoft Access displays a message.

ValidationRule property   By setting this property for fields, tables, or controls on forms, you can make sure data follows rules that you set. When the user updates a field or saves a record, Microsoft Access checks the data to make sure it fits with any validation expressions you've entered, and displays a message if it doesn't. You can specify the message that Microsoft Access displays by setting the ValidationText property.

BeforeUpdate event procedure   If you want to provide complex field validation that you can't write a validation expression for, you can write an event procedure that checks the data. Unlike other forms of validation in which Microsoft Access automatically displays a message, your BeforeUpdate event procedure must display a message and cancel the update.

The Contacts form already uses input masks. In this section, you'll add other validation, first setting properties in the Contacts table, and then creating a BeforeUpdate event procedure that checks data each time a user saves a record.

Require that each record have a complete name

To ensure that a field always has a value, you set the Required property in the table.

1   Close the Contacts form.

You have to close the Contacts form, because you can't modify the design of a table when the form is open.

2   Click the Database Window button on the toolbar.

3   Click the Tables tab, select the Contacts table, and then click Design.

Microsoft Access opens the table in Design view.

4   Click the FirstName field.

*Database
Window button*

5   In the lower half of the window, set the Required property to Yes.

Set the
Required
property
to Yes.

6   Click the LastName field, and set the Required property to Yes.

Now Microsoft Access won't allow the user to save a contact without entering both a first and last name.

Require that each record include a phone number

Because you often print a phone list, you'd like to make sure that users enter either a work phone number or a mobile phone number for every contact. If you wanted to require entry in both fields, you'd set the Required property as you did for the name fields. But because either one or both of the phone numbers is acceptable, you'll need to use a different strategy. To provide a validation rule that involves more than one field in a table, you set the table's ValidationRule property.

*Properties
button*

1   Click the Properties button on the toolbar.

2   In the property sheet, click the ValidationRule property, and then type **[WorkPhone] Or [MobilePhone]**.

This validation expression uses the Or operator to test whether the phone fields contain text. Logical operators such as Or treat everything as either true or false: fields that contain text are true, fields that don't are false. You can think of this expression as asking, "Is it true that either the WorkPhone field or the MobilePhone field contains text?"

If both phone fields are blank, then the entire expression is false, which tells Microsoft Access that the record is invalid. Note that you must include the brackets around the field names you use in the validation expression, or else the property sheet will interpret them as string expressions instead of field names.

89

3 Click the ValidationText property, and then type **You must enter either a work phone or a mobile phone.**

This is the message Microsoft Access displays if the record is invalid.

4 Close the property sheet.

5 Close the Contacts table, choosing Yes when Microsoft Access asks if you want to save changes, and choosing No when it asks if you want to check whether existing data follows the rules you set.

6 Minimize the Database window.

Test the validation rules

1 On the Contact Management Switchboard form, click Enter/View Contacts.

New Record button

2 Click the New Record button on the toolbar.

3 In the First Name field, type **Carl**.

4 On the Records menu, click Save Record.

Microsoft Access displays a message telling you that the Last Name field can't be null, and it doesn't let you save the record.

5 Click OK.

6 Click the Last Name field, and then type **Thorgerson**.

7 On the Records menu, click Save Record.

This time, Microsoft Access displays your phone number validation message—and it still won't let you save the record.

> **Microsoft Access** ⊠
>
> ⚠ You must enter either a work phone or a mobile phone.
>
>   OK   Help

8   Click OK.

9   Click the Work Phone field, and then type **212 555 1314** (because of the input mask, you don't have to enter the parentheses or the dash in the phone number).

10 On the Records menu, click Save Record.

> This time, you can successfully save the record in the Contacts table.

Validating Data Using an Event Procedure

So far, the validation you've added hasn't required any code. But what if you want to provide validation that works differently in different situations? You may want to remind users that addresses should always have a postal code. You could set the Required property for the PostalCode field in the Contacts table; then, every record would have to have this field filled in. But this would be too restrictive—some contact records won't have an address at all, so you don't always want to require a postal code.

To provide this type of custom validation, you write an event procedure that runs each time a record is saved. The procedure will check for a postal code, and then display a message if necessary.

 NOTE   When the wizard creates the Contact Management database, it formats the PostalCode field to hold U.S. ZIP codes only, not postal codes with other formats used in other countries. For this reason, the code you'll write in this section applies only to ZIP codes.

Create an event procedure that checks for a postal code

When the user tries to save a record in the Contacts table, the BeforeUpdate event occurs. In a BeforeUpdate event procedure, your code can either allow the record to be saved, or *cancel the event*, requiring the user to fix the problem and try again.

Design View button

1 Click the Design View button.

2 With the right mouse button, click the form selection box, and then click Properties on the shortcut menu.

3 Click the Event tab in the property sheet.

4 Click the BeforeUpdate property, and then click the Build button.

5 Select Code Builder, and then click OK.

Microsoft Access opens the form module for the Contacts form and creates the Form_BeforeUpdate event procedure.

```
Form_Contacts : Class Module                    _□X
Form                      ▼    BeforeUpdate              ▼
  Option Explicit

  Private Sub Form_BeforeUpdate(Cancel As Integer)
  |
  End Sub

  Private Sub Form_KeyDown(KeyCode As Integer, Shift As Integer)
  ' If key is CTRL+1, enter values for New York.

      If KeyCode = 49 And Shift = 2 Then    ' CTRL+1 was pressed
          City = "New York"
          StateOrProvince = "NY"
          Country = "USA"
```

You'll notice that the header for the BeforeUpdate procedure includes a Cancel argument. You'll use this argument in your event procedure to tell Microsoft Access whether to allow the user to save the record.

6 Enter the following Visual Basic code for the procedure:

```
Private Sub Form_BeforeUpdate(Cancel As Integer)
' If the user entered an address, check for a zip code.

    If Not IsNull(Address) And IsNull(PostalCode) Then
        MsgBox "You must enter a postal code.", vbExclamation
        PostalCode.SetFocus    ' Go back to PostalCode field.
        Cancel = True          ' Cancel saving the record.
    End If

End Sub
```

Let's walk through the procedure line by line.

The first line uses a complex condition—*Not IsNull(Address) And IsNull(PostalCode)*—to determine whether or not the record that the user is saving is acceptable. This condition uses the IsNull function, which returns True if the field in parentheses contains a value, and False if it contains no value (also known as the Null value). You can read the statement like this: "If the Address field doesn't contain Null (if it has a value) and the PostalCode field does contain Null (it doesn't have a value), then do the statements in the block."

If the user enters an address without a ZIP code, the next three lines run:

- The first line uses the MsgBox statement to display a simple message to the user. You've used this statement before, but here it has a second argument which you can use to tell Microsoft Access what type of box to display. The constant value vbExclamation tells Microsoft Access to display a message box with an exclamation point icon.

- The user must return to the PostalCode field to enter a ZIP code before saving the record. For convenience, the second line uses the SetFocus method to return the focus to this field automatically, so the user can just type in the ZIP code.

- The final statement sets the value of the Cancel argument to True to cancel the BeforeUpdate event. Every BeforeUpdate event procedure—like many other event procedures—includes the Cancel argument. Setting this argument to True is equivalent to saying, "Pretend that the user action that caused this event didn't happen." In this case, the user is trying to save the record, and canceling this event causes the record not to be saved. Instead, the user must enter a ZIP code and try again.

Test the new event procedure

Form View button

New Record button

1 On the Window menu, click Contacts : Form.

2 Click the Form View button on the toolbar.

3 Click the New Record button on the toolbar.

4 Fill in the fields as follows:

Field Name	Value
First Name	Karl
Last Name	Sigel
Address	200 Bourbon St.
City	New Orleans
State/Province	LA
Work Phone	404 555 3933

5 On the Records menu, click Save Record.

The BeforeUpdate event occurs, running the code in your event procedure. Because you filled in the Address field but not the Postal Code field,

93

the code in the procedure displays the message—complete with the exclamation point icon—telling you why the record can't be saved.

6 Click OK.

The code in your procedure continues, canceling the BeforeUpdate event. This returns you to the form without saving the record—you must now either undo the record or enter a ZIP code.

7 In the Postal Code field, type **70130**.

8 On the Records menu, click Save Record.

Asking the User a Question

Your procedure works just fine—if the user types an address but doesn't have the ZIP code, it is impossible to save the record. This is still awfully restrictive. To be more flexible, it would be nice to simply warn the user that there's no ZIP code, and then allow the record to be saved.

To do this, you'll learn a very important technique: using the MsgBox function to get a response from the user, and performing different actions based on the response.

Let the user leave the PostalCode field blank

1 On the Window menu, click Form_Contacts : Class Module.

2 Edit the code in the BeforeUpdate procedure to appear as follows:

```
Private Sub Form_BeforeUpdate(Cancel As Integer)
' If the user entered an address, check for a zip code.

    Dim strMessage As String
    Dim intOptions As Integer
    Dim bytChoice As Byte

    If Not IsNull(Address) And IsNull(PostalCode) Then
        strMessage = "You didn't enter a postal code. Save anyway?"
        intOptions = vbQuestion + vbOKCancel
        bytChoice = MsgBox(strMessage, intOptions)
```

```
        If bytChoice = vbCancel Then
            PostalCode.SetFocus    ' Go back to PostalCode field.
            Cancel = True          ' Cancel saving the record.
        End If
    End If
End Sub
```

The procedure now uses several new Visual Basic techniques:

■ The first three lines use Dim statements to tell Microsoft Access about three *variables* you're going to use in this procedure. A variable is a temporary place to store information in the computer's memory—similar to the memory function on a calculator. Each Dim statement includes the name of a variable, along with the type of data it will store. As the procedure continues, your code can assign values to the variables, retrieving the values at any time later in the procedure.

You'll notice that the name of each variable has a prefix that indicates the type of data it stores: "str" for string data, "int" for integer data, "byt" for byte data. You'll use this convention to name variables throughout the book.

■ The If...Then statement is the same as before, but the code block it runs if the user enters an address without a ZIP code is different. The first line in the block assigns a values to the strMessage variable. This variable stores the message you want to display, warning the user about the postal code and asking for a response. When you assign a value to a string variable, you surround the string data with quotation marks.

■ The next line assigns a value to the intOptions variable. This variable stores a number representing options for the MsgBox function. You can add the values of several constants to specify more than one option—here, for example, you've specified that you want the question-mark icon to appear in the box (vbQuestion), and that you want the box to include OK and Cancel buttons (vbOKCancel).

■ The next line uses the MsgBox function to display the question to the user. When you used the MsgBox statement previously, you placed the arguments to the statement—the message and options—after the statement, separated by a comma. Using the function, you do the same, but because it's a function, you surround the arguments with parentheses. In addition, the function returns a value that you want to store in the bytChoice variable. To assign the value of the function to the variable, you've put it after the variable name, separated by an equal sign (=). In effect, this line of code says, "Display the message text from the strMessage variable using the options from the intOptions variable, and put the result in the bytChoice variable." The result that the MsgBox function returns is a number representing which button the user chose in the message box, either OK or Cancel.

- The next few lines use another If...Then structure to perform an action based on the user's response to the question. If the user responds by clicking the Cancel button, the value that gets stored in the bytChoice variable will equal the constant value vbCancel, and the block of code runs.

- If the user responds by clicking Cancel, you want to move back to the PostalCode field and cancel the event so the user still has to enter a ZIP code. If the user responds with OK, the procedure skips this block of code, allowing the record to be saved without a ZIP code. Note that each If...Then structure ends with its own End If statement to indicate the end of that structure.

 TIP You may wonder how you can find out which constant values to use for specifying options for the MsgBox function and interpreting the response. You can read about all these constants in the Help topic for the MsgBox function, by clicking the MsgBox keyword in the Module window and pressing F1.

Test the procedure again

1   On the Window menu, click Contacts.

2   Click the Postal Code field's label, and press the DELETE key to delete the ZIP code.

3   On the Records menu, click Save Record.

> The BeforeUpdate event occurs, running your new code. This time, the code in the procedure displays the question—and includes OK and Cancel buttons so you can indicate a response.

```
Microsoft Access                    ×
  ?   You didn't enter a postal code. Save anyway?

         [   OK   ]     [ Cancel ]
```

4   Click Cancel.

> The code in your procedure continues, canceling the BeforeUpdate event. But suppose you realize that you don't have the ZIP code, and want to save the record anyway.

5   On the Records menu, click Save Record.

6   Click OK.

> This time, your response causes the code that cancels the BeforeUpdate event to be skipped, allowing the record to be saved as if the procedure weren't there at all.

As you can see, validation can be as simple or complex as necessary in your application. Even this procedure could be expanded to cover several different scenarios: if you had other rules for entering contacts in records, you would simply add additional blocks of code to the same BeforeUpdate event procedure to check all your rules before allowing the record to be saved.

Close the form and exit Microsoft Access

1 Close the Contacts form, clicking Yes when Microsoft Access asks if you want to save changes.

2 Close Microsoft Access.

Lesson Summary

To	Do this
Change a control's properties when a user moves to and from it	Write event procedures for the control's Enter and Exit events.
Perform actions after a user changes a control's value	Write an event procedure for the control's AfterUpdate event.
Perform actions when the user presses a key combination on a form	Write an event procedure for a form's KeyDown event, and set the form's KeyPreview property to Yes.
Validate data in code before a control value is accepted or a record gets saved	Write a BeforeUpdate event procedure for the control or form event. To cancel the update, set the Cancel argument to True.
Ask the user a question	Use the MsgBox function, along with constants that define its options. Store the value of the user's choice in a variable.

For online information about	On the Help menu, click Contents and Index, click the Index tab, and then
Declaring and using variables	Search for "variables"
Creating and using combo boxes	Search for "combo boxes"
Referring to fields, controls, and properties in Visual Basic code	Search for "expressions"

For more information on	In *Building Applications with Microsoft Access 97*, see
Declaring and using variables	Chapter 4, "Working with Variables, Data Types, and Constants"
Creating and using combo boxes	Chapter 3, "Using Forms to Collect, Filter, and Display Information"
Referring to fields, controls, and properties in Visual Basic code	Chapter 5, "Working with Objects and Collections"

Preview of the Next Lesson

In this lesson, you explored many events and learned a lot more about Visual Basic along the way. You've already used many Visual Basic programming techniques, but there are still quite a few you haven't explored. In the next part of the book—Lessons 5 through 7—you'll learn much more about the ins and outs of the Visual Basic language, and the tools you can use to get the most from it.

Part 2

Programming in Visual Basic

Write Your Own Functions

Estimated time
40 min.

In this lesson you will learn how to:

- Create a standard module.
- Write general Sub and Function procedures.
- Provide information to a procedure by adding arguments.
- Use general procedures in code and expressions on a form.

Watching small children learn to speak is fascinating. Long before they're aware of grammar or sentence structure, they manage to build sentences. Without any understanding of the rules of language, they nevertheless communicate. Of course, before you can read or write, you need to learn *something* about the language—still, you can get by pretty well with a rudimentary understanding of grammar and a limited vocabulary.

Although a far cry from anyone's native tongue, computer programming languages share many characteristics with human language. Both have an extensive vocabulary and complex rules of grammar to follow. But as you've seen in previous lessons, you can learn to get things done using Visual Basic, even create and customize applications, without bothering to learn much about the programming language. So far, you've been speaking the language without knowing the underlying rules.

You can get a good start with a language before studying any grammar, but you won't be likely to write *War and Peace*. In order to use a language with confidence, you need to understand how it works—the basic rules and components,

101

and how to combine them effectively. Now that you've gotten a taste of what you can accomplish by programming Microsoft Access, it's time to discover the bigger picture.

In this lesson, you'll learn about the fundamental building blocks of Visual Basic for Applications—modules and procedures—and how you fit them together to build flexible, well-organized applications. You'll pick up new vocabulary along the way, and you'll try using it in several different contexts. Then, throughout Part 2, you'll continue to explore the underlying rules of Visual Basic programming and try out all the tools Microsoft Access provides for crafting your modules.

Start the lesson

 Start Microsoft Access and open the 05Contac database in the practice files folder.

Understanding Modules and Procedures

In Part 1, you worked exclusively with event procedures on existing forms. Because forms are so central to Microsoft Access applications, this type of procedure is probably where you'll add most of the code you write. However, there is another important type of procedure you'll create in this lesson, called a *general* procedure. General procedures don't run automatically in response to events—instead, you have to run them yourself, either by referring to them in an expression on a form or report or by using them in Visual Basic code. General procedures come in two types: Sub procedures and Function procedures. Event procedures, by contrast, are all Sub procedures.

Why Create General Procedures?

You can think of general procedures as having a supporting role in your applications—while event procedures are the central force in Microsoft Access programming, general procedures are helpers along the way. You could accomplish most anything in Microsoft Access with event procedures alone, but using general procedures provides much better solutions as the complexity of your application increases. There are several ways you can use general procedures:

Perform complex operations that don't fit in an expression. If you've used expressions as property settings on forms and reports, you know that they can quickly become unwieldy. You can hide this complexity by creating your own function to perform the operation you need, and then referring to it in your expressions. Additionally, Visual Basic code can perform complex operations that aren't possible using expressions.

Reuse program code to repeat a task. Your event procedures often perform the same or similar actions at various times. For example, you might often display a message to the user. While you could copy the same code into every event procedure that uses it, this would be extremely inefficient. Instead, you can create a general procedure that performs a common task, and reuse it in every procedure that performs that task.

Break up programming tasks into manageable units. If you were to put all your code into event procedures, they could become very long, complicated, and difficult to understand. By creating separate procedures to perform each part of a large task, you can simplify your work and make each individual procedure easier to read and understand.

Standard Modules and Form Modules

You can put general procedures in one of two places: in a form or report module, where they share space with any event procedures you write; or in a *standard* module. Standard modules are separate database objects containing one or many procedures. They most often contain "utility" functions, so named because they are useful in many different circumstances. For example, one standard module might contain several general functions for working with dates in Visual Basic—you can copy such a module to any application in which you use dates.

If you add a general procedure to a form or report module, it belongs to that form or report. Most often, you'll use this type of procedure only in the form or report itself, either in expressions on the form or in other procedures in the same module. Create this type of procedure to perform a task that applies directly to the form—for example, to work with information in the fields on that form.

General procedures that you add to standard modules usually belong to the application as a whole. Create this type of procedure to perform a task that applies to more than one form or report—often, a task that could apply to any form or report.

Creating General Procedures in a Standard Module

A database can contain one or more standard modules, each of which can hold many procedures. You'll usually group all the procedures for a specific purpose into one module. In this section, you'll create a module to store two procedures that are used to display messages to the user.

Create a new standard module

1   In the Database window, click the Modules tab.

   Standard modules are regular objects in the Database window, just like tables and forms.

2   Click the New button.

Microsoft Access creates a new standard module and displays it in the Module window. From here, you can enter Visual Basic code and create general procedures.

Using the Declarations Section

A new module doesn't contain any procedures—however, like all modules, it has a special section called the *Declarations section*. In this section, you declare variables and constants, and enter other preliminary code that applies to the entire module. In a standard module, code in the Declarations section can even apply to all modules in the application.

As you can see, Microsoft Access automatically added two statements to the Declarations section of your module:

```
Option Compare Database
Option Explicit
```

These statements use the Option keyword to set options for the whole module. They are two of several available statements that begin with the Option keyword.

The Compare option determines the method Microsoft Access uses for comparing strings in your module, and can be set to Database, Text, or Binary. Using the Database option tells Microsoft Access to compare strings using the sort order set in your database, as opposed to the traditional Visual Basic sort order, which distinguishes between uppercase and lowercase letters. Because Option Compare Database makes sense for most applications in Microsoft Access, you should just leave this statement alone in your modules.

The Explicit option tells Microsoft Access to check all the variable names you use in the module, to make sure you've declared them. If you remove this option from the Declarations section of a module, Microsoft Access lets you enter just about anything in code—but doing this makes your code much more prone to errors, because a misspelling won't be caught before you run your code. Having the Option Explicit statement in your modules will help you avoid many headaches down the road.

Declaring Constant Values

One of the statements you can place in the Declarations section is the Const statement, which declares a *constant* for use in your code. A constant is like a variable, except that you can't change its value after you declare it. You've already used predefined constants such as vbCancel in previous lessons. Your own constants work the same way, except that you decide what name and value to give them. You can think of a constant as being a placeholder for a value, making it easier to refer to in your code.

Declare a constant for the name of your application

You might want to declare a constant to store the name of your application, which you plan to use in procedures in the module.

➤ Type **Const conAppName** = **"Contact Management"** and press ENTER.

This tells Microsoft Access that each time conAppName appears in code, it should be replaced with this string value. If you want to change the application name later, you'll only need to change it in one place, not throughout the module.

Here's what the completed Declarations section looks like:

105

NOTE Declaring a constant in the Declarations section makes the constant available throughout the module. If you plan to use a constant value in only one procedure, it makes more sense to declare it in the procedure itself.

On the other hand, if you plan to use a constant value in more than one module, you can make it available to the entire database by using the Global Const statement instead of Const. Place this statement only in the Declarations section of a standard module.

Creating a Sub Procedure

You've already seen how to create event procedures and write code for them in the Module window. Creating general procedures is much the same, except that you have more flexibility. While the attributes of an event procedure—its name, type, and arguments—are predefined by Microsoft Access, you choose all these attributes for the general procedures you create.

Create the DisplayMessage procedure

You'll create a general procedure that you can use to display a message to the user—a common task that the procedure will help make easier.

Insert Module
button

1   Click the arrow next to the Insert Module button on the toolbar (which displays the button face for the last button you selected here), and then click Procedure.

Microsoft Access displays the Insert Procedure dialog box, where you specify the name and type of the procedure you want to create.

2   In the Name box, type **DisplayMessage**.

3   In the Type box, select the Sub option.

4   Click OK.

Microsoft Access creates the new procedure and displays its Sub and End Sub lines in the Module window, just underneath the Declarations section for the module.

```
Module1 : Module                                    _ □ ×
(General)                        ▼   DisplayMessage            ▼
    Option Compare Database                              ▲
    Option Explicit

    Const conAppName = "Contact Management"


    Public Sub DisplayMessage()
    |
    End Sub
                                                     ▼
═ ≡ ◄                                              ► ╱
```

Add code to the procedure

1 Enter the following code for the procedure:

```
' Display an important message to the user.

    MsgBox "This is important.", vbExclamation, conAppName
```

This code uses the MsgBox statement to display your message. It specifies a MsgBox option by including the vbExclamation constant as the second argument, so that the message box will include the exclamation point icon. Additionally, it specifies a title for the message box by including the third argument—the constant value that provides the name of the application.

Save button

2 Click the Save button on the toolbar.

3 In the Module Name box, type **Messages**, and then click OK.

Microsoft Access saves the module in the Contacts database.

Test your procedure using the Debug window

You can test general procedures such as the DisplayMessage procedure by using the Immediate pane of the Debug window.

1 Click the Debug Window button on the toolbar.

Debug Window button

2 Type **DisplayMessage**.

```
Debug Window                                    _ □ ×
 Locals │ Watch │        <Ready>                    ...
 Expression          Value          Type          ▲
                                                   ▼
 DisplayMessage                                    ▲


                                                   ▼
◄ ─                                        ► ─
```

3 Press ENTER.

Your procedure runs, displaying a message on the screen.

```
Contact Management                    ×
  ⚠   This is important.

          ┌─────────┐
          │   OK    │
          └─────────┘
```

4 Click OK.

Adding Arguments to a Procedure

Your procedure works well so far, but it leaves something to be desired. The message it displays is always the same—and the user will get pretty tired of seeing it if it stays this way. What you want is a flexible procedure that allows you to specify which of several messages you want to display. You can achieve this by adding an argument to the procedure.

Add an argument to the DisplayMessage procedure

1 Close the Debug window.

2 Type **strMessage As String** within the parentheses in the Sub statement:

```
Public Sub DisplayMessage(strMessage As String)
```

This tells Microsoft Access that you want to be able to give some information to the DisplayMessage procedure, namely, the message you want to display. You're also saying that the piece of information you'll provide to the procedure will be a string, and that it will be called strMessage.

3 Edit the MsgBox line, replacing the message string with an argument—the strMessage variable you declared in the procedure's header:

```
MsgBox strMessage, vbExclamation, conAppName
```

Now, when Microsoft Access runs the MsgBox statement, it will use the value of strMessage instead of a string that's always the same.

Run your procedure using an argument

When you run a procedure and provide an argument value, it's referred to as *passing* the argument to the procedure.

Debug Window button

1 Click the Debug Window button on the toolbar.

2 Type **DisplayMessage "I can say anything I like!"** and press ENTER.

Your procedure runs, using the string value you passed for the strMessage argument.

> **Contact Management**
>
> ⚠ I can say anything I like!
>
> [OK]

3 Click OK.

Creating a Function

The procedure you created performs an action, but it doesn't provide any information back to the program—this is the nature of a Sub procedure. A much more common type of general procedure is a *function*. Using a function procedure allows you to *return* a value to the procedure that runs the function. You've probably already used lots of built-in functions in Microsoft Access, such as the IsNull function, to get information back about something. Now you'll create your own function.

Create a procedure that asks a question

In Lesson 4, you used the MsgBox function to ask for confirmation before saving a record. Now you'll create a general function, called Confirm, that performs this same task for any action that needs confirmation. The function returns a different value depending on the choice the user makes in the message box.

Insert Procedure button

1 Close the Debug window.

2 Click the Insert Procedure button on the toolbar.

3 In the Name box, type **Confirm**, and then click OK.

109

Because the default type of procedure is Function, Microsoft Access creates a new function and displays its Function and End Function statements.

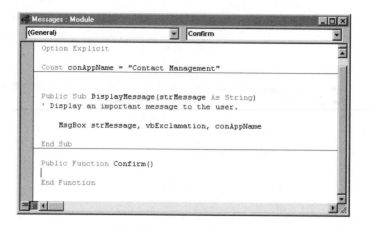

4 Type **strMessage As String** within the parentheses of the Function statement, and type **As Boolean** at the end:

```
Public Function Confirm(strMessage As String) As Boolean
```

Let's take a close look at this function declaration:

- The Public keyword before the Function statement says that this function can be used from anywhere in the application. If you had used the Private keyword instead, you could only run the Confirm function from within the Messages module.

- The argument declaration in parentheses tells Microsoft Access that you'll pass the message you want to display to the procedure, as you did for the DisplayMessage procedure.

- The As clause at the end of the Function statement tells Microsoft Access that you want the function to return a certain type of value. Because you want the Confirm function to return either True or False depending on the user's choice, you'll use the Boolean data type for the function—variables of the Boolean type can have one of only two values, True or False.

5 Type the following code into the procedure between the Function and End Function statements:

```
' Ask the user to confirm an action, returning True or False.

Dim bytChoice As Byte

bytChoice = MsgBox(strMessage, vbQuestion + vbOKCancel, conAppName)
```

```
If bytChoice = vbOK Then
    Confirm = True
Else
    Confirm = False
End If
```

Here's what the code does:

- First, it uses the Dim statement to declare the variable bytChoice, which will store the number returned by the MsgBox function.

- Next, it calls the MsgBox function, passing it the strMessage argument and specifying options using the predefined constants vbQuestion and vbOKCancel, which tell Microsoft Access to display the message with a Help (question mark) icon and to include OK and Cancel buttons.

- Finally, the function uses an If...Then statement to check whether the user chose OK—the condition in the statement compares the bytChoice variable to the predefined constant vbOK. If the condition is true, the return value of the Confirm function gets set to True; otherwise, it gets set to False. To specify the value you want a function to return, all you have to do is type the function name followed by an equal sign and the value you want it to return. Of course, the value it returns must be consistent with the data type of the function, in this case Boolean.

Test the Confirm function

Now you can try out the Confirm function. To display the value of a function in the Debug window, you type a question mark (?) before the function name. Also, remember to enclose the arguments to a function in parentheses.

Debug Window button

1 Click the Debug Window button on the toolbar.

2 Type **?Confirm("Is it OK?")** and press ENTER.

Your procedure runs, using the string value you passed for the strMessage argument and displaying the message box according to the options you specified in your function.

Contact Management   ✕
❓   Is it OK?
[OK]   [Cancel]

3 Click OK.

The Debug window displays the return value of the Confirm function.

```
Debug Window                                    _ □ ×
Locals | Watch |          <Ready>                      ...
Expression          | Value        | Type            ▲
                                                     ▼

DisplayMessage                                       ▲
DisplayMessage "I can say anything I like!"
?Confirm("Is it OK?")
True
                                                     ▼
◄                                                  ►
```

Because you chose OK, the Confirm function returned True.

4 Press the BACKSPACE key six times to move back to the end of the line that calls the Confirm function, and then press ENTER.

5 Click Cancel.

This time, the function returns False, indicating that you didn't confirm the action.

6 Close the Debug window.

7 Close the Module window, clicking Yes when Microsoft Access asks if you want to save changes to the Messages module.

You've created two useful general procedures, DisplayMessage and Confirm, that you can use in code throughout your database. Moreover, you could copy the Messages module to other databases you create, so you wouldn't have to redo this work in future applications. This is the advantage of standard modules—they're like a box of tools you can use when you need them, and you can carry them around wherever you go, increasing your programming productivity.

Using General Procedures on a Form

The next step is to put your new procedures to work. And because they're general procedures, declared as public, you can use them anywhere in your application. In this section, you'll simplify the code in the Contacts form's module by using general procedures where appropriate.

Open the Contacts form's module

In Part 1, you opened the Contacts form's module by setting event properties in the property sheet. However, an easy way to view the Visual Basic code for a form is to click the Code button.

1 In the Database window, click the Forms tab, and then click the Contacts form.

Code button

2 Click the Code button.

Microsoft Access opens the Contacts form in Design view, and then opens its module and displays the existing procedures in the module. From here, you can browse through procedures or add new Visual Basic code.

```
Form_Contacts : Class Module                                    _ □ ×

Form                          ▼   BeforeUpdate                      ▼

Option Compare Database
Option Explicit

Private Sub Form_BeforeUpdate(Cancel As Integer)
' If the user entered an address, check for a zip code.

    Dim strMessage As String
    Dim intOptions As Integer
    Dim bytChoice As Byte

    If Not IsNull(Address) And IsNull(PostalCode) Then
        strMessage = "You didn't enter a postal code. Save anyway?"
        intOptions = vbQuestion + vbOKCancel
        bytChoice = MsgBox(strMessage, intOptions)

        If bytChoice = vbCancel Then
```

The first event procedure shown in the module is the Form_BeforeUpdate procedure, to which you added code in Lesson 4. It displays a message if a user fails to enter a ZIP code for an address. If the user clicks Cancel in the message box, it cancels the update so the record isn't saved.

Edit the code to use the Confirm function

This procedure performs a simple action, but it uses several variables and lines of code that aren't really related to the task at hand—they're related to the problem of displaying a message box that asks the user a question. Now that you have a general function that does this for you, you can simplify this event procedure.

1 Replace the three Dim lines with a single Dim statement:

```
Dim blnOK As Boolean
```

This line of code declares a variable called blnOK, which stores the response you get from the Confirm function. Because the Confirm function returns a Boolean value (either True or False), you declare the variable with the Boolean data type.

2 Replace the three lines that set up and display the message (after the first If...Then statement) with the following line:

113

```
blnOK = Confirm("You didn't enter a postal code. Save anyway?")
```

This line calls the Confirm function, passing it the message you want to display and storing its return value—True if the user chose OK, False if Cancel—in the blnOK variable.

3 Replace the second If...Then statement, which tests what button the user chose, with the following line:

```
If Not blnOK Then        ' User chose Cancel.
```

This line checks to see whether the user chose the OK or the Cancel button. Because the value of blnOK is True if the user chose OK, the condition *Not blnOK* is True if the user chose Cancel. If the user chose Cancel, the code in the If...Then block runs, moving the focus to PostalCode and canceling the update.

The following illustration shows the much simplified BeforeUpdate event procedure:

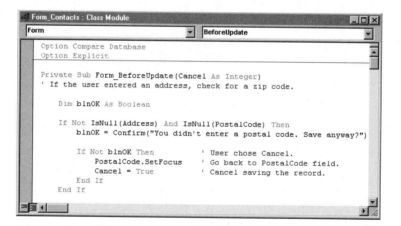

Try the procedure

*Form View
button*

1 Switch to the Contacts form.

2 Click the Form View button on the toolbar.

3 Click the Postal Code field's label to select the text in the field, and then press DELETE to delete the ZIP code.

4 On the Records menu, click Save Record.

The BeforeUpdate event occurs, running your new version of the event procedure. The event procedure works just as it did before, displaying the message that asks if you want to save. This time, however, your general Confirm procedure displays the question.

114

5 Click OK.

Creating General Functions in a Form Module

You've created general functions, and you're using one of them on the Contacts form. Now, suppose you have some ideas for functions that would be useful on the Contacts form, but that would apply only to the form itself. For example, you might want to write functions that manipulate text values on the form.

There's no reason to put this type of procedure in a standard module, because no other form could use it. Additionally, from a standard module, it would be harder to work with values on the form: every time you referred to it, you'd have to specify the form name so that Microsoft Access would know which controls you were referring to. Instead, you should put this type of procedure in the form module.

In this section, you'll create two general functions designed specifically for the Contacts form.

Create the FullName function

The Contacts table has separate fields for last name and first name—and for good reason: in a database that has a single field for names, it's very difficult to search and sort by last name. But suppose you're finding that you often need a way to refer to the full name of the current contact, either in expressions or in code. You can write a very simple general function for the form that returns the full name, so you'll have a simple way to refer to it.

1 Switch to the Contacts form's module.

Up to now, you've created a procedure by clicking a toolbar button. But you don't have to use a command to create a new procedure—you can also create a procedure by typing its header in the Module window.

2 Press CTRL+END to move to the end of the module.

3 Type the following function header:

```
Private Function FullName() As String
```

When you press ENTER, the new procedure gets created, and Microsoft Access automatically adds an End Function statement for it (you might need to scroll down in the window to see this line). As its procedure header declares, the FullName function returns a string value. The function is private to the Contacts form module, because you won't need to call the function from outside the form.

4   Type the following line of code for the function:

```
FullName = FirstName & " " & LastName
```

This line concatenates the value of the FirstName field with a space, followed by the value of the LastName field, and specifies that this is the value for the function to return.

Use the FullName function in an expression

The Contacts form has a calculated field that displays the full name of the contact—it's at the top of page 2 of the form. The ControlSource property of this field is set to an expression that combines the two name fields. But now that you have a function to perform this task, you can refer to the function as the source of the control. This is one of the common situations for including a private function in a form module—when you need to refer to a calculation in expressions on the form.

1   Switch to the Contacts form window.

2   Click the Page 2 button in the form footer.

Contacts	
Contact Name	Hardy Griffin
Contact Type	Client
Email Name	
Referred By	
Notes	

This field displays the full name of the current contact in the form.

Now you'll change the control to use your new function.

3   Click the Design View button on the toolbar.

4   Scroll down a bit in the form, and then click the Contact Name text box.

5   If the property sheet isn't open, click the Properties button on the toolbar.

6   In the property sheet, click the Data tab.

Design View button

Properties button

The ControlSource property has a long setting, which you can simp... by using your new function.

Text Box: Contact Name

| Format | Data | Event | Other | All |

Control Source . . . . . =[FirstName] & " " & [LastName]
Input Mask . . . .
Default Value . . . . . .
Validation Rule . . . . .
Validation Text . . . . .
Enabled . . . . No
Locked . . . . Yes
Filter Lookup . . . . . . Database Default

7 Change the ControlSource property setting to **=FullName()**.

This setting tells Microsoft Access to run your function each time it re-freshes this control, and display the return value of the function in the control.

8 Close the property sheet.

9 Click the Form View button on the toolbar.

Form View button

10 Click the Page 2 button in the form footer.

The Contact Name control still shows the full name, but now it uses your function to fill in the name.

In this case, you could have done without the function—after all, the wizard wrote the control's expression for you. But now that you have a function, you can use it in expressions or code throughout the form.

Create the FullAddress function

You might want to combine the address fields for a contact into a single value, such as the full address you'd type on an envelope. But unlike the FullName function, which you'll only use on the Contacts form itself, you may want to call this function from outside the form—to put the address on another form or report, for example. To make a function available outside the form, you declare it using the Public keyword.

1 Switch to the Contacts form's module.

2 Click below the End Function line in the FullName function, and then type the following function (except the End Function line, which Microsoft Access enters automatically after you type the function header):

117

```
Public Function FullAddress() As String
' Return a string containing the full name and address.

    ' If no name or address, return an empty string.
    If IsNull(LastName) Or IsNull(Address) Then
        FullAddress = ""
    Else
        ' Build the address string.
        FullAddress = FullName & vbNewLine & _
            Address & vbNewLine & _
            City & ", " & _
            StateOrProvince & " " & PostalCode
    End If
End Function
```

Here are some things to notice in the function:

■ First, the function uses the If...Then statement to determine whether there are LastName and Address values on the form. If there aren't, it returns an empty string (""). If there are, it builds the address string by concatenating the contact's name, address, city, state, and postal code. (Note that this function applies to U.S. addresses only.)

■ Take a closer look at the Else statement, which builds the address string. Because the code is much too long to fit on a single line, it's broken up into four lines using the Visual Basic line-continuation character, the underscore (_). Any time you want to continue a line of code on a second line, you can type a space followed by this character, and then continue on a new line—Microsoft Access interprets the code as if it were all on one line.

■ The Else statement uses the FullName function you already created to represent the first and last names. You'll recall that in the expression for the ContactName control, you had to include an equal sign before the function, and then follow the function name with a pair of parentheses; in code, by contrast, you can run a function that has no arguments by simply entering its name.

■ The code then goes on to concatenate the fields in the address, separating them with correct formatting. In order to format the address on three separate lines, it uses the Visual Basic constant vbNewLine, which is a short way of specifying a carriage return character followed by a linefeed character. It places the vbNewLine value after the name and address, places a comma and a space after the state, and includes a space before the postal code. This whole string value gets assigned to the return value of the FullAddress function.

Try the FullAddress function from the Debug window

Now that the function is complete, you can use it in expressions or code throughout the form. For example, you could create a control on the form that displays the full address. But because you declared the FullAddress function using the Public keyword, you should also be able to use it from outside the Contacts form—for example, from the Debug window.

Debug Window button

1   Click the Debug Window button on the toolbar.

The Debug window still displays the text you assigned earlier.

2   Type **?Forms!Contacts.FullAddress**.

The expression *Forms!Contacts* refers to the Contacts form. To use a public function of a form, you enter the form reference, followed by a period (.), followed by the function name (and its arguments, if any, in parentheses).

3   Press ENTER.

The FullAddress function runs, combines the address fields for the current record on the Contacts form, and displays the function's return value in the Debug window.

```
Debug Window                              _ □ X

Locals  Watch            <Ready>              ...

Expression          Value          Type        ▲


                                                ▼

?Forms!Contacts.FullAddress                     ▲
Hardy Griffin
115 Leary Wy.
Seattle, WA
                                                ▼
◄                                       ►
```

 NOTE   Since the FullAddress function refers to the values of several fields on the Contacts form, the form must be open in Form view whenever you use the function. If the Contacts form is in Design view instead of Form view, the previous procedure causes an error. If you encountered an error running the FullAddress function, switch the Contacts form into Form view and then go back to the Debug window and try again.

Try the FullName function from the Debug window

As you've seen, there's no problem running a public function from outside the form. But what about the FullName function, which you declared using the Private keyword?

1   Type **?Forms!Contacts.FullName** and press ENTER.

An error message appears, telling you that there was an object-defined error. In plain English, this means that you asked the form to do something it isn't allowed to do—and it responds, "Sorry, that's private!"

2   Click OK.

As you can see, you can't refer to a private function from outside its module. Note, however, that if a public function in the module uses the private function, you can end up running the private function from elsewhere. This is the case with the FullAddress function, which uses the FullName function in its code—so although FullName isn't directly available from the Debug window, we actually ran it courtesy of the FullAddress function, because FullName is available to any other function in the Contacts form's module.

So Many Options, So Few Rules

Microsoft Access gives you nearly unlimited freedom as a programmer to put code all over the place—in standard modules, form and report modules, and event procedures—and to specify various options, such as public and private procedures. How do you decide where to put your code and how to declare it? Here are some guidelines:

Break procedures into separate tasks.   Try to follow the rule of one procedure per task—your applications will be much easier to maintain. If you're writing code for an event procedure and it's getting complex, consider writing a general function for each subtask.

Generalize procedures whenever possible.   If you can write a procedure so that it could apply to any form or report, do so—and put it in a standard module. One way to achieve this is to add arguments to the procedure, so you can provide the specifics when you call the procedure.

Put object-specific procedures in the object's module.   For tasks or procedures that you know will only be used by a single form or report, be sure to put them in the form or report modules where they belong. You'll avoid having stray procedures, and it will be easier to refer to objects, properties, and controls on the form.

Choose private over public to avoid conflicts.   In a form or report module, declare procedures using the Private keyword unless you have a reason to call them from outside the form. In a standard module, most procedures will need to be declared using Public, because you'll want to use them throughout your database; however, if they're only used to perform subtasks for other procedures in the module, be sure to declare them using Private. Making procedures private whenever possible uses less memory, and can help avoid conflicts.

Close windows and exit Microsoft Access

1 Close the Debug window.

2 Close the Contacts form's Module window.

3 Close the Contacts form, clicking Yes when Microsoft Access asks if you want to save changes.

4 Close Microsoft Access.

The Many Ways to Declare Variables

Like procedures, the variables you use can be public or private, and can live in various places in your database. How variables work depends entirely on where and how you declare them. So far, all the variables you've used have been private variables, declared using the Dim keyword inside a procedure—and used only in that procedure. When the procedure finishes running, a variable declared in this way disappears, along with its contents.

There are several other ways to declare variables that you'll want to keep in mind:

Module-level To declare a variable that you'll use throughout a module, use the Dim statement in the Declarations section of the module—outside any one procedure. The variable will keep its value between procedure calls. Use this type of variable when several procedures in the module all work with the same data.

Public To declare a variable that you'll use throughout your application, use the Public statement instead of the Dim statement, placing it in the Declarations section of any module. The variable will keep its value during the entire time your application is running. You can declare a public variable in a form or report module, but you'll have to include the object's name in every reference to the variable that occurs outside that object. Public variables are useful for application-wide information, such as the names of the application users.

Static Variables you declare within a procedure normally lose their values when the procedure ends. However, if you want Microsoft Access to preserve the value of a variable between calls to the procedure, replace the Dim keyword with the Static keyword. This is useful for a procedure that accumulates a value each time it is called.

In later lessons, you'll use some of these techniques. However, except in special cases, you should stay in the habit of using only private, procedure-level variables—they take up space in memory only while their procedure is running, and they don't conflict with variables of the same name in other procedures.

Lesson Summary

To	Do this
Create a standard module	In the Database window, click the Modules tab, and then click the New button.
Add a general procedure to a module	In the Module window, click the Insert Procedure button. Or, click anywhere outside a procedure and type a Sub or Function statement declaring the procedure.
Provide information to a procedure	Include arguments, along with their data types, in parentheses in the Sub or Function statement declaring the procedure.
Return information from a function	Include the return data type of the function in the declaration. In the function, assign the value you want to return to the function name.
Call a Function procedure and pass arguments	Assign the function name to a variable, including arguments, if any, in parentheses after the function name.
Call a Sub procedure and pass arguments	Type the procedure name followed by the arguments (without parentheses).
Use a general function in a property setting	Type an equal sign followed by the function name, including arguments in parentheses (or just parentheses if there aren't any arguments).
Declare and use a constant	Type the Const statement, followed by a name, the equal sign, and the value of the constant. To use the constant, simply include its name in place of its value.

For online information about	On the Help menu, click Contents and Index, click the Index tab, and then
Using variables	Search for "variables"
Using constants	Search for "constants"
Declaring Sub and Function procedures	Search for "declaring procedures"
Working with string values and other data types	Search for "data types"

For more information on	In *Building Applications with Microsoft Access 97*, see
Using variables and constants	Chapter 4, "Working with Variables, Data Types, and Constants"
Declaring Sub and Function procedures	Chapter 2, "Introducing Visual Basic"
Working with string values and other data types	Chapter 4, "Working with Variables, Data Types, and Constants"

Preview of the Next Lesson

Up to this point, you've written code and seen the results of your efforts, but you haven't actually *seen* the code run. In the next lesson, you'll try out tools in the Module window that let you watch your Visual Basic code in action—and help you find any mistakes you've made along the way. Additionally, you'll learn how to deal with errors or unexpected events that occur while your application is running.

Monitor and Debug Your Code

Estimated time
35 min.

In this lesson you will learn how to:

- Watch Visual Basic code run line by line.
- View the values of variables in your code.
- Compile procedures to ensure that they follow the rules.
- Find and fix programming errors using Visual Basic debugging tools.

In trying to stay on course to reach a destination, a navigator uses various tools to keep track of the vessel's location and heading—and keeps a constant eye on the chart. Because of obstacles, wind conditions, or currents, changes in course are common, and a navigator has to anticipate problems and adjust accordingly. A change in course doesn't necessarily indicate a mistake; it's just part of the job.

When you program in Visual Basic, you have to anticipate that errors will pop up here and there, both while you're programming and when you run your application. Microsoft Access comes equipped with many tools that, like a ship's compass or direction finder, help you keep track of where your application is and where it's heading. In this lesson, you'll learn to monitor your Visual Basic code as it runs, and to understand what's really happening inside that computer when your application is running. You'll use tools in Microsoft Access to find bugs and then fix them and test to make sure they're taken care of.

Start the lesson

 Start Microsoft Access and open the 06Contac database in the practice files folder.

Stepping Through Code Line by Line

In previous lessons, you've written quite a bit of Visual Basic code, and seen the results of running your procedures. But so far, you haven't actually *seen* the code run—you've taken it on faith that your code was running behind the scenes. In this section, you'll see your code run for the first time.

The Visual Basic Module window provides tools that let you stop your code while it's running, and step through Visual Basic statements one by one. This way, you can see what's really going on in your code.

Open the Messages module

In order to watch code run, you first need to open it up and tell Microsoft Access where you want to start watching it. First, you'll open the Messages module and move to the Confirm function, which you created in Lesson 5.

1   In the Database window, click the Modules tab.

2   Double-click the Messages module.

   Microsoft Access opens the Module window and displays your code.

3   Scroll down in the Module window to view the Confirm function.

Setting a Breakpoint to Stop Running Code

When you want Microsoft Access to stop running your code midstream so you can take a look at it, you set a *breakpoint* at the line of code you want to check. A breakpoint tells Microsoft Access, "When you get to this line—but before you run it—stop everything and display the code." It's like calling time out in a basketball game: the action stops so you can regroup, consider what you're doing right or wrong, and make adjustments. Then, when the time-out is over, you allow your code to continue, letting the game go on as before.

Set a breakpoint at the beginning of a procedure

You'll set a breakpoint at the very beginning of the Confirm function, on the Function statement itself. This way, you can take a look at the function each time it runs. To set and clear breakpoints, you use the gray margin that runs down the left side of the Module window.

➤ Click the gray margin to the left of the Confirm function header line (the line that begins with Public Function Confirm).

Click the margin to set a breakpoint for this line.

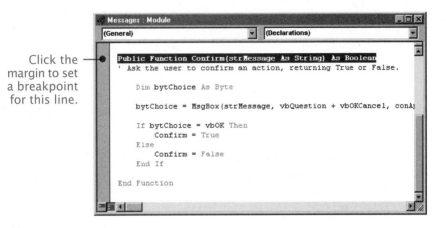

A red dot appears in the margin, and the line of code changes to white text on red. This indicates that Microsoft Access will stop when it encounters this code—in other words, as soon as it tries to run the Confirm function.

 TIP If you set a breakpoint on the wrong line of code, click the red dot to clear the breakpoint, and then click next to the correct line.

Run the procedure

Now try running the Confirm function from the Debug window.

*Debug
Window button*

1 Click the Debug Window button.

2 In the Immediate pane of the Debug window, type **?Confirm("Isn't it wonderful?")**, and press ENTER.

The Confirm function runs, but as soon as it starts, Microsoft Access encounters the breakpoint you set. It then switches back to the Confirm function in the Module window. When you view running code, you'll notice that Microsoft Access displays a *current statement indicator*:

127

a yellow arrow in the margin, and a yellow background highlighting the current statement.

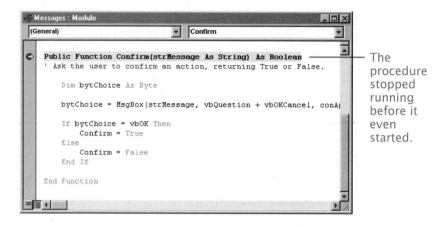

The procedure stopped running before it even started.

Step through the code one line at a time

Nothing is happening right now because of the breakpoint—but in a sense, your code is still running. Information about the procedure, such as the values of local variables and arguments, is stored in your computer's memory. Microsoft Access is ready to continue running the function as soon as you say so. You'll use the Step Into command, which tells Microsoft Access to run one line of code, and then display the Module window again and return control to you.

1 Click the Step Into button.

When you click the button, Microsoft Access moves the current statement indicator to the statement that uses the MsgBox function. Note that Microsoft Access skips over two lines of code: the comment statement and the Dim statement. Because these lines of code don't actually perform an action, they never become the current statement.

Step Into button

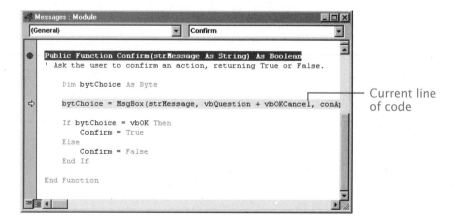

Current line of code

This line of code uses the MsgBox function to display a message to the user, and assigns the return value of the function to the bytChoice variable. When you start the code running again, you can expect to see the message on the screen.

2 Click the Step Into button again.

Microsoft Access runs the current statement, which displays your message on the screen.

3 Click OK.

When you answer the question in the message box, Microsoft Access finishes running the statement by assigning your choice to the bytChoice variable. It then returns to the Module window and moves the current statement indicator to the next line of code: the If...Then statement that determines whether you clicked the OK button.

4 Click the Step Into button again.

Because the condition in the If...Then statement is true—the bytChoice variable is equal to the vbOK constant—Microsoft Access moves to the line of code directly underneath the If...Then statement.

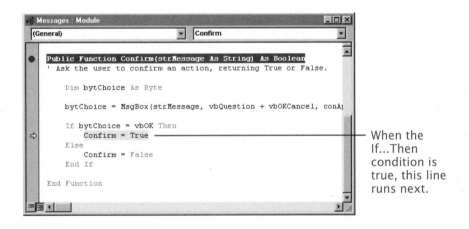

When the If...Then condition is true, this line runs next.

5 Click the Step Into button again.

Microsoft Access sets the return value of the Confirm function to True, and then skips over the Else block, moving the current statement indicator to the End If statement.

```
Messages : Module                                    _ □ ×
(General)                        ▼   Confirm                    ▼

● Public Function Confirm(strMessage As String) As Boolean
  ' Ask the user to confirm an action, returning True or False.

      Dim bytChoice As Byte

      bytChoice = MsgBox(strMessage, vbQuestion + vbOKCancel, conA

      If bytChoice = vbOK Then
          Confirm = True
      Else
          Confirm = False
⇨     End If ─────────────────────────────────────────
                                                                  ── Microsoft
  End Function                                                       Access skips
                                                                     to this line.
```

Here's where you can really see the value of stepping through your code. If the condition in the If...Then statement were false—if you'd chosen Cancel instead of OK—Microsoft Access would have taken a different path through the code. By stepping through your code, you can see exactly which lines of code actually run, rather than trying to guess what's happening in your procedures.

6 Click the Step Into button two more times.

The last two statements in the function run. When you step past the End Function statement, the Debug window becomes active again. This is where you started running the code—before it was stopped by the breakpoint—so this is the place Microsoft Access returns you to when the code finishes running.

```
Debug Window                                         _ □ ×
Locals | Watch |        <Ready>                           ...
Expression            Value            Type            ▲



                                                       ▼
?Confirm("Isn't it wonderful?")                        ▲
True



◄ |                                                    ▼
```

The Debug window displays the return value of the function, which is True.

7 Close the Debug window.

8 In the margin, click the red dot next to the line with the breakpoint (the Confirm function's header line).

This clears the breakpoint you set, so that Microsoft Access will allow the Confirm function to run without interruption in the future.

Stepping from One Procedure to Another

So far, you've stepped through code in just one procedure. But in Lesson 5, you learned to separate your code into a procedure for each task. When you step through code in your application, Microsoft Access can automatically step into each procedure you call so you can follow the progression of your code.

To see this, you'll step through the BeforeUpdate event procedure on the Contacts form. This event procedure calls the Confirm function, so you'll get to see how Microsoft Access runs both procedures.

Open the Contacts form's module and set a breakpoint

Before you can step through the code in an event procedure, you need to set a breakpoint in the function.

Database Window button

Code button

1 Click the Database Window button on the toolbar.

2 In the Database window, click the Forms tab.

3 Select the Contacts form, and then click the Code button.

Microsoft Access opens the Contacts form in Design view, and displays the form's module in the Module window. The first procedure in the window is the Form_BeforeUpdate event procedure.

4 Resize the Module window so it displays most of the code in the procedure (drag the upper left corner of the window to make it larger).

5 In the gray margin, click next to the fifth line in the procedure—the one that calls the Confirm function.

This sets a breakpoint on the statement, so code will stop running there.

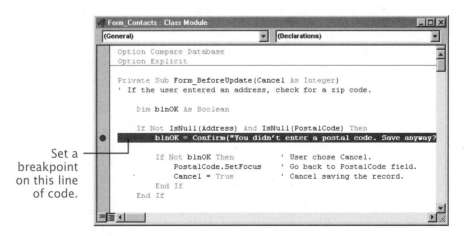

Set a breakpoint on this line of code.

Step through the event procedure

To run an event procedure on a form, you don't use the Debug window—instead, you make the event occur on the form, and the event procedure runs automatically.

Form View button

1 Switch to the Contacts form.

2 Click the Form View button.

3 Click the Postal Code field, and delete the value in the field.

4 On the Records menu, click Save Record.

The BeforeUpdate procedure runs, and when Microsoft Access encounters the breakpoint you set, it displays the event procedure in the Module window.

```
Form_Contacts : Class Module                               _ □ ×

Form                    ▼    BeforeUpdate                  ▼

Option Compare Database
Option Explicit

Private Sub Form_BeforeUpdate(Cancel As Integer)
' If the user entered an address, check for a zip code.

    Dim blnOK As Boolean

    If Not IsNull(Address) And IsNull(PostalCode) Then
        blnOK = Confirm("You didn't enter a postal code. Save anyway?

        If Not blnOK Then              ' User chose Cancel.
            PostalCode.SetFocus        ' Go back to PostalCode field.
            Cancel = True              ' Cancel saving the record.
        End If
    End If
End Sub
```

The procedure runs until it reaches the line of code with the breakpoint.

This line of code, the next statement that will run, calls the Confirm function in the Messages module. When you step through this statement, Microsoft Access will pass control to the Confirm function.

Step Into button

5 Click the Step Into button.

Microsoft Access switches to the Messages module window and displays the Confirm function.

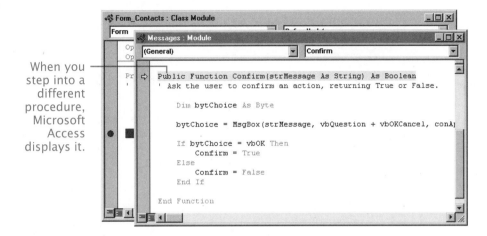

When you
step into a
different
procedure,
Microsoft
Access
displays it.

Now that you're in the Confirm function, you could step through code line by line. Instead, you'll use another new technique to run several lines of code at once, stepping through the entire Confirm function.

*Step Out
button*

6 Click the Step Out button.

The Step Out command tells Microsoft Access to run code until it finishes the current procedure, then pause again when it returns to the procedure that called it. When you click the button, the code in the Confirm function displays your message, asking whether you want to save the record without a postal code.

7 Click Cancel.

When the Confirm function ends, Microsoft Access returns control to the Form_BeforeUpdate event procedure—remember, this is the procedure that called the Confirm function. Starting up where it left off, it moves the current statement indicator to the If...Then statement after the line that called the function.

After
Microsoft
Access
returns from
another
procedure,
code
continues
running
where it
left off.

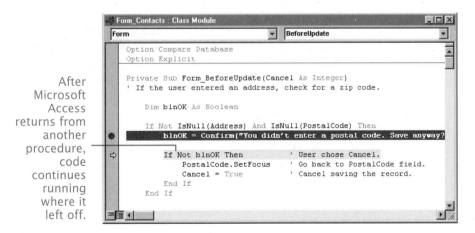

You can now continue stepping through the event procedure, or just tell Microsoft Access to continue.

Go/Continue button

8   Click the Go/Continue button.

The BeforeUpdate event procedure finishes running.

9   On the Window menu, click Contacts.

Because you chose the Cancel button in the message box, your code didn't allow the record to be saved—the pencil icon is still displayed in the record selector. In the next section, you'll try to save the record again.

NOTE   When you're stepping through code in an event procedure, you can't switch back to the form until the event procedure finishes running. If you want to stop code from running, use the End command (Run menu) to end the procedure. Additionally, if an error occurs while you're stepping through code, you may seem to be "stuck" in the procedure. If you can't fix the error and move on, use the Reset command (Run menu) to stop all code from running and reset all variables.

Monitoring Variables and Other Values

Stepping through your code can help you figure out where it's going. But as your application progresses, the values of variables and fields stored in the computer's memory change, affecting how your application works. To really understand what's happening as your code runs, you'll want to find out the values of variables and fields along the way. You need a window into the computer's brain.

Using the debugging tools built into Microsoft Access, you can find out the value of a variable, control, or other expression. In fact, you've already done this: in Lesson 3, you used the Debug window to find out the value of a property. However, there are more efficient ways to monitor values while your code is running, such as using the *Locals pane* (the top pane) of the Debug window. In the Locals pane, Microsoft Access displays the values of all variables and objects that apply to the currently running procedure—the *local* variables and objects, as they're called. As code runs, the Locals pane automatically reflects the changing values of the variables it shows.

Step through the event procedure again

To see how the Locals pane works, you'll run the form's BeforeUpdate procedure one more time by trying to save the record again with the Postal Code field blank. Then, you'll monitor the value of a variable while the procedure runs.

1   On the Records menu, click Save Record.

When Microsoft Access encounters the breakpoint you set in the BeforeUpdate event procedure, it displays the Module window. Now that the procedure is running, you can check the Debug window to see the value of the blnOK variable, which the procedure uses to determine which choice you make in the message box.

Debug Window button

2   Click the Debug Window button.

The top half of the Debug window—the Locals pane—lists three objects, the third of which is the blnOK variable. As you can see, the blnOK variable is currently set to False.

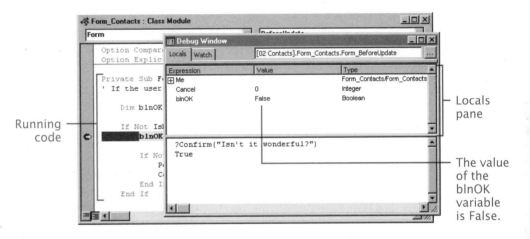

TIP   In the Locals pane, you may notice the entry for "Me" listed above the two variables. This entry, which you'll find at the top of the Locals pane whenever an event procedure is running, represents the current Form or Report object—in this case, the Contacts form—with all its controls and properties. Using this entry, you can view properties of the form and its controls as you monitor your application. To display properties of the form, click the small box with a plus sign to the left of the Me entry. This expands a long list of properties and objects belonging to the form. To view the properties of controls on the form, locate them in the expanded list and click their plus signs.

You're ready to step through the event procedure and watch its variables. In the previous run through this code, you stepped into the code of the Confirm function. This time, you'll learn how to save time by skipping *over* procedures that you aren't interested in. To run a line of code without stepping into the procedure it calls, use the Step Over command—it works just like the Step Into command, except that it runs procedures without pause.

135

Step Over button

3 Click the Step Over button on the toolbar.

The Confirm function runs, displaying its message box.

4 Click OK.

Microsoft Access displays the BeforeUpdate event procedure again—although you stepped over the Confirm function, you are still stepping through code line by line. The Confirm function in the line you just stepped over should have set the blnOK value based on your choice in the message box.

5 Switch back to the Debug window.

As you can see, the Locals pane shows that the blnOK variable is now set to True—indicating that you chose OK in the message box.

The value of the blnOK variable is now True.

You can now continue stepping through the event procedure.

6 Click the Step Over button again.

Because the value of the variable is True—which means that *Not blnOK* is False—the If...Then block doesn't run.

The current statement indicator skips to this line.

7 Click the Step Over button three more times.

The BeforeUpdate event procedure finishes running, allowing the record to be saved in the Contacts form.

Other Techniques for Monitoring Code

The Locals pane of the Debug window is useful when you want to monitor the value of a variable or other object continuously while your code runs. But there are several other techniques you can use for monitoring the progress of your code.

Set watch expressions in the Watch pane. The Locals pane shows only the variables and objects in the current procedure. Sometimes, you may want to view the values of variables or objects outside the current procedure—variables shared by your entire application, for example. To specify exactly what data you want to monitor, use the Add Watch or Quick Watch command (Debug menu). Then, click the Watch tab in the Debug window to see the values of each expression you've specified.

Send values or messages to the Debug window. If there is a certain point in your code where you want to check the status of your procedure or the value of a variable, you can send a message to the Debug window by using the Print method of the Debug object. Anywhere you want to send output to the Debug window, insert a line and type Debug.Print followed by the expression you want to display. For example, you might add the following line of code in the BeforeUpdate procedure instead of using a watch expression:

```
Debug.Print "The Confirm function returned: "; blnOK
```

This way, each time the procedure runs, it reports the value of blnOK in the Debug window. You don't need to set a breakpoint or step through code at all—you can just check the Debug window after the procedure finishes running.

Display message boxes. If you want to report on the progress of a procedure while it runs, but you don't want to check the Debug window each time, you can instead display messages to yourself using the MsgBox function. For example, you could place the following line of code in the BeforeUpdate procedure:

```
MsgBox "The Confirm function returned: " & blnOK
```

Change code as it runs. In most programming systems, you can't change code while it's running. But in Microsoft Access, you have the flexibility to change the values of variables or code itself while you step through line by line. Suppose you're monitoring a variable and you

continued next page

Other Techniques for Monitoring Code, *continued*

notice it doesn't have the value you expect. If necessary, you can add a line of code to your procedure and continue running it.

Set the current statement. Normally, when stepping through code, you don't control the order in which Visual Basic statements occur. However, if you're stepping through code and would like to change which statement runs next, you can use the Set Next Statement command (Debug menu). This is especially useful if you change a line of code that didn't work as expected, and you want to run it again without restarting the procedure.

The strategy you select to monitor and debug your code depends on what problems you're trying to diagnose and how often you need to check what's happening. As you program in Visual Basic, you'll learn which techniques are most appropriate for each debugging task.

Finding and Fixing Bugs in Your Code

The procedures you've stepped through so far aren't broken—although you've learned more about how they work by monitoring them more closely, they seem to be working just fine. But what if code isn't working as you'd planned? This is when Module window tools come in especially handy. In this section, you'll learn to check your Visual Basic code as you enter it, and then fix any errors you find.

Most of your contacts are in either New York City or Seattle, and you'd like to make it easier for users to enter addresses from these cities. One approach is to write an event procedure that runs after you enter a postal code, filling in the correct City and State values. This way, users who know about the shortcut can skip over the City and State fields when they're entering New York City or Seattle addresses. While you're at it, you'll also have the event procedure fill in the Country field if the user enters a U.S. postal code.

Write an event procedure that fills in values for you

You want to set the City, State, and Country fields each time the user enters a value in the PostalCode field. To do this, you need to create an event procedure for the control's AfterUpdate event.

1   In the Object box at the top of the Module window (on the left), select PostalCode.

2   In the Procedure box (on the right), select AfterUpdate.

The Module window shows the PostalCode_AfterUpdate event procedure.

Object box → **PostalCode** ... **AfterUpdate** ← Procedure box

```
Form_Contacts : Class Module

        ' If no name or address, return an empty string.
     If IsNull(LastName) Or IsNull(Address) Then
         FullAddress = ""
     Else
            ' Build the address string.
         FullAddress = FullName & strNewLine & _
            Address & strNewLine & _
            City & ", " & _
            StateOrProvince & " " & PostalCode
     End If
  End Function

  Private Sub PostalCode_AfterUpdate()
  |
  End Sub
```

3 Type the following code for the event procedure:

```
' If New York or Seattle postal code, fill in city and state.

Select Case PostalCode
    Case "10000" To "10200"
        City = "New York"
        State = "NY"
    Case "98100" To "98199"
        City = "Seattle"
        State = "WA"

End Select
```

So far so good! This code introduces a new Visual Basic statement for controlling the flow of code: the Select Case statement. You use this statement when you want to perform one of several different actions based on the value of a single variable or expression. Each Case statement underneath it introduces a different block of code—which block of code runs depends on which value the Select Case expression has. As you've seen before, indenting each block of code helps to show how the statement works.

In this example, you're telling Microsoft Access, "Okay, look at the value of the PostalCode field—if it's between 10000 and 10200 (most New York City addresses), run this first block of code; if it's between 98100 and 98199 (most Seattle addresses), run this second block of code." You can set up as many "cases" as necessary; if you want, you can finish with the Case Else statement followed by a block of code, which runs if none of the cases match the value of the Select Case expression.

Next, you'll add code that checks whether the postal code is a U.S. ZIP code, and fills in the Country field if it is a U.S. ZIP code.

139

4 Just above the line with the End Select statement, enter the following line of code:

```
If PostalCode > "00000" And < "99999" Then
```

When you press ENTER, the text of this line turns red and a message appears. You made an error! (Of course, you were only following instructions.) The error message, "Expected: expression," tells you that Visual Basic requires an expression—such as a variable—that's missing somewhere in this line.

5 In the message box, click OK.

Now that you've cleared away the message, you'll notice that the "<" symbol is highlighted—this is the point in the line that Microsoft Access doesn't like—and the line is still shown in red text.

```
                                                                        Microsoft
         End If                                                         Access
End Function                                                            highlights
                                                                        the spot
Private Sub PostalCode_AfterUpdate()                                    where it
' If New York or Seattle postal code, fill in city and state fields.    identifies a
                                                                        problem.
    Select Case PostalCode
        Case "10000" To "10200"
            City = "New York"
            State = "NY"
        Case "98100" To "98199"
            City = "Seattle"
            State = "WA"
    If PostalCode > "00000" And   "99999" Then

    End Select
```

You may not have known it, especially if you're a good typist, but every time you've entered a line of code in the Module window, Microsoft Access has checked to make sure it follows the rules. In this case, you've entered something that isn't allowed, even though it looks like it should work. The line seems to say, "If the PostalCode field is greater than five zeros and less than five nines, then..." Why doesn't it work? Unlike the English language, where you can skip the subject if it's repeated after a conjunction such as "and"—as in "Buzz went to the moon and returned"—the Visual Basic language requires you to repeat the subject. In other words, you have to say, "If the PostalCode field is this and the PostalCode field is that..."

Fix the error and finish the procedure

Before going any further, you should fix the error. Incidentally, if you don't fix a line of code that contains a syntax error, Microsoft Access continues to display the line in red text to indicate that it isn't valid.

1 Press the LEFT ARROW key, type **PostalCode**, and then click the next line.

No error this time!

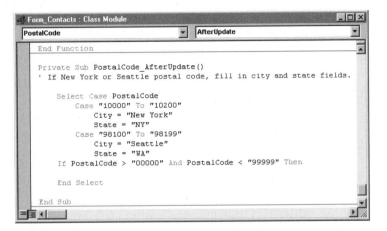

2 Enter the following two lines of code underneath the If...Then statement:

```
Country = "USA"
Title.SetFocus
```

These two lines set the value of the Country field and then move the focus to the Title field, because the user no longer needs to enter a value in the Country field.

Types of Errors

Errors are bound to occur when you write or run code—which is why Microsoft Access offers so many tools to help you deal with them. Still, it isn't always easy to figure out what's wrong. To know where to look, it helps to know the types of errors that can occur. Most errors fall into the following categories:

Syntax errors   When you type a keyword incorrectly or leave off punctuation in code, Microsoft Access displays a message as soon as you try to leave the line. Usually, the message tells you exactly what is wrong with the line of code. Until you fix a line of code with a syntax error, Microsoft Access displays the line in red.

Invalid references   If you misspell a variable, field name, or proce-dure, or if you forget to declare a variable you use, Microsoft Access dis-plays an error when you try to run the code.

continued next page

Types of Errors, *continued*

Incomplete code If your code isn't complete—for example, if you have an If...Then statement block without an End If statement—Microsoft Access displays an error when you try to run the code.

Logic errors If your code runs without errors but doesn't do what you had planned, you've probably made an error in the logic of your program. Remember, the computer only does what you tell it—you can't make any assumptions about how things will work! The toughest kind of error to figure out, a logic error requires that you step through code to watch what's happening, and then correct any mistakes you find.

Run-time errors There are many errors that Microsoft Access can't detect until your application is running. For example, if your code passes an invalid value as the argument to a Visual Basic function, an error occurs and code stops running. A run-time error sometimes indicates that your code needs rethinking—especially if you made incorrect assumptions about how the user interacts with your application. In many cases, however, run-time errors are to be expected. Later in the lesson, you'll see how your code can respond to them before an error message disrupts your application.

You'll see examples of all these types of errors in this lesson—and you're guaranteed to keep seeing them, just about every time you program. However, as you gain experience with Visual Basic programming, you'll become better at avoiding errors or handling them as they come up.

Telling Microsoft Access to Check Your Code

You've already seen how Microsoft Access checks each line of code you enter to make sure that it doesn't contain any errors. But many errors aren't obvious in a single line. To see them, you have to look at the line of code in the context of the rest of the procedure or application. Although it doesn't do so automatically while you enter code, Microsoft Access does check your procedures thoroughly before it runs them. It checks for various types of consistency—for example, whether the variables you've used in your code are all declared, and whether the procedures you call exist in your application. This process is called *compiling*, because it involves putting together information from various sources in your application, preparing to run the code.

One way to compile a procedure is to try running it. But you won't always want to wait until you run your code to make sure it's all right—that would be like checking to see if you have air in your tires only *after* leaving on a long trip. Fortunately, you can ask Microsoft Access to compile your procedures at any time.

Compile your event procedure and resolve errors

Believe it or not, there are a couple of errors in the PostalCode_AfterUpdate procedure. If you try to run the procedure as it is, it won't work. To find out what they are, you'll ask Microsoft Access to compile your code.

*Compile Loaded
Modules button*

1 Click the Compile Loaded Modules button.

Microsoft Access displays the error message "Variable not defined." This message means, more or less, that Microsoft Access isn't familiar with an expression in your code.

2 In the message box, click OK.

The expression it can't figure out is highlighted in the Module window. In this case, the "variable" that Microsoft Access doesn't recognize is *State*.

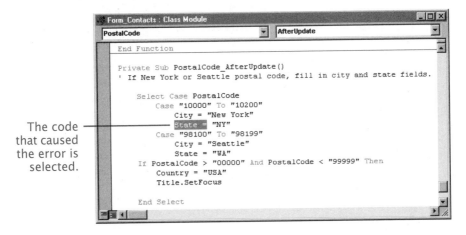

The code that caused the error is selected.

3 In this line of code, you're not actually referring to a variable at all. You're trying to refer to the State field on the Contacts form. The reason for this error? The field is actually called *StateOrProvince*—a simple mistake, but one we'll need to correct before going on. In cases like this one where you've misspelled something, you'll notice that Microsoft Access isn't always as helpful as it could be. At least it isn't judgmental, just matter-of-fact. Click the end of the word *State* and type **OrProvince**.

4 Two lines down, at the other reference to *State,* click the end of the word and type **OrProvince**.

Now that you've fixed the error, you should compile again to make sure that everything's just right.

5 Click the Compile Loaded Modules button again.

It's not just right. This time, the message Microsoft Access displays is "Case without Select Case." This message indicates that at least one block of code in the procedure isn't set up correctly, and Microsoft Access encountered a Case or End Select statement when it expected something else. Here is the problem: You used the If...Then statement, included a block of code after it, but didn't include the End If statement to indicate the end of the block. To successfully compile and run this procedure, you'll have to make sure each block of code has a beginning and an end (just as a parenthetical remark has an opening and a closing parenthesis).

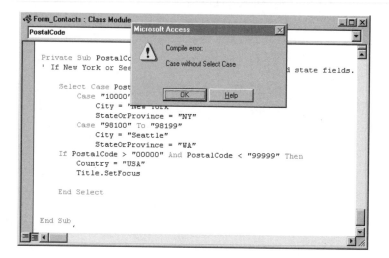

6   Click OK.

The statement that's selected is the one immediately *after* the point where Microsoft Access expects to see the End If statement.

7   Click the blank line above the End Select statement and type **End If**.

8   Click the Compile Loaded Modules button once again.

No surprises this time; your house is in order.

> **TIP**   In any Visual Basic error message, you can click the Help button to see a Help topic giving you more information about the error and how to fix it.

Run the event procedure from the Contacts form

Now that the code compiles fine, you can test the procedure to see if it works correctly. You'll want to step through the code, so you should set a breakpoint in the event procedure.

1 In the Module window, click the gray margin next to the Select Case line.

The now familiar breakpoint indicator appears in the margin.

2 Switch to the Contacts form.

3 Click the New Record button on the toolbar.

4 Fill in the fields in the record as follows:

New Record button

Field Name	Value
First Name	Katherine
Last Name	Ransel
Address	102 W. 86th St.
Postal Code	10024

5 Press TAB to leave the Postal Code field.

When you leave the field, your event procedure runs. When Microsoft Access reaches the breakpoint, it suspends the running code and brings the Module window to the front.

Before you step through the code, you'll check to see what the PostalCode value is. Earlier in the lesson, you checked values using the Debug window. Here, you'll use an even easier method. When code is suspended as it is now, you can point to any variable in the Module window to bring up a *Data Tip*—a small box that tells you the current value of the variable.

6 Point to the PostalCode variable anywhere in the event procedure.

A Data Tip appears just underneath the variable, showing the value you entered for the PostalCode field: 10024.

When code is running, Data Tips display the current value of variables or fields you point at.

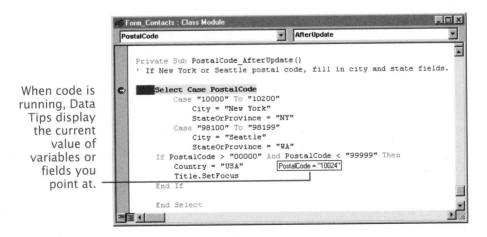

145

Now that you've verified that the value of the Select Case expression is 10024, step through the code and watch what happens.

Step Into button

7 Click the Step Into button on the toolbar.

The current statement indicator moves to the Case statement for the first block of code, where it will check whether the value 10024 falls in the range of 10000 to 10200.

8 Click the Step Into button again.

As expected, the current statement indicator moves into the first block of code, because the value 10024 does fall in the range of 10000 to 10200. When you allow it to continue, Microsoft Access will run the two lines underneath the Case statement, which set the City and StateOrProvince values for New York City.

```
Form_Contacts : Class Module                            _ □ ×
PostalCode                    ▼    AfterUpdate                ▼

    Private Sub PostalCode_AfterUpdate()
    ' If New York or Seattle postal code, fill in city and state fields.

        Select Case PostalCode
            Case "10000" To "10200"
                City = "New York"
                StateOrProvince = "NY"
            Case "98100" To "98199"
                City = "Seattle"
                StateOrProvince = "WA"
        If PostalCode > "00000" And PostalCode < "99999" Then
            Country = "USA"
            Title.SetFocus
        End If

        End Select
```

9 Click the Go/Continue button on the toolbar.

10 Switch to the Contacts form.

Go/Continue button

The City and State Or Province fields are filled in as you'd planned. However, look at the Country field. Your code was supposed to set it for you, but it doesn't have a value. Something in the event procedure isn't working correctly.

Fix a bug in your code

To figure out the problem, you need to run the event procedure again. This time, you'll try a different postal code, and see what happens in the code.

1 Click the Postal Code field and type **02134**.

2 Press TAB.

The PostalCode_AfterUpdate event procedure runs and stops at the breakpoint.

Step Into button

3 Click the Step Into button twice.

Microsoft Access steps over the Case statements, because the postal code you entered doesn't fall in the range.

4 Click the Step Into button a third time.

As you expected, the two lines underneath the second Case statement didn't run. But look where the current statement indicator jumped to: it skipped over not only the two lines under the Case statement, but also the entire block of code that sets the Country field, and ended up on the End Select statement at the very end of the procedure.

Microsoft
Access
skipped
from here...

...to here,
skipping over
the block of
code you
want it to run.

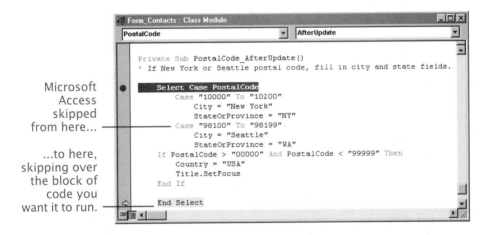

```
Form_Contacts : Class Module

PostalCode                          AfterUpdate

    Private Sub PostalCode_AfterUpdate()
    ' If New York or Seattle postal code, fill in city and state fields.

        Select Case PostalCode
            Case "10000" To "10200"
                City = "New York"
                StateOrProvince = "NY"
            Case "98100" To "98199"
                City = "Seattle"
                StateOrProvince = "WA"
        If PostalCode > "00000" And PostalCode < "99999" Then
            Country = "USA"
            Title.SetFocus
        End If

    End Select
```

You've found the mistake in the code. Because the block of code is between the second Case statement and the End Select statement, Microsoft Access assumes it is part of that "case," and runs it only when the postal code is in that range. To make the If...Then block run independently, you need to move it completely outside the Select Case...End Select structure.

5 If the End Sub statement isn't showing in the Module window, scroll down to bring it into view.

6 Click to the left of the If...Then statement (but *not* in the gray margin) and drag down to the End If statement to select the entire block of code.

The four lines appear highlighted.

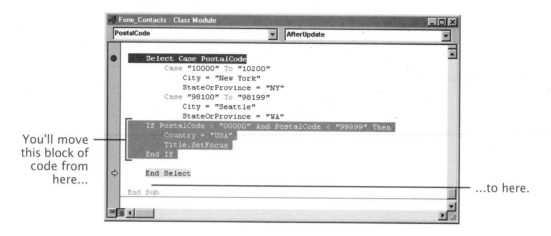

You'll move this block of code from here...

...to here.

To move code in the Module window, you just drag it to the new location.

7 Click the highlighted block of code, and then drag it down below the End Select line and release the mouse button.

Now this block will run independently of the Select Case block.

Retest the procedure

Debugging your code is all about testing and retesting your procedures—and it's time to test it once more. First, however, you'll need to stop the code that's currently running and clear the breakpoint so the procedure can run without interruption.

1 Click the Reset button on the toolbar.

Reset button

Microsoft Access ends the procedure and resets all variables.

2 On the Debug menu, click Clear All Breakpoints.

3   Switch to the Contacts form.

4   Click the Postal Code field, and then type **10024**.

5   Press TAB.

This time, the Country field gets filled in with the value "USA," and the focus moves to the Title field. The bug is fixed!

As you continue to program in Visual Basic, you're guaranteed to get all sorts of unexpected results from your code: some because of typos, some because of mistakes in program logic, and still others because of misunderstandings about how Microsoft Access works. But using the tools available in the Debug window—along with a healthy dose of patience and diligence in testing and retesting your procedures—you'll be able to solve these problems and get your application working just right.

Close the form and exit Microsoft Access

1   Close the Contacts form, clicking Yes when Microsoft Access asks if you want to save changes to the form.

2   On the File menu, click Exit.

Lesson Summary

To	Do this	Button
Stop a procedure from running so you can monitor its progress	Set a breakpoint at the line where you want to stop the code from running. (Click the gray margin to the left of the line of code.)	
Step through code in a procedure line by line, moving into the procedures that your code calls	Click the Step Into button (or press the F8 key).	
Step through code line by line, skipping over the procedures that your code calls	Click the Step Over button.	
Continue running code until the current procedure ends; then pause to step through code again	Click the Step Out button.	
Continue running code until it finishes (or encounters a breakpoint or error)	Click the Go/Continue button.	

Lesson Summary, *continued*

To	Do this	Button
View the value of a variable while code is running	While code in the Module window is running, point to the variable to see a Data Tip. Or, to view all local variables and objects in the Locals pane, click the Debug Window button.	
Run one of several different blocks of code based on the value of a single expression	Use the Select...Case statement.	
Check your code to make sure the structure and all the syntax are correct	Compile your code using the Compile Loaded Modules command or the Compile All Modules command (Debug menu).	

For online information about	On the Help menu, click Contents and Index, click the Index tab, and then
Using tools in the Module window	Search for "Module window"
Finding and fixing bugs in your code	Search for "debugging code"
Controlling the flow of code in your application	Search for "control flow"

For more information on	In *Building Applications with Microsoft Access 97*, see
Using tools in the Module window	Chapter 2, "Introducing Visual Basic"
Finding and fixing bugs in your code	Chapter 8, "Handling Run-Time Errors"
Controlling the flow of code in your application	Chapter 2, "Introducing Visual Basic"

Preview of the Next Lesson

In this lesson, you discovered more about how your procedures work, and learned to find programming errors. In the next lesson, you'll learn about errors that can't be fixed—errors due to unexpected conditions or actions the user takes, that occur while the application runs. Instead of fixing your code, you'll learn how to write code that anticipates such errors and handles them accordingly.

Respond to Errors and Unexpected Conditions

Estimated time
35 min.

In this lesson you will learn how to:

- Replace standard Microsoft Access error messages with your own.
- Write code that responds to errors and unexpected conditions.
- Add a value to a combo box list.

If you've ever been on a trip into the wilderness, you know that there's quite a bit of work involved in preparation. You need to be ready for anything. Confusing trails make it easy to get lost, unexpected weather can catch you off guard, and even a minor injury can be a big deal away from civilization. For safety, you bring maps, a compass, first aid supplies, and extra food and clothing in case of a prolonged stay. Most of the time, you won't take advantage of your precautions—but who wants to be stuck in the middle of nowhere without these bases covered? You don't mind the risks, of course; it wouldn't be any fun if it were as safe as sitting in your living room!

Planning for the unexpected has its application in Visual Basic programming as well. The nature of an event-driven system like Microsoft Access is that your application waits around for things to happen. Most of them are what you expect: the user adds data here, clicks a button there. But computer users have a way of trying everything, and sooner or later, someone will try something you didn't anticipate. Although the errors that can occur in your application are less exciting than being stuck in the wilderness, it nevertheless pays to prepare your application for anything before sending it out into the wild world of daily use.

The Visual Basic language provides sophisticated ways to control what happens when errors occur. Normally, errors can interrupt your application, causing it to appear unpolished or even making it unusable. In this lesson, you'll learn to respond to special events that occur when users perform unexpected actions on your forms. Additionally, you'll learn to use Visual Basic statements to intercept errors that occur while your procedures are running. Overall, you'll discover strategies for making your application foolproof—so that whatever comes its way, it can respond gracefully and effectively.

Start the lesson

➤ Start Microsoft Access and open the 07Contac database in the practice files folder.

Replacing Standard Error Messages

There are many errors that can occur when users interact with the forms in your application. Some of these errors will come as a complete surprise, and there may be nothing you can do about them. On the other hand, you occasionally *intend* to have a specific error occur. For example, suppose you set the Required property to Yes for a field in a table, and then the user tries to leave the field blank when entering data. As you would expect, Microsoft Access displays an error message saying that the field can't be blank. In Lesson 4, you did this very thing for the LastName and FirstName fields in the Contacts table.

If you expect that users will commonly encounter a specific error in a form, such as the error for leaving a required field blank, you'll want to ensure that the message they receive makes sense to them, so they can fix the problem and continue with their work. But the standard error messages Microsoft Access displays won't always make sense to your users. In this section, you'll learn to replace the standard error messages that occur on your forms with your own messages. Specifically, you'll respond to the error that occurs when a user leaves a required field blank, creating an event procedure that displays your own message for this situation.

Responding to the Error Event

Each time an error occurs in a form, the form's Error event occurs. You can place code in this event procedure to display a message, or even to fix the problem that's causing the error. But to respond, you'll need to know what error has occurred. For this purpose, the Error event procedure includes an argument called DataErr, which contains the code number of the error that occurred. You'll use this number to determine whether it's the error you're expecting, so you can respond appropriately.

But first, you must do a little detective work. You need to find out what the code number is for the error you want to respond to. To do this, you'll add code to the Error event procedure telling Microsoft Access to display the error number in the Debug window. Then, you'll cause the error to occur so you can discover the number. After you know the code number of the error that occurs when the user leaves a required field blank, you'll change the code to respond to this specific error.

Find out the code number for an error in a form

You'll first open the Contacts form, and then add a line of code to the Error event procedure.

1 In the Database window, click the Forms tab.

2 Click the Contacts form, and then click the Design button.

3 If the property sheet isn't open, click the Properties button on the toolbar.

*Properties
button*

4 Click the Event tab in the property sheet.

5 Select the OnError property, and then click the Build button.

```
Form                                        ×
Format | Data | Event | Other | All |
On Dbl Click . . . . . . .
On Mouse Down . . . .
On Mouse Move . . . .
On Mouse Up . . . . . .
On Key Down . . . . . .  [Event Procedure]
On Key Up . . . . . . . .
On Key Press . . . . . .
Key Preview . . . . . . .  Yes
On Error . . . . . . . . .                  ▼ ...  ──── Click the
On Filter . . . . . . . . .                              Build button.
On Apply Filter . . . . .  [Event Procedure]
On Timer . . . . . . . . .
Timer Interval . . . . .  0
```

6 Click Code Builder, and then click OK.

Microsoft Access displays the Form_Error event procedure in the Module window.

```
Form_Contacts : Class Module                        _ □ ×
Form                          ▼   Error                      ▼
                End If
         End If

      End Sub

      Private Sub Form_Error(DataErr As Integer, Response As Integer)
      |
      End Sub

      Private Sub Form_KeyDown(KeyCode As Integer, Shift As Integer)
      ' If key is CTRL+1, enter values for New York.

         If KeyCode = 49 And Shift = 2 Then     ' CTRL+1 was pressed.
            City = "New York"
            StateOrProvince = "NY"
```

153

Note the two arguments in the Sub header for the Form_Error procedure, DataErr and Response.

7 Press TAB and type the following line of code:

```
Debug.Print "DataErr = "; DataErr
```

Debug Window button

8 Click the Debug Window button.

This opens the Debug window so your code will have somewhere to send its message.

Cause the error to occur

Now you'll jump back to the Contacts form and cause the error to occur by trying to save a record without a name.

1 Switch to the Contacts form.

2 Click the Form View button on the toolbar.

Form View button

3 Press DELETE to delete the data in the First Name field.

Delete the data in this field.

4 Press TAB.

Because the First Name field is required, Microsoft Access displays an error message.

154

As you can see, the error message isn't all that friendly—but you'll replace it with your own message.

5 Click OK.

When you caused the Error event to run the event procedure, your code sent a message to the Debug window. Let's take a look.

6 On the Window menu, click Debug Window.

```
┌─────────────────────────────────────────────────────┐
│ ▣ Debug Window                             _ □ X      │
├─────────────────────────────────────────────────────┤
│ Locals │ Watch │          <Ready>              ...    │
├─────────────────────────────────────────────────────┤
│ Expression          │ Value        │ Type       │ ▲  │
│                                                  │    │
│                                                  │    │
│                                                  │    │
│                                                  │    │
│                                                  │ ▼  │
├─────────────────────────────────────────────────────┤
│   DataErr =  3314                                │ ▲  │
│                                                  │    │
│                                                  │    │
│                                                  │    │
│                                                  │ ▼  │
├─────────────────────────────────────────────────────┤
│ ◄ │                                          ► │ /   │
└─────────────────────────────────────────────────────┘
```

The error number for this error—leaving a required field blank—is 3314.

7 Close the Debug window.

8 Press ESC to undo your change.

Displaying Your Own Message for a Specific Error

Now that you know the error number, you can write code to respond to the error. In the Error event procedure, you'll check to see if the error is due to the user leaving a required field blank. If it is, you'll display an appropriate message; if not, you'll allow Microsoft Access to display the standard error message.

In addition to the DataErr argument that provides you with the number of the error that occurred, the Error event procedure has another argument: the Response argument. You use this argument to tell Microsoft Access how to proceed after your code runs. You have two options: you can tell Microsoft Access to display the standard message for the error, or you can tell it to ignore the error (because you've either solved the problem or displayed your own custom error message).

Write code that displays a custom error message

You'll replace the Debug.Print code you wrote before with code that displays your own message.

1   Switch to the Contacts form's module.

The Module window still shows the Form_Error event procedure.

```
Form_Contacts : Class Module                    _ □ ×
Form                    ▼    Error                ▼
            End If
        End If

    End Sub

    Private Sub Form_Error(DataErr As Integer, Response As Integer)
        Debug.Print "DataErr = "; DataErr
    End Sub

    Private Sub Form_KeyDown(KeyCode As Integer, Shift As Integer)
    ' If key is CTRL+1, enter values for New York.

        If KeyCode = 49 And Shift = 2 Then      ' CTRL+1 was pressed.
            City = "New York"
            StateOrProvince = "NY"
```

2   Enter the following Visual Basic code for the procedure, replacing the line containing Debug.Print with the lines of code shown here:

```
Private Sub Form_Error(DataErr As Integer, Response As Integer)
' If error is because of name, display a custom error message.

    Const conErrFieldRequired = 3314

    If DataErr = conErrFieldRequired Then
        DisplayMessage "You must fill in First Name and Last Name."
        Response = acDataErrContinue
    Else
        Response = acDataErrDisplay    ' Display standard message.
    End If
End Sub
```

Let's walk through the procedure line by line:

- The Const statement declares a constant value for the error code you discovered. This helps to make your code more readable, because it clarifies what the number 3314 means. You can use the constant conErrFieldRequired in place of the number later in the procedure.

- The condition in the If...Then statement checks whether the DataErr value passed to the event procedure is equal to the error value conErrFieldRequired. If it is, the procedure runs the first block of code, displaying your custom message.

■ The DisplayMessage line of code uses the general procedure you created in Lesson 5 to display a message box. The message tells users what to do to solve the problem: fill in both the first and the last name before saving the record.

■ The next line sets the Response argument of the Error event procedure, using the predefined constant acDataErrContinue. Setting the Response argument to this value tells Microsoft Access to skip displaying the standard error message—which is what you want in this case, because you displayed your own message.

■ The Else block of code, which runs if the error is something other than the one you want to respond to, sets the Response argument to acDataErrDisplay. This tells Microsoft Access to display the standard error message for the error, because you don't know what the error is.

Try the new message

If you cause the error again, it should display your new message.

1 Switch to the Contacts form.

2 Click the label of the First Name field to select the data in the field.

3 Press DELETE to delete the data in the field.

4 Press TAB.

   Microsoft Access displays the new error message.

5 Click OK.

6 Press ESC.

This simple use of the Error event shows how you can make life easier for users by anticipating problems they may encounter. Of course, this code responds only to a single error. By writing more complex code for the Error event, you can respond to errors in various ways. For example, you might want to use a Select...Case statement to branch to several different blocks of code, providing your own error message for several errors. Or you might write code to help the user solve the problem—for example, your code could enter a required value automatically so that the record could be saved. The possibilities are endless; the main thing to remember is that when an error occurring in a form causes confusion, the Error event procedure is there as a resource to help you solve the problem.

Responding to a Combo Box Error

While the Error event helps you respond to many errors, there's one error that you respond to using a different event—an error that commonly occurs if you use combo boxes on your application's forms. Combo boxes and list boxes are one of the most powerful features of Microsoft Access, because they provide a way to look up values stored in different tables. In this section, you'll learn how to make them work even better by responding to the NotInList event.

The Contacts form has a lookup field courtesy of the Database Wizard: the Contact Type field. This field displays values from the Contact Types table, so you can easily specify the type of each contact you enter by selecting from the list. For many fields, you'll want to ensure that only certain values are entered in the list. Combo boxes do this automatically if their LimitToList property is set to Yes—if you try to type a value in the Contact Type field that isn't in the list, you get an error.

Try typing a new value in the Contact Type field

Suppose you want to enter the contact type for the first record in the Contacts form.

1   Click the Page 2 button in the Contacts form footer.

2   Click the Contact Type field, and then click the drop-down arrow next to the combo box.

You don't see the contact type you want.

3   Click the drop-down arrow again to close the list, and then type **Vendor** and press ENTER.

Microsoft Access displays an error message, telling you that this value isn't in the list.

4 Click OK.

5 Press ESC.

This error message is a form of validation; Microsoft Access makes sure you don't enter an incorrect value. But what if you want users to be able to add their own contact types? They could do this by opening the Contact Types form, but this would interrupt their task of entering a contact. Ideally, you'd like them to do this easily from within the Contacts form. What you want to do is run an event procedure any time the user enters a value that isn't in the list. You can do this by responding to the NotInList event, which occurs when the user tries to enter the value—but before the error message tells the user the value must be in the list.

Let users add a contact type to the list automatically

When a user enters a contact type value that isn't in the list, you want to ask if the user really wants this value to appear in the list permanently. To ask the question, you'll use the Confirm function you wrote in Lesson 5. If the user does want to add the new type, you'll use Visual Basic code to add the value to the Contact Types table behind the scenes.

Design View button

1 Click the Design View button.

2 Scroll down in the form window so you can see the ContactTypeID combo box.

3 Click the ContactTypeID control.

Microsoft Access displays the event properties for the ContactTypeID control.

4 Click the OnNotInList property, and then click the Build button.

5 Select Code Builder, and then click OK.

Microsoft Access opens the form module for the Contacts form and creates the ContactTypeID_NotInList event procedure.

```
Form_Contacts : Class Module                        _ □ ×
ContactTypeID                   ▼   NotInList                        ▼
    Option Compare Database
    Option Explicit

    Private Sub ContactTypeID_NotInList(NewData As String, Response
    |
    End Sub


    Private Sub Form_BeforeUpdate(Cancel As Integer)
    ' If the user entered an address, check for a zip code.

        Dim blnOK As Boolean

        If Not IsNull(Address) And IsNull(PostalCode) Then
            blnOK = Confirm("You didn't enter a postal code. Save ar
```

You'll notice that the header for the NotInList procedure includes two arguments: NewData and Response. The NewData argument contains the value the user entered in the field—the value that isn't yet in the list. The Response argument lets you tell Microsoft Access what to do after your procedure ends, just like the Response argument you saw earlier in the Error event procedure.

6 Enter the following Visual Basic code for the procedure:

```
Private Sub ContactTypeID_NotInList(NewData As String, Response As Integer)
' Ask the user whether to add a value to the list.

    Dim strMessage As String
    Dim dbsContacts As Database
    Dim rstTypes As Recordset

    strMessage = "Are you sure you want to add '" & NewData & _
        "' to the list of contact types?"

    If Confirm(strMessage) Then

        ' Open the Contact Types table and add the NewData value.
        Set dbsContacts = CurrentDb()
        Set rstTypes = dbsContacts.OpenRecordset("Contact Types")
        rstTypes.AddNew
        rstTypes!ContactType = NewData
        rstTypes.Update
        Response = acDataErrAdded      ' Requery the list.
    Else
        Response = acDataErrDisplay    ' Display the error.
    End If
End Sub
```

This event procedure uses the same type of code you've seen before to ask the user a question. However, there are several important new elements:

- The procedure has three Dim statements declaring variables you're going to use later in the procedure. The first declares a string variable you'll use to store your message to the user. The other two are *object variables*—so named because they store whole database objects, not just values—which you'll use when you add a record to the Contact Types table. The first of these is dbsContacts, a Database-type variable that will store information about the database; the second is rstTypes, a Recordset-type variable that will represent the Contact Types table when you add records.

- The line that sets the value of the strMessage variable concatenates string values with the ampersand (&) operator. In this case, the line of code combines your message text with the value of the NewData variable, so the message can include the new value in the question it asks: "Are you sure you want to add "*this value*" to the list of contact types?"

- The condition in the If...Then statement is actually a call to your own Confirm function, which asks the user a question and returns True or False. If the Confirm function returns True, it means the user chose OK in the message box, and the first block of code runs.

- The key to this procedure is the block of code that runs if the user chooses OK. These five lines are known as *data access object* (DAO) code, because they utilize methods and statements belonging to the DAO code library, which you use when working directly with databases. For example, the first line uses the Set statement to assign an object to the dbsContacts variable—in this case it assigns the current database object, which is returned by the CurrentDb function. Before you can work with data in Visual Basic, you have to open a database in this way.

- The next line uses the OpenRecordset method of the new database object to open the Contact Types table. To add or edit records using Visual Basic, you need to open a recordset object, either a table or a query. The Set statement assigns the recordset object to the rstTypes variable. As with other methods, you type the method after the object, separated by a period.

- The next line uses the AddNew method of the rstTypes recordset to add a record to the end of the table.

- The next line assigns the value of the NewData argument, which is the value the user wants in the list, to the ContactType field in the table. To refer to the value of a field in a recordset, you follow the recordset name with the field name, separated by an exclamation point (!).

- The final line of DAO code uses the Update method to save the change to the recordset, adding the new record to the Contact Types table.

- After your procedure adds the record to the table, the last task is to tell Microsoft Access how to proceed. Setting the Response argument to the constant acDataErrAdded tells Microsoft Access that you've added the value, and you want it to requery the list box so that the value will show up in the list.

■ The line after the Else keyword runs if the condition is False, in which case it sets the Response argument to acDataErrDisplay. This setting tells Microsoft Access that you didn't add the value, and that you want it to display the standard error message and require the user to enter a value in the list.

The NotInList procedure gives a simple example of DAO code for manipulating a database—in later lessons, you'll learn advanced techniques for working with databases in Visual Basic. But this procedure does the trick for now: it adds a new record to the list. Perhaps most importantly, it allows your users to avoid a potentially annoying error message every time they try to type something in this box.

Try the NotInList event procedure

1   Close the Module window.

2   Click the Form View button on the toolbar.

3   Click the Page 2 button in the form footer.

4   Click the Contact Type field, and then type **Vendor** and press ENTER.

The NotInList event occurs, and your event procedure displays the message box, asking if you want to add your entry to the list.

Form View button

5   Click OK.

Your code opens the Contact Types table, adds the new record, and then tells Microsoft Access to requery the list to include your new value.

6   Click the drop-down arrow next to the Contact Type box.

The list now includes your new entry.

Adding a record to the list behind the scenes is just one possible strategy for responding to the NotInList event; you may need to choose another based on your application's needs. For example, if the records shown in a combo box list are just part of a complete set of records that includes other values—a list of contacts' names, perhaps, taken from a complete table with addresses and phone numbers—you couldn't add records automatically. In a case like this, your NotInList event procedure might display another form where users could enter contact information.

Creating Error-Handling Routines

Up to this point, you've learned how to respond to errors that occur due to users' actions on a form, particularly when they enter data that isn't allowed. These errors are easy to respond to, because form events occur whenever they happen. When you program in Visual Basic, there's an even more important class of errors: those that happen as a result of actions your code performs, rather than as a result of users' actions. Some errors occur because of mistakes in the code you've written; these you should fix. But others happen not because of an error in your code, but just because your code can't anticipate every possible condition that might be in place when it runs.

For example, suppose your code works with a database on a network, and the network suddenly goes down. Obviously, this would cause an error. Or what if your code makes changes to a database, but the user opens the database using the read-only option so that changes can't be made? These unexpected conditions will cause run-time errors, and would normally cause your application to stop abruptly, showing a message that would mean very little to a user who doesn't know about programming.

Fortunately, Visual Basic provides a mechanism with which you can respond to any type of error that occurs while your code is running. It's called *error handling*. Error handling allows you to avoid abrupt interruptions of your application whenever unexpected things happen. By handling errors, you can either solve problems that come up and move on with your business, or give the user appropriate feedback about the problem and bow out gracefully. In this section, you'll learn how to use the On Error GoTo statement along with other Visual Basic statements to respond to run-time errors.

Handling Errors That Occur When Your Application Is Read-Only

When testing your application, it's a good idea to think of all the different conditions that might arise when users run it. One situation is that the user might open the application database in read-only mode. This isn't a common case, but it is certainly possible, and you want your application to be able to cope with it gracefully. Fortunately, when users open an application as read-only, Microsoft Access automatically forbids them to change data in forms—you don't have to do anything special to make it work. You only have to worry if your code itself tries to make changes to data.

But guess what? In Lesson 4, you wrote code that sets the value of controls on the form. It's the Form_KeyDown procedure, which sets city, state, and country values on the form for New York City whenever a user presses CTRL+1. If the data can't be updated—for example, if the database is read-only—this code will cause a run-time error.

Set up a run-time error in your code

Before you write code to handle this error, let's see what happens if you don't handle it at all. Rather than closing the database and reopening it in read-only mode, you'll simulate this condition by making just the data in the Contacts form read-only. To do this, you can set the RecordsetType property for the form to Snapshot.

Design View button

1 Click the Design View button on the toolbar.

2 Click the Data tab in the property sheet.

3 Click the RecordsetType property, and select Snapshot from the list of values.

4 Click the Form View button on the toolbar.

Form View button

5 Press CTRL+1.

An error occurs—and not one you'd like your users to see.

```
Microsoft Access                         [X]

Run-time error '3326':

This Recordset is not updatable.

   [ Debug ]  [ Continue ]  [ End ]  [ Help ]
```

As with all run-time errors, you have two choices: Debug or End (you can also get Help on the message, but eventually you still have to choose one of the other two options). If you click Debug, Microsoft Access opens the Module window and displays the procedure that caused the error, highlighting the specific line of code that caused it. If you click End, the procedure that caused the error stops running.

Note the code number of the error at the top of the dialog box text: 3326. You'll use this number in your error-handling code.

6 Click Debug.

The Module window shows the existing Form_KeyDown event procedure, which you wrote in Lesson 4.

```
Form_Contacts : Class Module                              _ □ ×

Form                        ▼   KeyDown                      ▼

    End Sub

    Private Sub Form_KeyDown(KeyCode As Integer, Shift As Integer)
    ' If key is CTRL+1, enter values for New York.

        If KeyCode = 49 And Shift = 2 Then      ' CTRL+1 was pressed
⇨           City = "New York"
            StateOrProvince = "NY"
            Country = "USA"
        End If

    End Sub

    Private Sub Combo47_Enter()
```

This line of code caused the error, because data in the form is read-only.

NOTE When you click the Debug button in a run-time error message, the procedure stops running temporarily, but doesn't end. It's just as if you'd set a breakpoint on the statement that caused the error—except that you can't keep stepping through this code unless you first take care of the error. If you want to end the procedure that caused an error, rather than stop and view it, click the End button in the run-time error message.

Add error-handling code to the event procedure

Because you want to avoid having users see an error message like this—especially one that lets them dive right into your code—you'll add error-handling code to the procedure. But first you'll want to reset the code that you left running when the error occurred.

Reset button

1   Click the Reset button on the toolbar.

2   Edit the existing KeyDown event procedure to appear as follows:

```
Private Sub Form_KeyDown(KeyCode As Integer, Shift As Integer)
' If key is CTRL+1, enter values for New York.

On Error GoTo Err_Form_KeyDown

    Const conErrNotUpdatable = 3326

    If KeyCode = 49 And Shift = 2 Then   ' CTRL+1 was pressed.
        City = "New York"
        StateOrProvince = "NY"
        Country = "USA"
    End If
```

```
     Exit_Form_KeyDown:
         Exit Sub

     Err_Form_KeyDown:
         If Err.Number = conErrNotUpdatable Then
             DisplayMessage "Can't edit record; data is read-only."
         Else
             DisplayMessage Err.Description
         End If
         Resume Exit_Form_KeyDown
     End Sub
```

Here's what the code does:

- The On Error GoTo statement says that if an error occurs while the procedure is running, Microsoft Access should jump to the line labeled Err_Form_KeyDown, rather than halting the code and displaying an error message.

- The Const statement declares a constant value for the error code you saw earlier (3326), which signifies the "Recordset not updatable" error.

- The Exit_Form_KeyDown line is a *label*, a name followed by a colon that you can use to identify a line of code you want Microsoft Access to jump to. The Exit Sub statement below the label makes sure that if the procedure runs normally without error, it will exit after running the main code, rather than continuing with the error-handling code below. You should always add the Exit Sub or Exit Function statement before error-handling code, so the error-handling code won't run unless an error actually occurs.

- The Err_Form_KeyDown label introduces the error-handling code, and provides a place for Microsoft Access to jump to if an error does occur.

- The If...Then statement on the next line checks to see if the error is in fact the one you expected. It uses the Number property of the Err object, which always contains the number of the last error that occurred in your application.

- If the error is caused by read-only data, the following line displays your custom message using the DisplayMessage Sub procedure you created in Lesson 5. If the error is caused by something else you didn't expect, the line under the Else statement displays the standard Microsoft Access error message, which you can find using the Description property of the Err object.

- Finally, the Resume statement in the last line tells Microsoft Access that your error-handling code is finished, and that you want to continue running your procedure at the line labeled Exit_Form_KeyDown. Resuming at this line runs the Exit Sub line, causing the procedure to end.

Now, if this procedure can't set values in the form for any reason, the user will receive a message explaining the problem, but your application will continue running instead of ending abruptly with an error message.

Step through the error-handling code

To try out the new error-handling code, you'll cause the error to happen again. However, before you start, you'll set a breakpoint in the procedure so you can step through and see how it works.

1   Set a breakpoint on the sixth line of the procedure—the line that sets the City field to "New York"—by clicking the gray margin to the left of the line.

Now the procedure will stop at this line, regardless of whether an error occurs.

2   Switch to the Contacts form.

3   Press CTRL+1.

The KeyDown event procedure runs, reaches your breakpoint, and appears again in the Module window. The next statement to run will try to set a value in the form. Because data in the form is still read-only, you can expect that this statement will cause an error.

Step Over button

4   Click the Step Over button.

Instead of moving to the next statement, the current statement indicator jumps all the way down to the line below the label Err_Form_KeyDown—the line you specified in the On Error GoTo statement at the beginning of the procedure.

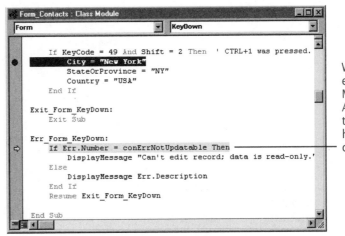

When the error occurs, Microsoft Access jumps to your error-handling code.

In effect, the error-handling code you wrote is now interrupting the normal flow of code—you might say your procedure is in "error-handling mode."

5 Click the Step Over button twice.

Your code displays the error message.

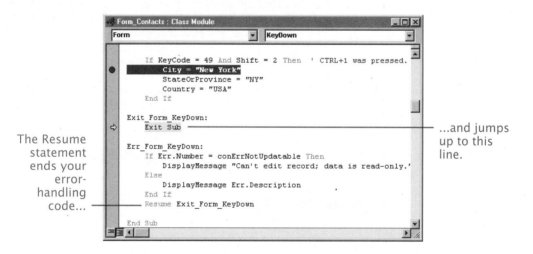

6 Click OK.

7 Click the Step Over button two more times.

When your error-handling code finishes running, the Resume statement sends the current statement indicator up to the line under the Exit_Form_KeyDown label: the Exit Sub line.

The Resume statement ends your error-handling code...

...and jumps up to this line.

```
Form_Contacts : Class Module
Form                          KeyDown

        If KeyCode = 49 And Shift = 2 Then  ' CTRL+1 was pressed.
            City = "New York"
            StateOrProvince = "NY"
            Country = "USA"
        End If

Exit_Form_KeyDown:
        Exit Sub

Err_Form_KeyDown:
        If Err.Number = conErrNotUpdatable Then
            DisplayMessage "Can't edit record; data is read-only."
        Else
            DisplayMessage Err.Description
        End If
        Resume Exit_Form_KeyDown

    End Sub
```

8 Click the Step Over button a final time.

9 Close the Module window.

Stepping through your error-handling code helped to show you how this technique works. For your users, this is all hidden—but the important difference is that now they won't see the run-time error message that appeared before your error-handling code was in place.

Anticipating Other Problems That Cause Errors

Having data turn out to be read-only is just one of many unexpected conditions that can occur in your application—the possibilities for errors are endless. And there are plenty of other procedures in the application that don't yet have error-handling code in them. To be thorough, you would want to provide error-handling code in every procedure you write, so that users will never see your application halt abruptly with an error message. However, most procedures you write won't perform any actions that are likely to cause errors. To save time and effort, you can concentrate on providing error handling only where errors are likely to occur.

Although by no means complete, the following list shows a few actions for which you should be sure to provide error handling. You should anticipate that errors could occur any time your code attempts to do any of the following:

- Access any file on disk, directly or indirectly
- Run queries or change data in a database
- Set properties of objects
- Perform mathematical calculations

Additional Error-Handling Techniques

You've seen one simple way to handle errors using the On Error GoTo statement. But there are several other techniques you can use to handle errors. Here's a sampling:

Resume code at the statement that caused the error. If your code can diagnose and solve the problem that occurred, you'll want to allow your code to continue running with the statement that caused the error. By using the Resume statement on a line by itself at the end of your error-handling code, you can tell Microsoft Access to return to the line that caused the error and try it over again.

For example, if your code tries to access a file on a floppy disk drive and an error occurs because the disk isn't in the drive, your code could display a message telling the user to insert the correct disk. At the end of the error-handling code, you'd use the Resume statement so that the statement that tried to access the disk could run again.

Skip over the statement that caused the error. If the statement that causes an error is not critical to your application, you can use the Resume Next statement to tell Microsoft Access to continue running code at the statement *after* the one that caused the error. In this type of situation, you might even *expect* the error to occur on a regular basis, and you want the statement to run only if it doesn't result in an error.

continued next page

Additional Error-Handling Techniques, *continued*

For example, suppose you have a procedure that sets a value on a form that may or may not be open. If the form is open, the line of code that sets the value runs as expected. If it's not, the line causes an error—but because you don't want to set the value unless the form is open, you're content to simply skip the statement altogether using Resume Next.

Tell Microsoft Access to ignore errors temporarily. If you know that an error is likely to occur on a particular statement and you don't want to suspend the running code at all, you can use the On Error GoTo Next statement to suspend error handling altogether. This causes Microsoft Access to skip over a line that causes an error as if the error didn't occur. For example, if you want to set a property for a control only if the control has the property, you could use On Error GoTo Next before setting the property so that an error won't occur if the property doesn't exist.

If you use this strategy, you'll usually want to check the Err.Number value immediately following the statement to determine what error occurred, if any. Additionally, be sure to turn error handling back on by including another On Error GoTo statement, or additional errors could occur without your knowledge, causing problems in your application.

The technique you choose will depend on the types of errors you anticipate and what you want to do with them. If you don't know how you want to handle an error, the best fallback position is the strategy you used in this lesson: display the description of the error in a message box, and then exit the procedure.

Close the form and exit Microsoft Access

1   Close the Contacts form, clicking Yes when Microsoft Access asks if you want to save changes to the form.

2   On the File menu, click Exit.

Lesson Summary

To	Do this
Respond when an error occurs in a form	Write an event procedure for the form's Error event, using the DataErr argument to determine which error occurred.
Respond when the user enters a value in a combo box that isn't in the list	Write an event procedure for the control's NotInList event. To add the value to the combo box list automatically, use DAO code to add a new record to the table that the list comes from.

To	Do this
Specify the action Microsoft Access should perform after the Error or NotInList event procedure finishes	Set the Response argument to one of the following constants: acDataErrContinue, acDataErrDisplay, or acDataErrAdded.
Specify error-handling code to run if an error occurs in your code	Include the On Error GoTo statement at the beginning of your procedure, followed by a line label where error-handling code begins.
Determine the last run-time error that occurred in your code	Include Err.Number in your procedure. For a description of the error, use Err.Description.
Continue running your procedure after error-handling code finishes	Include the Resume statement at the end of your error-handling code.

For online information about	**On the Help menu, click Contents and Index, click the Index tab, and then**
Handling errors in forms and code	Search for "error handling"
Using combo boxes	Search for "combo boxes"
Using list boxes	Search for "list boxes"
Using data access object (DAO) code to work directly with databases	Search for "recordsets"

For more information on	**In Building Applications with Microsoft Access 97, see**
Handling errors in forms and code	Chapter 8, "Handling Run-Time Errors"
Using combo boxes and list boxes	Chapter 3, "Using Forms to Collect, Filter, and Display Information"
Using data access object (DAO) code to work directly with databases	Chapter 9, "Working with Records and Fields"

Preview of the Next Lesson

Throughout Part 2, you learned Visual Basic programming techniques for writing, debugging, and polishing your code, while working with the Contacts database created by the Database Wizard. With these techniques at your disposal, you're ready to move forward to create an application from scratch. In Part 3, you'll learn to put together all the pieces of a complete user interface, working with a custom application rather than one created by the Database Wizard. In Lessons 8 and 9, you'll start by working with your own dialog boxes and pop-up forms, both powerful tools for interacting with users of your applications.

Creating a Custom Application

Lesson

8

Gather Information in a Dialog Box

Estimated time
45 min.

In this lesson you will learn how to:

- Create an unbound form to act as a dialog box.
- Find a record in a form's recordset.
- Filter records in a report using criteria the user selects.

Have you noticed that every other phone number you call these days has some sort of automated answering system? "Welcome to our automated information center. If you're using a touch-tone phone, please press 1 now." It's becoming rare to talk to an actual person, unless of course you first jump through all the required hoops: "To wait to talk to an actual human being, please stay on the line...." If you're like me, you've chosen to wait for the good old human representative more than a few times!

These systems save companies lots of money, and often provide just the information callers need. But even as we become more accustomed to them, it's clear that they're much less flexible than most human beings. Automated answering systems are limited—for now, anyway—by the keypad provided on your telephone. They don't always have the options you need at a given time, and you have to answer several questions to get where you want to be.

Like a telephone answering system, your database applications need to help users get to information. Fortunately, your computer's interface is much more flexible than a telephone, but you'll still consider the same types of challenges and pitfalls. You need to ask users questions about what they want to do—establish a dialogue with them—and respond to their input. Of course, the conversations you have can exchange quite a bit more information than pressing 0 through 9 on a telephone keypad.

One of the tools you have for conversing with the user is the *dialog box*, a form you can present on the screen to provide information and ask questions. In this lesson, you'll learn to communicate with your application's users by creating dialog boxes and accessing the information the users provide in them.

Start the lesson

 Start Microsoft Access and open the 08Subscr database in the practice files folder.

Creating an Application on Your Own

In Parts 1 and 2 of this book, you enhanced a database that you created with the Database Wizard. But as a Microsoft Access developer, you're likely to need databases that the wizard doesn't create. Your applications may need to store a type of data that the wizard doesn't handle, or you may just want to communicate with users in your own way. In Part 3, you'll create an application user interface on your own.

When you create an application from scratch, you need to plan in advance the features you want it to have. First, you create the tables that will store all the information you need. Then, you begin creating forms, reports, and other objects that make up the interface for your application. Finally, you'll tie all the objects together by writing Visual Basic code. Along the way, you might use many different wizards and builders to help you—even if you bypass the Database Wizard, you can get help creating parts of your application by relying on other wizards, such as the Table Wizard and the Command Button Wizard.

View the tables in the Subscription database

Starting in this lesson, you'll work with an application that stores subscriptions to a publication. The Subscription practice database already has tables full of subscriber data, and even some of the forms and reports you'll need—but you'll create additional objects and the Visual Basic code that makes it work. First, however, you should take a look at what's already in the Subscription database.

1   In the Database window, click the Tables tab.

The Subscription database contains two tables, Subscribers and Payments. If you'd designed this database from scratch, you would have created these tables and chosen their fields either by running the Table Wizard or by using Table Design view.

Relationships button

2   Click the Relationships button on the toolbar.

Microsoft Access displays the Relationships window, showing the fields in the Subscribers and Payments tables and the relationship between the two tables.

Relationships	□
Subscribers	**Payments**
SubscriberID	PaymentID
FirstName	SubscriberID
LastName	PaymentDate
CompanyName	YearlyRate
Address	YearsPaid
City	PaymentMethod
State	CreditCardName
ZipCode	CreditCardNumber
Phone	ExpirationDate
PaidThrough	CreditCardAuthorizatic

This line indicates that the two tables are related based on values in the SubscriberID field.

As you can see, the Subscribers table includes fields for name and address information—everything you'll need to send mailings to subscribers. The Payments table includes fields that store each payment received from a subscriber. There is a *one-to-many* relationship between the tables, because for each subscriber, there can be many related payment records.

3   Close the Relationships window.

These two tables are all that's required for this database. But for a more complex application, you may need many tables that relate in different ways.

Open the Subscribers form

Most applications have a *main form*—the place where users spend most of their time viewing and entering data. In the Subscription database, the main form is the Subscribers form, which is already provided for you in the practice database.

1 In the Database window, click the Forms tab.

2 Double-click the Subscribers form.

To create a form like this for your own application, you can use the Form Wizard. After you create a form and let the wizard lay out the fields for you, you may want to open the form in Design view to rearrange and resize fields, or perhaps to add formatting or pictures to give the form a custom look. Then, you may want to add additional capabilities to the form; for example, in the next section, you'll add a useful command button to the form.

Using Dialog Boxes in Your Applications

So far, the only interaction you've learned to have with the user is through message boxes, which are a simple type of dialog box. You've displayed a message, and the user has responded by clicking a button. But message boxes all look the same, and are limited to one, two, or three buttons. By creating a custom dialog box form, you can include any combination of controls and buttons you want. What all dialog boxes have in common, however, is that they pop up on top of the user's work and wait for a response.

Dialog boxes are especially useful for the following:

Presenting users with a custom message box If you want to display a message that has a custom appearance or special command buttons—with text other than Yes, No, OK, or Cancel—you can't just rely on the MsgBox function. For example, you might want a dialog box to allow four or more actions, or to include command buttons with icons on them.

Asking questions before opening a form or report When you provide a way for users to open a form or report, you may want to allow them to specify options. For example, you might want to ask users which records they want to view or in which order to display them.

Allowing users to specify general options for your application
A dialog box can have many controls for entering diverse types of information in one place. For example, you might want to allow users to customize the appearance or behavior of your application by collecting their preferences in a dialog box called Options and then saving them in a table.

Gathering additional information for a menu command   If your application uses custom menu bars, you may want one of the commands to open a dialog box to get details on how to proceed. Microsoft Access itself, like most Windows applications, has several dialog boxes accessible from menus and toolbars. In Lesson 10, you'll learn to create custom menu bars and toolbars that perform actions such as opening a dialog box.

There are as many uses for dialog boxes as there are types of applications. In this lesson, you'll create two common kinds of dialog boxes, and learn all the basic techniques you need to create a dialog box for any purpose.

Creating a Dialog Box to Go to a Specific Record

In this section, you'll create a dialog box that helps users jump to a specific record in the Subscribers form. In the dialog box you'll add a list box to display the available records, and you'll write code for a new button to display the record that the user selects.

You've already written code to help users locate a record: in Lesson 3, you created a combo box to do this. But by using a dialog box, you can keep this tool out of the way of users, giving you more room on the form—and more flexibility in how users select the records they're looking for. When a user clicks a button on the Subscriber Form, your dialog box will pop up.

Users can select the record they want from a list in the dialog box.

Create the GoToRecord dialog box form

A dialog box is a special type of form: instead of displaying data in its controls, it allows the user to set the control values so you can collect information. A form that doesn't display data is called an *unbound* form, because it isn't bound to a table or query—its RecordSource property is blank. You create unbound forms from scratch in Design view, because there's no wizard to create them for you.

*Database
Window button*

1 Click the Database Window button on the toolbar.

2 Click the New button.

Microsoft Access displays the New Form dialog box. Design view is selected by default, so you don't have to choose a method for designing the form. And because you want the form to be unbound, you won't select a table or query either.

3 Click OK.

Microsoft Access creates a blank form and displays it in Design view. As you can see by the Design view rulers, the new form's Detail section is 5 inches wide and 2 inches long.

4 Click the right side of the Detail section of the form and drag to resize it to 4½ by 2 inches.

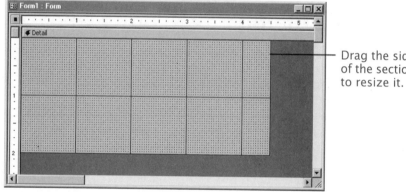

Drag the side of the section to resize it.

*Save
button*

5 Click the Save button on the toolbar.

6 Type **GoToRecordDialog**, and then click OK.

Microsoft Access saves the form in the database.

Use a wizard to create the Select Subscriber list box

Now you're ready to add controls to the dialog box to get the user's input. The primary control for the dialog box is a list box from which the user can select a subscriber's record. You'll create this control using the List Box Wizard.

*Control
Wizards tool*

1 In the toolbox, make sure the Control Wizards tool is selected, and then click the List Box tool.

2 Click near the top of the form.

*List Box
tool*

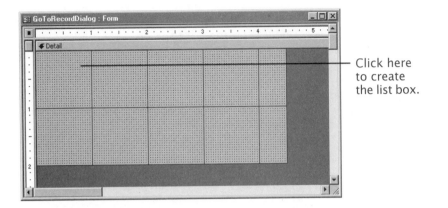

Click here to create the list box.

The List Box Wizard starts, asking how you want the list box to get the values it displays.

3 Select the first option, I Want The List Box To Look Up The Values In A Table Or Query, and then click Next.

The wizard asks which table you want the list box to get values from.

4 Click Subscribers, and then click Next.

The wizard asks which fields you want to include in the list box.

5 Double-click the LastName field to add it to the Selected Fields list, followed by the FirstName, City, and State fields (in that order), and then click Next.

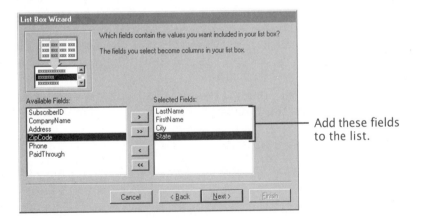

Add these fields to the list.

The wizard displays the list of subscribers as it will appear in the list box.

6 Resize the columns of data:

■ Double-click the right side of the FirstName column selector to have it fit the data and field name.

181

- Drag the right side of the City column selector to make it slightly wider than the data shown.

- Double-click the right side of the State column selector to have it fit the data and field name.

Use the column selectors to resize columns as shown.

7 Click Next.

The wizard asks what label you want for your combo box.

8 Type **Select Subscriber:** and then click Finish.

The wizard creates the list box and places it on your form. Behind the scenes, the wizard sets properties for the list box so it will display the data you specified. It also automatically includes the SubscriberID field—the primary key field in the Subscribers table—as a hidden field in the list box. Users won't see this field, but the list box will be based on it, and you'll use its value to set the current record in the Subscribers form.

Notice that the wizard gave the list box the default name List0. You'll use this name in code when referring to the value of the list box.

Position the list box on the dialog box form

The list box isn't quite right yet. Before you test it, you'll want to make a few adjustments.

1 Point to the upper left corner of the list box's label and drag it just above the upper left corner of the list box.

2 Double-click the right side of the label, resizing it to fit the text.

3 Click and drag the list box to move it near the upper left corner of the form.

4   Drag the bottom right corner of the list box to make it slightly wider (increase the width by about ¼ inch) and nearly as long as the Detail section of the form.

The form should look like this:

> GoToRecordDialog : Form
>
> Detail
>
> Select Subscriber
> Unbound

To test your list box, you can switch to Form view.

Form View button

5   Click the Form View button on the toolbar.

The list box shows records from the Subscribers table.

> GoToRecordDialog : Form
>
> Select Subscriber
>
> | Griffin | Hardy | Seattle | WA |
> | O'Halloran | Kevin | New York | NY |
> | Stepanian | Kara | Boston | MA |
> | Hunting | David | New York | NY |
> | Christensen | Bonnie | Dallas | TX |
> | O'Keefe | Maura | New York | NY |
> | Geloff | Kevin | Seattle | WA |
> | MacDougall | Rob | Los Angeles | CA |
> | Sundberg | Deborah | Atlanta | GA |
> | Doyle | Judy | New York | NY |
> | Greenman | Gilbert | New York | NY |

Modify the list box to sort by last name

You may have noticed that the records in the form aren't sorted alphabetically—unfortunately, the List Box Wizard doesn't do this for you. It would be quite a bit easier for users to find the records they want if the subscribers were in order. To sort the records, you'll need to modify the RowSource query that the wizard created for your list box.

Design View button

1   Click the Design View button on the toolbar.

2   On the GoToRecordDialog form, click the list box to select it.

183

Properties
button

3 If the property sheet isn't open, click the Properties button to display it.

4 Click the Data tab in the property sheet.

5 Click the RowSource property, and then click the Build button.

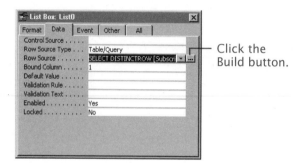

Click the
Build button.

Microsoft Access displays the query for the list box in a Query Builder window.

6 Select the Sort row underneath the LastName field, and then click the drop-down arrow and select Ascending from the list.

Set the sort order for the LastName field to Ascending.

7 Select the Sort row underneath the FirstName field, and then click the drop-down arrow and select Ascending from the list.

8 Close the Query Builder window, clicking Yes when Microsoft Access asks if you want to save changes to the RowSource property.

Now records in the list box will be sorted by last name, and if there are duplicate last names, by first name as well. The list box is ready to go!

9 Close the property sheet.

Add a button to change records in the Subscribers form

You'll try out the list box soon enough—first, you need to add buttons and Visual Basic code to the dialog box to make it work. The most important item to add is the button that actually finds the selected record in the Subscribers form.

Control Wizards tool

Command Button tool

1 In the toolbox, click the Control Wizards tool to deselect it, and then click the Command Button tool.

2 Click near the top of the form, just to the right of the list box.

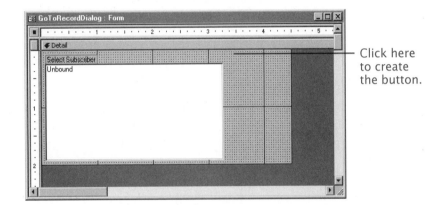

Click here to create the button.

Microsoft Access creates the button, giving it a default caption such as Command2.

Properties button

3 Click the Properties button on the toolbar, and then click the All tab in the property sheet.

4 Click the Name property and type **ShowRecord**.

5 Click the Caption property and type **&Show Record**.

6 Set the Default property to Yes.

With the Default property set to Yes, the button will be selected automatically if the user presses ENTER while in the dialog box.

7 Set the Enabled property to No.

Setting the button's Enabled property to No disables it, so the user can't click it when the dialog box first opens. You wouldn't normally want to disable a button, but in this case, there's a good reason to do so. When you first open a form that has a list box, the list box doesn't have a value—nothing is selected. Until the user selects a subscriber in this list box, you don't want the ShowRecord button to be available. Later, you'll add code that enables the button as soon as the user selects something in the list.

8 Close the property sheet.

9 With the right mouse button, click the ShowRecord button, and then click Build Event.

10 Double-click Code Builder.

Microsoft Access displays the event procedure for the button's Click event.

```
Form_GoToRecordDialog : Class Module
ShowRecord                        Click

Option Compare Database
Option Explicit

Private Sub ShowRecord_Click()

End Sub
```

11 Add the following code to the procedure (except the Sub and End Sub lines, which are already there):

```
Private Sub ShowRecord_Click()
' Find the selected record, then close the dialog box.

    Dim rst As Recordset

    ' Store the recordset for the Subscribers form.
    Set rst = Forms!Subscribers.RecordsetClone

    ' Locate the record for the selected subscriber.
    rst.FindFirst "SubscriberID = " & List0

    ' Set the form's Bookmark property to move to the record.
    Forms!Subscribers.Bookmark = rst.Bookmark

    ' Close the dialog box.
    DoCmd.Close acForm, "GoToRecordDialog"
End Sub
```

This code changes the current record in the Subscribers form to the one the user has selected in your list box. Let's look at this code more closely.

- The Dim statement creates a recordset-type variable called *rst*. You'll use this variable to represent the set of subscriber records in the Subscribers form.

- The second line of code begins with the Set statement. This line contains an expression—*Forms!Subscribers.RecordsetClone*—that refers to the records shown in the Subscribers form. Every form has a RecordsetClone property that you can use to get a copy of the form's underlying recordset. As you've seen before, you refer to a form other than the current form by preceding the form name with the Forms keyword, followed by an exclamation point. And to refer to a property, you separate the object and its property with a period.

  A recordset-type variable is an *object* variable—it stores an object rather than a simple value—which means you must use the Set statement to assign an object to it. In plain English, the whole line says: "Create a copy of the set of records in the Subscribers form and assign it to the rst variable so I can refer to it later."

- Recordset objects have many methods that help you work with them. In Lesson 7, you learned how to add a record to a recordset by using the AddNew method. The third code line uses a new method, FindFirst, to move to a specific record in the recordset. To use a method, you follow the object variable with its method, separated by a period, as in rst.FindFirst.

  The FindFirst method takes an argument that specifies the criteria you want to use to find the record. As you recall, when you created the List0 list box, you specified that its value should be based on the subscriber ID for the selected subscriber. Now, you want this argument to specify that the value you're looking for in the recordset is the one that's selected in the list box. Using the ampersand (&) operator, this line combines the string *SubscriberID =* with the list box value.

  All put together, this line of code says, "In the recordset stored in the rst variable, find the first record where the SubscriberID field contains the same value as the List0 list box."

- Normally, your next step would be to check whether Microsoft Access found the record you were looking for. In this case, however, you know that the record is there, because the list box contains the same records as the Subscribers form. So the current record in the rst recordset is now the one the user selected in the list box.

  It's important to note that finding the record doesn't automatically change the record shown in the Subscribers form. This is because you're actually working with a *copy* of the recordset, which you

187

stored in the rst variable using the RecordsetClone property. To actually move to the record you want, the next line of code sets the Bookmark property of the Subscribers form. Forms and recordsets both have a Bookmark property, which is a special value Microsoft Access uses to keep track of which record is current—just as if the record were the page you had reached in a book. When two recordsets contain the same records, you can synchronize one recordset with another by setting its Bookmark value to the same value as the other's.

At the risk of oversimplification, you can read the Bookmark line as saying, "In the Subscribers form's set of records, move to the same record that's current in the rst recordset object."

■ Now that you've moved to the record the user specified, the work of the dialog box is complete. The next line of code uses the Close method of the DoCmd object to close the dialog box. The arguments for the Close method specify which object to close. Using the predefined constant acForm, you tell Microsoft Access that the object to close is a form; with the second argument, you give the name of the form to close, GoToRecordDialog.

Add code to enable the ShowRecords button

As you recall, you made sure the ShowRecords button is disabled by default, because no item is selected in the list when the dialog box first appears. As soon as the user selects a value in the list, you want to enable the button. You can do this by responding to the list box's AfterUpdate event, which occurs whenever the user changes the value of the list box.

1 Switch back to the GoToRecordDialog form.
2 Click the list box control to select it.
3 Click the Properties button on the toolbar, and then click the Event tab in the property sheet.

Properties button

4 Click the AfterUpdate property, and then click the Build button.

188

5 Double-click Code Builder.

Microsoft Access displays the List0_AfterUpdate event procedure.

6 Add the following code to the procedure:

```
Private Sub List0_AfterUpdate()
' Once a record is chosen in the list, enable the ShowRecord button.

    ShowRecord.Enabled = True

End Sub
```

The line of code in this procedure sets the Enabled property for the ShowRecord button to True—just as if you'd set the property to Yes in the property sheet—so the button appears enabled and the user can click it.

Add code to respond when the user double-clicks an entry in the list

To make your dialog box easier to use, there's one other event that you can respond to. When the user double-clicks a value in the list box, you want to respond as if the ShowRecord button had been clicked immediately afterward. This way, a user can avoid the added step of clicking the button after selecting a subscriber.

1 In the Module window's Procedure box, select DblClick.

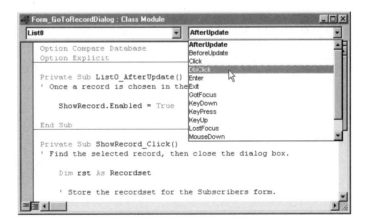

Microsoft Access displays the List0_DblClick procedure in the Module window.

2 Add the following code to the procedure:

```
Private Sub List0_DblClick(Cancel As Integer)
' When the user double-clicks, act as though
' the ShowRecord button was chosen.

    If Not IsNull(List0) Then
        ShowRecord_Click
    End If

End Sub
```

The line in the middle of this procedure tells Microsoft Access to run the ShowRecord_Click event procedure. You can run a procedure in the current module by simply entering the name of the procedure on a line by itself. When Microsoft Access encounters this line, it jumps to the ShowRecord_Click procedure, running it just as it would have if the ShowRecord button had actually been clicked.

The If...Then statement in this procedure is a safety measure. It checks to make sure the List0 list box has a value; if it doesn't, the button shouldn't be enabled, so you wouldn't want to run its event procedure. Normally, when the user double-clicks the list box, this action sets a value for the list box. However, by double-clicking the list box label, it is possible to make the DblClick event occur when the list box has no value. If the List0 control doesn't have a subscriber selected, the value of the expression *Not IsNull(List0)* is False, so the code in the procedure does nothing.

Check your Visual Basic code for errors

You've written quite a bit of code for the dialog box! It's a good idea to get in the habit of compiling your code from time to time—this lets Microsoft Access catch any errors right away and saves you from being interrupted when you run your code.

Compile Loaded Modules button

1 Click the Compile Loaded Modules button on the toolbar.

If Microsoft Access encounters any errors, it identifies them for you—otherwise, it does nothing (other than preparing your code to run). Of course, if there are errors, you should fix them and compile your code again.

Save button

2 Click the Save button on the toolbar.

3 Close the Module window.

4 Close the property sheet.

Add a Cancel button to close the form

Your dialog box is almost complete! But in addition to a button that performs an action, such as the ShowRecord button you created, every dialog box should have a Cancel or Close button, in case the user has a change of heart and doesn't really want to do anything. In this case, you just need a button to close the GoToRecordDialog form, performing no action at all. The easiest way to create this button is by using the Command Button Wizard.

Control Wizards tool

Command Button tool

1 In the toolbox, click the Control Wizards tool to select it, and then click the Command Button tool.

2 Click the right side of the form, just underneath the left side of the ShowRecord button.

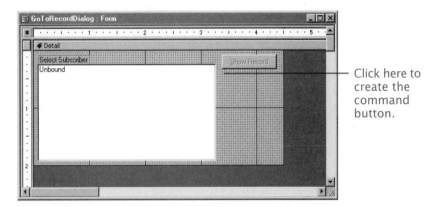

Click here to create the command button.

The Command Button Wizard starts, asking what action you want the button to perform.

3 Select Form Operations from the Categories list, select Close Form from the Actions list, and then click Next.

The wizard asks whether you want a picture or text on your button.

4 Select the Close Form text from the Text box, type **Cancel** to replace the text, and then click Next.

The wizard asks what you want to name the button.

5 Type **Cancel**, and then click Finish.

The wizard creates the Cancel button.

6 Drag the bottom right corner of the Cancel button to make it the same size as the ShowRecord button.

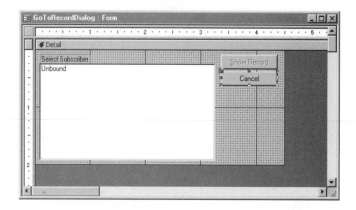

Now that the button is complete, there's one more step. With most any Cancel or Close button on a dialog box, you want users to be able to press ESC in lieu of clicking the button. To make this possible, you just set the button's Cancel property to Yes—identifying it to Microsoft Access as the Cancel button for the form.

7 Click the Properties button on the toolbar, and then click the Other tab in the property sheet.

Properties button

8 Set the Cancel property to Yes.

The button is finished—and you're ready to put the final touches on your dialog box.

Set properties for the dialog box

Although a dialog box is a form like any other, you want it to look and be-have differently in many ways. First, you'll take a look at the form as it stands now, with its default property settings. Then, you'll change several properties to make it work the way you want.

Form View button

1 Click the Form View button on the toolbar.

The list box shows records in alphabetical order, and everything seems to be in its place. Notice, however, that like any ordinary Microsoft Access form, this form has several features used for moving around in a set of records—navigation buttons, scroll bars, and a record selector—all things that dialog boxes *don't* customarily have.

A dialog box shouldn't have these navigation features.

Each of these features has a corresponding form property you can set to remove it from your form.

Design View button

2 Click the Design View button on the toolbar.

3 On the Edit menu, click Select Form.

4 In the property sheet, click the Format tab.

5 Set the following properties to the values shown:

Property	Value
Caption	Go To Record
ScrollBars	Neither
RecordSelectors	No
NavigationButtons	No
AutoCenter	Yes
BorderStyle	Dialog

These settings will make your dialog box look much like any other Windows 95 dialog box—a thin border, a simple title, and no extra navigation tools. However, there are two additional properties you'll want to set so that your dialog box *works* the way a dialog box should.

6 In the property sheet, click the Other tab.

7 Set the Popup property to Yes.

This setting makes your dialog box into a pop-up form: it will appear on top of all other windows, including Microsoft Access itself.

8 Set the Modal property to Yes.

This setting makes your dialog box *modal*, which means that users won't be able to click outside of the dialog box while it's open. Most dialog boxes are modal: you intend that the user will complete the action—such as locating a record—and then close the dialog box to move on to the next task.

9   Close the property sheet.

10   Close the GoToRecordDialog form, clicking Yes when Microsoft Access asks if you want to save changes to the form.

Add a button to the Subscribers form to open the dialog box

Now that your dialog box is complete, the only thing left is to hook it up to the Subscribers form. To do this, you'll add a button using the Command Button Wizard.

1   Switch to the Subscribers form, which is still open behind the Database Window.

2   Click the Design View button on the toolbar.

3   Scroll down in the form to display the Form Footer section.

4   In the toolbox, click the Command Button tool.

5   Click the left side of the form footer.

Design View button

Command Button tool

Click here to create the command button.

The Command Button Wizard starts, asking what action you want the button to perform.

6   Select Form Operations from the Categories list, select Open Form from the Actions list, and then click Next.

The wizard asks which form you want to open. Because the GoToRecordDialog form is already selected, you don't have to click it.

7   Click Next.

The wizard asks whether you want a picture or text on your button.

8   Select the Open Form text in the Text box, type **&Go To Record** to replace the text, and then click Next.

The wizard asks what you want to name the button.

9 Type **GoToRecord**, and then click Finish.

The wizard creates the button, including an event procedure that automatically opens your dialog box whenever the button is clicked.

10 Click the Save button on the toolbar.

Save button

Try the new dialog box

No more waiting—you're finally ready to click that button and try out the dialog box!

Form View button

1 Click the Form View button on the toolbar.

2 Click the Go To Record button.

The Go To Record dialog box appears.

Baugher	Janée	New York	NY	
Christensen	Bonnie	Dallas	TX	
Demerais	Darren	Seattle	WA	
Doyle	Judy	New York	NY	
Geloff	Kevin	Seattle	WA	
Greenman	Gilbert	New York	NY	
Griffin	Hardy	Seattle	WA	
Hunting	David	New York	NY	
MacDougall	Rob	Los Angeles	CA	
Mahoney	Michael	Denver	CO	
O'Halloran	Kevin	New York	NY	

As you can see, the form no longer looks like an ordinary Microsoft Access form—it has a thin border, and no navigation tools. Because the form is modal, if you try to click on a Microsoft Access menu or on the Subscribers form behind it, your computer beeps and nothing happens. The only actions you can take are to move or close the dialog box, or to select a record in the list box and click a button.

And notice that the Show Record button is disabled because you haven't yet selected a subscriber in the dialog box.

3 In the Select Subscriber list box, click the entry for Judy Doyle.

The Show Record button is now enabled—when you set the value of the list box, the AfterUpdate event procedure ran, and your code set the Enabled property.

4 Click the Show Record button.

Your event procedure for the button changes the current record in the Subscribers form's recordset to the record for Judy Doyle, and then closes the dialog box. It works!

5 Click the Go To Record button again.

This time, you can test the double-clicking feature you added.

195

6 In the Select Subscriber list box, double-click the entry for Gilbert Greenman.

The Subscribers form now shows this record—your event procedure for the list box's DblClick event took care of it.

Finally, you should test the Cancel button in the dialog box.

7 Click the Go To Record button again, and then click any entry in the list box.

8 Click the Cancel button.

The Subscribers form still shows the same record—as expected, the dialog box has no effect if you click Cancel.

9 Close the Subscribers form.

As you've seen, quite a bit of work goes into creating a custom dialog box. (As you practice, you'll learn ways to make it easier.) It's worthwhile, though, when you consider how polished your applications can look by using custom dialog boxes to meet users' needs.

TIP To save time when creating a dialog box for your own application, you may want to copy or import an existing dialog box form and start work from there. Because many dialog boxes have similar controls and property settings, you'll be well on your way—and much happier than if you'd started from scratch.

Hiding a Dialog Box and Referring to Its Controls

When you click the ShowRecord button on the GoToRecordDialog form, it's the code behind the button that performs an action using the information you enter. After it changes records in the Subscribers form, the same event procedure then closes the dialog box.

However, there's another possible strategy that you could use for this dialog box, one that might prove easier to implement for some dialog boxes. Rather than close a dialog box when the user finishes with it, your code can instead simply hide the dialog box, making it look like it's closed. To do this, you set the dialog box's Visible property to False. The advantage to this strategy is that you can still refer to values on the dialog box from code you've written in other forms. In this case, for example, you could hide the GoToRecordDialog form—set its Visible property to False—and then add code to the Subscribers form that would move to the specified record. From that code, you could refer to the list box value in the dialog box, even though it would no longer be in view.

Hiding a Dialog Box and Referring to Its Controls, *continued*

> The strategy you did use—performing actions from code in the dialog box form itself—usually results in code that's easier to follow. On the other hand, in cases where you want to continue referring to values the user entered long after the dialog box is "gone," it might make more sense to simply hide the dialog box form. However, if you do hide a dialog box and leave it open, you'll usually want to close that form later in your application. What's more, you'll need to watch out for code that assumes the dialog box form is open behind the scenes, unless you make sure that it stays open.

Filtering Data in a Report

Because the task of selecting a subset of data is so important in database applications, one common use for a dialog box is to specify criteria for filtering records. Microsoft Access provides a powerful interface for filtering records in forms, so your applications can rely on standard filtering tools in many cases. In other cases, however, you'll want to provide a custom method for selecting records. This is especially true for selecting records to include in reports, because filtering records for reports is much less straightforward than it is for forms. In this section, you'll add code to a dialog box that helps users select which records to include in a report.

As you might imagine, the most critical reports in a database of mailing addresses are the reports that print mailing labels. The Subscription database includes two reports called BigMailingLabels and SmallMailingLabels. These reports were created using the Label Wizard, which helps you lay out and print names and addresses on standard mailing label paper. However, users of the Subscription database don't want to print a label for every subscriber every time. By providing a custom dialog box, you'll help them select the subset of labels they want.

Try the SmallMailingLabels report

Before working on the dialog box, let's preview one of the mailing label reports by itself.

1   In the Database window, click the Reports tab.

2   Double-click the SmallMailingLabels report.

197

Microsoft Access displays the report in Print Preview, showing several subscribers' names and addresses.

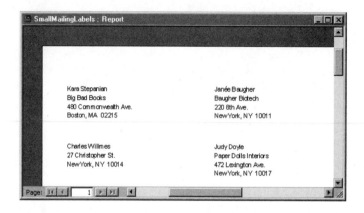

3 Click anywhere on the page of the report to zoom out.

All 20 subscribers' names and addresses are shown. This could be useful if you want to send a mailing to everyone who's ever subscribed—not too many people at this point. But as the database grows and the mailing labels span many pages, users will need a way to print only the labels appropriate for a particular mailing.

4 Close the report window.

Open the MailingLabelsDialog form in Design view

The Subscription database contains a dialog box for filtering records in the report. This form was created for you using many of the same steps you followed to create the GoToRecordDialog form. Now you'll add the Visual Basic code to make it work.

1 In the Database window, click the Forms tab.

2 Click the MailingLabelsDialog form, and then click the Design button.

The first thing you may notice on this form are the two tabs at the top that say "Mailing Type" and "Label Type." This is a special type of control you may not have tried yet, called a *Tab control*. You can put a Tab control on any form where you want to keep options or fields separate— it's like having several pages on the form, except that users simply click the tabs at the top to move from page to page.

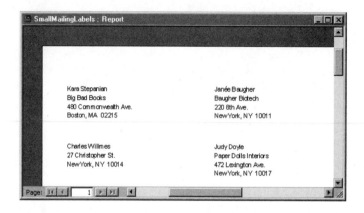

NEW
for
97

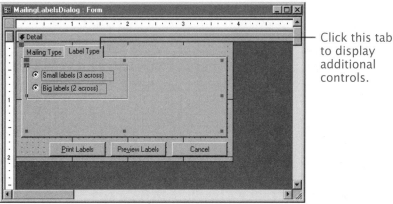

The form uses a Tab control to keep the printing options organized.

On the Mailing Type tab, you can see an option group that allows the user to select which group of subscribers to include in a mailing. There are three options: the first includes all subscribers who are paid to the current date, the second includes all subscribers who need to make a payment in the next three months in order to stay current, and the third includes subscribers who recently failed to pay and are no longer receiving issues. You'll use this control to filter the records that print in the mailing label reports.

3 Click the Label Type tab.

Click this tab to display additional controls.

This tab contains an option group that allows the user to choose small or large mailing labels. You'll use this control to determine which of the two reports to use, BigMailingLabels or SmallMailingLabels.

Finally, the form has three command buttons, which are outside the Tab control so they always appear at the bottom of the dialog box: one to print mailing labels, one to preview them, and a third that closes the dialog box without doing anything.

199

Add code for the PrintLabels button

The PrintLabels button doesn't yet have a Click event procedure to do the job. When a user clicks this button, you want the code to open one of the two mailing labels reports—that much will be easy using the OpenReport method of the DoCmd object. But you don't want the report to display all the subscriber records, as it did when you opened it from the Database window. Instead, your code needs to interpret the selected option in the option group, and then filter the subscriber records according to the user's selection.

1 With the right mouse button, click the PrintLabels button, and then click Build Event on the shortcut menu.

2 Double-click Code Builder.

Microsoft Access opens the Module window and displays the PrintLabels_Click event procedure.

3 Add the following code to the procedure:

```
Private Sub PrintLabels_Click()
' Open a mailing labels report with a filter, then close the dialog.

    Dim strFilter As String, strReportName As String

    ' Determine which set of subscribers user wants.
    Select Case MailingType
    Case 1       ' Journal mailing -- all current subscribers.
        strFilter = "PaidThrough >= Date()"
    Case 2       ' Subscriptions expiring within 3 months.
        strFilter = "PaidThrough >= Date() And PaidThrough < Date() + 90"
    Case 3       ' Subscriptions that expired in past 3 months.
        strFilter = "PaidThrough < Date() And PaidThrough > Date() - 90"
    End Select

    ' Determine which mailing labels user wants.
    If LabelType = 1 Then
        strReportName = "SmallMailingLabels"
    Else
        strReportName = "BigMailingLabels"
    End If

    DoCmd.OpenReport strReportName, acViewNormal, , strFilter
    DoCmd.Close acForm, "MailingLabelsDialog"

End Sub
```

This code covers mostly familiar territory, but it uses a couple of new techniques. Here's how it works:

- At the end of this procedure, you specify both the name of the report you want Microsoft Access to open, and filter criteria—a description of the records you want to see in the report. The Dim statement at the beginning of the procedure defines two string variables, strReportName and strFilter, for storing the name and criteria.

- Each criteria string you specify in this procedure refers to a field in the Subscribers table called PaidThrough. This field stores the last month in which a subscriber should receive an issue (assuming that the subscriber doesn't make another payment). Each time a subscriber makes a payment, the field is updated to reflect the new month.

- Each criteria string also uses the Date function, a Microsoft Access function that returns the current date stored by the computer system. By comparing the value of this function with the values in the PaidThrough field, you can determine whether any given subscriber is "paid up."

- The Select Case statement begins a Select Case...End Select block, which allows you to specify three different statements to run, depending on which option the user selected in the option group. The statement uses the expression MailingType because that's the name of the option group control on the form.

- The first Case block, Case 1, runs if the user selected the first option in the group (MailingType is 1). For this option, you want to include all subscribers who have paid through the current date—in other words, subscribers whose PaidThrough date is the same as or later than the current date. The criteria string is:

```
"PaidThrough >= Date()"
```

- In the second Case block, you want to include all subscribers who need to make a payment within three months if they want their subscriptions to continue. To specify this condition, you make two comparisons, combining them with the And operator—this way, Microsoft Access makes sure both comparisons are true for records it includes in the report. This criteria string includes subscribers whose PaidThrough date the same as or later than the current date *and* whose PaidThrough date is less than 90 days from now:

```
"PaidThrough >= Date() And PaidThrough < Date() + 90"
```

As this expression demonstrates, adding or subtracting an integer value to a date expression changes the date value by that many days.

- In the third Case block, you want to include all subscribers who've let their subscriptions expire—but only those who have done so in the past three months. The criteria string includes subscribers whose PaidThrough date is earlier than the current date (they're no longer paid up) *and* whose PaidThrough date is within the past 90 days:

```
"PaidThrough < Date() And PaidThrough > Date() - 90"
```

- The If...Then block checks the option the user chose in the LabelType option group—the one on the second tab of the dialog box—which determines the report to be printed. If the user chose the Small Labels option (number 1 in the option group), the next statement sets the strReportName variable to SmallMailingLabels. Otherwise, the user must have chosen the Big Labels option, so the statement following the Else keyword sets the variable to BigMailingLabels.

- After your code sets the strFilter variable to the appropriate criteria and the strReportName variable to the appropriate report, it's time to use this information to open the report. The line after the End Select statement uses the OpenReport method of the DoCmd object, specifying the strReportName variable for the report name argument.

    The second argument to the OpenReport method lets you specify whether to open and print the report (specified using the acViewNormal constant) or preview the report (specified using the acViewPreview constant). The fourth argument—you skip the third argument by including two commas in a row—is the WhereCondition argument, with which you specify the criteria string Microsoft Access will use to filter records in the report. This is where you put your variable, strFilter, which contains the filter string you set in the Select...Case block.

- The last statement in the procedure uses the Close method of the DoCmd object to close the dialog box form.

    When you click the PrintLabels button, your code will select a filter string, open the report to print the set of labels the user wants, and close the dialog box.

Copy the code for the PreviewLabels button

Print Preview is a powerful Microsoft Access feature that you can easily take advantage of in your applications—and Windows users have come to expect it. Whenever you provide the option to print a report, it's also a good idea to allow previewing. Fortunately, the code you'll use for the PreviewLabels button is nearly identical to the code for printing a report. In fact, you'll just copy the code to the other button's event procedure, and then make a small modification to allow previewing.

1 Select all the code between the Sub and End Sub lines in the PrintLabels event procedure (click at the beginning of the second line and drag to just before the last line).

2 Press CTRL+C.

3 In the Module window's Object box (on the left), select PreviewLabels.

Microsoft Access displays the PreviewLabels_Click event procedure.

4 Press CTRL+V.

5 Edit the line that contains the OpenReport method (toward the end of the procedure) to use the acViewPreview constant instead of the acViewNormal constant:

```
DoCmd.OpenReport strReportName, acViewPreview, , strFilter
```

Using this constant for the View argument of the OpenReport method tells Microsoft Access to display the form in Print Preview rather than printing it directly.

6 Close the Module window.

7 Close the MailingLabelsDialog form, clicking Yes when Microsoft Access asks if you want to save changes.

Try the dialog box

Now that the dialog box is finished, you can use it to open the report.

1 In the Database window, double-click the MailingLabelsDialog form.

The dialog box appears, allowing you to select an option for your mailing labels.

2   Select the second option, Invoice Mailing.

3   Click the Label Type tab.

4   Click the second option, Big Labels.

5   Click Preview Labels.

Your event procedure runs, opening the BigMailingLabels report in Print Preview.

6   Click anywhere on the report to zoom out.

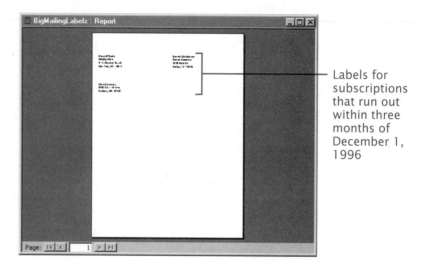

Labels for subscriptions that run out within three months of December 1, 1996

Because your code opens the report using the filter string *PaidThrough >= Date() And PaidThrough < Date() + 90* it includes just a few of the subscribers—those whose subscriptions haven't yet expired as of today's date, but that will expire within three months. (Note that depending on the current date setting on your computer, you might see different subscribers in the report or even no subscribers at all. To include subscribers, change their PaidThrough date in the table to within three months of the current date.)

7   Close the report.

If you want to try out the other filters on the report, repeat this procedure, selecting the first and third options in the dialog box.

Other Ways to Change the Records in a Form or Report

The code you wrote uses a straightforward way of filtering the records in a report: specifying an OpenReport WhereCondition argument when opening the report. However, there are other ways you can change the records that appear in a report.

Base the report on a query.   If you always want to display the same subset of records in a report, or if you want the records to appear in a specific order, create a query that displays records as you want them, and then set the report's RecordSource property to the query. This way, you don't have to write any code to filter records.

Set the report's Filter and FilterOn properties.   If you want to change records that are displayed in a report that's already open in Print Preview, you can use Visual Basic code to set the report's Filter property to a criteria string. Then set its FilterOn property to True to apply the filter.

Set the report's OrderBy and OrderByOn properties.   If you want to change the sort order of a report that's already open in Print Preview, you can set the report's OrderBy property to the name of the field you want to sort, and then set its OrderByOn property to True to apply the sort.

All these techniques work for forms as well as reports—in fact, in the next lesson you'll learn how to use the Filter property in forms.

Exit Microsoft Access

   On the File menu, click Exit.

Lesson Summary

To	Do this
Create a dialog box form	Create a blank form in Design view, add controls, and then set properties on the Format and Other tabs to make the dialog box appear and work as you want it to. Add buttons that perform desired actions.
Create a list box	Use the List Box Wizard in Form Design view, specifying the fields you want the list box to display.

Lesson Summary, *continued*

To	Do this
Move to a specific record in a form	Get a copy of the form's underlying recordset using the RecordsetClone property, and then move to the record using the FindFirst method. Finally, set the form's Bookmark property to the Bookmark value for the copy of the recordset.
Open a report to print specific records	Use the OpenReport method of the DoCmd object, specifying a filter string for the WhereCondition argument. In the filter string, specify criteria for one or more fields in the underlying table or query for the report.
Create a tabbed form to organize various fields and options	Add a Tab control to the form and set its properties and size, and then add the controls you want to each tab. If there are controls such as command buttons that you want to show at all times, add them to the form, but not on the Tab control.

For online information about	On the Help menu, click Contents and Index, click the Index tab, and then
Creating dialog boxes	Search for "dialog boxes"
Filtering records in forms and reports	Search for "filters"
Using data access object (DAO) code to work with recordsets, or finding records in a recordset	Search for "recordsets"
Using bookmarks	Search for "Bookmark property"
Using the Date function	Search for "date"

For more information on	In *Building Applications with Microsoft Access 97*, see
Creating dialog boxes, or filtering records in forms and reports	Chapter 3, "Using Forms to Collect, Filter, and Display Information"
Using data access object (DAO) code to work with recordsets, finding records in a recordset, or using bookmarks	Chapter 9, "Working with Records and Fields"
Using the Date function	Chapter 2, "Introducing Visual Basic"

Preview of the Next Lesson

In this lesson, you began adding features to the Subscription database, a custom application created from scratch. In Lesson 9, you'll learn to link the forms of an application together, helping users jump from one task to another and putting the information they need at their fingertips. As Part 3 progresses, you'll complete the custom user interface for the Subscription database, learning techniques you can use to create your own custom database applications.

Navigate Through Your Application

Estimated time
35 min.

In this lesson you will learn how to:

- Display records in a pop-up form.
- Synchronize the records in one form with records the user selects in another form.
- Requery a form to display current data.

In a relay race, the performance of each individual team member is important, but the transitions are critical. When a runner hands off the baton to a team-mate, that's the moment when seconds are gained or lost. Relay teams train extensively to make transitions as efficient as possible, and arrange each of the runners in the position that is most beneficial to the team.

No matter how well your forms and reports work on their own, it's the way they work together that makes your database applications powerful and easy to use. As when planning for a relay race, you'll need to consider the ways your objects "hand off" from one to another. To make the transitions seamless, you can use Visual Basic code to customize the way a new object starts and how it works with other objects. Of course, the structure of an application is much more flex-ible than the structure of a relay race, so there are even more variables to con-sider—because of the flexibility of event-driven applications, users can take any number of paths through your application, and you'll need to anticipate all of them.

In this lesson, you'll learn techniques for handing off control from one form or report to another—passing the baton, so to speak. You'll write event procedures that check which other forms are currently open, copy values and set properties from one form or report to another, and update objects at appropriate times. By anticipating how users will run the course, you'll see how to make your application work smoothly.

Start the lesson

 Start Microsoft Access and open the 09Subscr database in the practice files folder.

Making Forms Work Together

In an ideal world, everything computer users need to do their work would be in one place—in a database application, for example, it would be nice if all the data you needed were on a single form. In all but the simplest applications, however, you'll need several objects to handle the different types of information required, and the tasks the user needs to complete. For example, you'll have forms for entering information, forms for summarizing information, and still other forms that help users accomplish a specific task. How you organize these objects depends on what information and tasks are most important to users. In planning your application, you'll want to prioritize these items and decide how to best serve everyone's needs.

Most relational database applications store information in separate but related tables. For example, in the Subscription database, the Subscribers and Payments tables contain related information. In presenting this information on the screen, you can take several different approaches—some approaches work on their own, while others require Visual Basic code to make them work. Here are some of the ways you can organize data in an application, and factors you'll need to consider when using them:

Place subforms on forms to display related records.   The subform control provides a powerful way to display related records in a single form without writing any code. For example, you could use a subform to display a list of subscriber payments—on the same form that displays subscriber information. You can set up this type of subform using the Subform Wizard, or create form and subform at once using the Form Wizard. However, in many cases there won't be enough room on the screen to display all the information you need on the main form as well as all the related information contained in a subform. Additionally, subforms can be less intuitive for entering data, especially when space is limited. Still, because Microsoft Access handles the relationships between form and subform automatically, you may want to use this approach when you want all related information to appear in one place.

Build forms and reports based on multiple-table queries.   By designing queries that combine information from two or more tables, you can easily present data from several tables on a single form or report. Whenever possible, Microsoft Access allows users to update all the information in a query, automatically making changes in the underlying tables—but beware: some fields in multiple-table queries aren't updatable, so users can sometimes encounter unintelligible error messages when trying to make changes. And as with subforms, you won't always have room on a single form for all the fields you need to display. For forms and reports in which you summarize information, however, queries are indispensable tools for combining data from multiple tables.

Create a separate form for each table. By making separate forms for data in related tables, you present a very straightforward model to users: "Here is where you view and enter information about this; for other types of information, click these buttons." This approach requires users to switch from one place to another more frequently—between a main form and a pop-up form, for example—but it gives you the most screen space and flexibility for each form. When you do have several forms, however, users will expect them to work together intelligently. For example, if you've chosen a value in one form, you shouldn't have to choose it again in another form. As you'll see, it's important to link objects together using Visual Basic event procedures.

Separate data entry and data display. In some cases, you'll want to provide more than one form for the same information, each of which is used for a different task. Forms that allow you to enter new data often need different controls and features than those for finding or summarizing data. But as you increase the number of forms that make up your user interface, your application becomes much more complex. In some cases, you'll want to limit what users can do in a given form, making some forms or controls read-only and carefully controlling the paths users can take through your application.

In this lesson, we'll focus on the last two techniques, connecting separate forms in the Subscription database to display and enter related information. In the process, you'll learn to write Visual Basic code that links objects together in custom ways. In your own applications, you'll most likely draw from all these approaches—using subforms and queries to combine some of your application's data, while linking together a series of forms when it makes sense to keep information separated into different chunks.

Displaying Related Records in a Pop-Up Form

In any database that contains more than one table, you'll commonly have records in one table that are related to records in another. For example, in the Subscription database, each subscriber has one or more related payment records documenting the payments that the subscriber has made. When users are viewing records in a main form, such as the Subscriber form, they'll commonly want to see related records on the screen. One way to show related records is in a *pop-up* form, a special type of form that always remains on top of other windows. In this section, you'll add a pop-up form that displays the payment history for the current subscriber (the subscriber currently selected in the Subscribers form).

Open the PaymentHistory form

The practice database already includes the PaymentHistory form, which displays payment records. By default, the form shows payments for all subscribers together in one list.

1   In the Database window, click the Forms tab.

2   Double-click the PaymentHistory form.

Date	Yearly Rate	Years Paid	Total Amount
8/2/95	$24.00	0.5	$12.00
8/29/95	$24.00	1	$24.00
9/16/95	$24.00	1	$24.00
11/2/95	$18.00	1	$18.00
11/16/95	$24.00	1	$24.00

Record: 1 of 25

This simple form has the Payments table as its record source, and has four fields. The TotalAmount field is not actually in the Payments table—it's a calculated field, which means that its ControlSource property is set to an expression. The expression multiplies the YearlyRate value by the YearsPaid value to show the total.

Display the PaymentHistory form as a pop-up form

When users view the PaymentHistory form, they'll want it to remain on top of other windows so they can see it while they work in the Subscribers form. To make it work this way, you'll set its Popup property to Yes. You'll also set properties to make the form read-only, so that users can view payments in the form, but not change them.

*Design View
button*

1   Click the Design View button on the toolbar.

2   If the property sheet isn't displayed, click the Properties button on the toolbar.

3   Click the Other tab in the property sheet.

4   Set the Popup property to Yes.

*Properties
button*

5   Click the Data tab in the property sheet.

6   Set the AllowEdits, AllowDeletions, and AllowAdditions properties to No.

7   Close the PaymentHistory form, clicking Yes when Microsoft Access asks if you want to save changes.

Add a button to the Subscribers
form to open the PaymentHistory form

The PaymentHistory form is designed to work hand in hand with the Subscribers form. To make the pop-up form accessible, you'll add a button that opens it, displaying the payment records for the current subscriber. You can use the Command Button Wizard to create the button and its event procedure.

1 In the Database window, select the Subscribers form, and then click the Design button.

The form opens in Design view. (If the property sheet is in the way, drag it to the lower right corner of the screen.)

2 Scroll down in the form to display the Form Footer section.

3 In the toolbox, make sure the Control Wizards tool is selected, and then click the Command Button tool.

Control Wizards tool

4 Click the form footer just to the right of the Go To Record button.

Command Button tool

Click here to create the button.

The Command Button Wizard starts, asking what action you want the button to perform.

5 Select Form Operations from the Categories list, select Open Form from the Actions list, and then click Next.

The wizard asks which form you want to open.

6 Select PaymentHistory, and then click Next.

The wizard asks whether you want to display specific information in the form. This gives you the chance to filter records in the pop-up form to include only the payments for the current subscriber.

7 Select Open The Form And Find Specific Data To Display, and then click Next.

The wizard asks which field in the Subscribers form contains matching data in the PaymentHistory form. Because the Subscribers and Payments tables are related based on the SubscriberID values in each record, you'll specify this field.

8   Select SubscriberID in both list boxes, click the button between the lists to create a link between them, and then click Next.

Select fields in both lists...

...and then click here to link them.

The wizard asks whether you want a picture or text on your button.

9   Select the Open Form text in the Text box, type **&Payment History** to replace the text, and then click Next.

The wizard asks what you want to name the button.

10 Type **PaymentHistory** and then click Finish.

The wizard creates the button.

Try the new button

Now you can use your new button to open the pop-up form.

Form View button

1   Click the Form View button on the toolbar.
2   Click the Payment History button.

The button's Click event procedure runs, opening the Payment History pop-up form.

The form shows only three records: the past payments made by Hardy Griffin, whose subscriber record is displayed in the Subscriber form.

Change records in the Subscriber form

When the PaymentHistory pop-up form is open, you can still work in the Subscribers form—the pop-up form isn't modal like a dialog box. Let's see what happens when you change subscriber records.

1   Click anywhere on the Subscribers form. (If necessary, you can first drag the PaymentHistory form out of the way so that you can see the name of the current subscriber.)

2   Press the PAGE DOWN key several times to change records.

    The same three records are displayed in the PaymentHistory form, regardless of which subscriber record you're viewing. When the user changes records in the Subscribers form, you'd like the PaymentHistory form to display payment records for the currently selected subscriber—in other words, you'd like the pop-up form to stay *synchronized* with the main form.

3   Close the PaymentHistory pop-up form.

Add code to keep the pop-up form synchronized

To make the pop-up form stay synchronized, you need to update the records it displays each time the user changes records in the main form. To do this, you'll add an event procedure to the Subscribers form that makes sure the pop-up form displays related payment records as you move from one subscriber to another.

Design View button

1   Click the Design View button on the toolbar.

2   On the Edit menu, click Select Form.

3   In the property sheet, click the Event tab.

4   Click the OnCurrent property, and then click the Build button.

Click the Build button.

5   Double-click Code Builder.

Microsoft Access opens the Module window and displays the form's Current event procedure. The code you add to this procedure will run any time the user changes from one record to another in the Subscribers form.

6 Enter the following code for the procedure:

```
Private Sub Form_Current()
' Synchronize the PaymentHistory form if it's open.

    If IsOpen("PaymentHistory") Then
        Forms!PaymentHistory.Filter = "SubscriberID = " & _
            Nz(SubscriberID, 0)
    End If

End Sub
```

The If...Then statement in this code uses a special function called IsOpen to check whether the PaymentHistory form is open. This is an important step, because unless the user has opened the pop-up form, attempting to change the records it displays would cause an error. The IsOpen function returns True if the form is open, causing the line of code in the If...Then block to run. The IsOpen function is included in the practice database in the Miscellaneous module; for more information, see "Looking into the IsOpen Function," on page 218.

If the PaymentHistory form is open, the next line actually synchronizes the form. To do this, it sets the pop-up form's Filter property, referring to the property by using the expression *Forms!PaymentHistory.Filter*. For the property setting, the code combines the text *SubscriberID =* with the actual SubscriberID value currently on the Subscribers form. For example, if the current subscriber's ID is 4, it sets the Filter property to *SubscriberID = 4* and the pop-up form displays only the payment records for that subscriber.

The line also uses the Nz function ("Nz" stands for Null-zero), which converts the SubscriberID value to zero in the unlikely event that it is null (has no value). This is necessary because if the value is Null—which occurs if the user moves to the new (blank) record in the Subscriber form—the Filter would get set to *SubscriberID =* with nothing to the right of the equal sign and an error would occur. This way, if the SubscriberID value is Null, the Filter gets set to *SubscriberID = 0* and the pop-up form displays no records (because no subscriber is number 0).

Add code to close the pop-up form automatically

The PaymentHistory pop-up form only works as an auxiliary tool for the Subscribers form. If the user closes the Subscribers form while the pop-up form is still open, you may as well close the pop-up form. To do this, you can add code to the Subscribers form's Close event procedure.

1 In the Procedure box at the top of the Module window (on the right), select the Close event.

The Module window shows the blank Form_Close event procedure.

2 Enter the following code for the procedure:

```
Private Sub Form_Close()
' Close the PaymentHistory pop-up form if it's open.

    If IsOpen("PaymentHistory") Then
        DoCmd.Close acForm, "PaymentHistory"
    End If

End Sub
```

Like the code you wrote to synchronize the two forms, this procedure uses the IsOpen function to check whether the PaymentHistory form is open. If it is, the Close method of the DoCmd object closes the form.

3 Close the Module window.

4 Click the Save button on the toolbar.

Save button

Test the synchronized form

The pop-up form should now work properly, even if you change records. When you close the Subscribers form, the pop-up form should close as well.

1 Click the Form View button on the toolbar.

2 Click the Payment History button in the form footer.

The Payment History pop-up form appears, again showing the three payments for the current subscriber.

Form View button

3 Click anywhere on the Subscribers form, and then press the PAGE DOWN key several times to change subscriber records.

Each time you change records, your event procedure runs, setting the pop-up form's Filter property and causing it to display a different set of payments—those related by the SubscriberID value to the current subscriber. As you can see, most subscribers have made only one or two payments.

As you change subscribers...

...your code filters the pop-up form to show payments for the current subscriber.

4   Close the Subscribers form.

Your Close event procedure runs, closing the pop-up form automatically.

Looking into the IsOpen Function

The Subscription database includes a standard module called Miscellaneous, which contains three general procedures provided as part of the practice application. The first two are the procedures you wrote in Lesson 5 to display message boxes. The third is the IsOpen function, which you just used in the Subscribers form's Current event procedure to check whether the PaymentHistory form is open. Because it's so useful, you may want to include the IsOpen function in other applications you create.

Here's the code, which you can also view by opening the Miscellaneous module in the Subscription database:

```
Public Function IsOpen(ByVal strFormName As String) As Boolean
' Returns True if the specified form is open in Form view.

    Const conDesignView = 0
    Const conObjStateClosed = 0

    IsOpen = False
    If SysCmd(acSysCmdGetObjectState, acForm, strFormName) <> _
            conObjStateClosed Then

        If Forms(strFormName).CurrentView <> conDesignView Then
            IsOpen = True
        End If
    End If
End Function
```

Looking into the IsOpen Function, *continued*

As its function declaration states, the IsOpen function accepts as an argument the name of a form and returns a *Boolean* value: either True or False, depending on whether the specified form is open or not. Early in the function, a line of code sets the return value to False—assuming the form is *not* open—and then the function goes on to check whether to change this value to True.

The procedure uses If...Then statements to check two conditions:

Is the form in Microsoft Access's list of open objects?
Microsoft Access keeps an internal list of all the objects that are open. The SysCmd (read as "SIS-command") function is a built-in function that lets you ask for information about the system and its status. By calling this function, you can find out whether a form is open.

You pass three arguments to the SysCmd function: a constant that specifies the type of information you want, in this case the state of an object; the type of object you're interested in, in this case a form; and a string containing the name of the object, in this case the string variable that was passed to the IsOpen function. The SysCmd function returns a number that indicates the status of the form, and this code compares the return value with a constant value indicating that the object is closed. If the return value doesn't equal (<>) the value for a closed object, the code continues; otherwise, the IsOpen function returns False.

Is the form in Design view?   If the form is in Design view, you want the IsOpen function to return False, because most code that refers to a form in Design view would cause errors. Forms have a property called CurrentView, which stores a number representing the current view of the form. This code compares the current view to the constant value that indicates Design view, and then sets the function's return value to True if the property doesn't equal that value.

The expression that refers to the CurrentView property uses a technique you haven't seen yet. So far, you've used the exclamation point operator to refer to a form in the database, as in *Forms!Subscribers.* An alternative method for referring to a form—and the method you must use when the form name is contained in a variable—is to say *Forms("Subscribers").* To refer to the form that was passed to the function, this code uses the expression *Forms(strFormName).*

Because this function is provided for you in the practice database, you don't need to concern yourself too much with how it works—you can simply call it whenever you want to check whether a form is open. As you've seen, the expression *IsOpen("NameOfForm")* gives you the information you need. To take advantage of the techniques you learn in this lesson, simply copy or import this function into any application that needs to refer to one form from another.

Opening a Form to Add Related Records

A pop-up form is useful for showing a small amount of information that you want to keep on top of other forms. However, most forms you present to users won't be pop-up forms, because you'll want users to be able to switch from one form to another, bringing the current form to the front. Any time you provide the user with ways to switch between forms, you'll want to consider how the forms work together. As was the case with the PaymentHistory pop-up form, you'll often need to create event procedures to get the results you want.

In this section, you'll work with a form designed for entering new payments into the Subscription database. The form is called EnterPayment, and is already in the practice database, ready for you to use. Anticipating that users will jump to this form from the PaymentHistory form, you'll add code that makes the two forms work together well.

Add a button to open the EnterPayment form

Because users will often want to enter a payment for a subscriber while viewing data in the Subscribers form, your first step is to add another button to the Subscribers form. As before, you'll use the Command Button Wizard.

1   In the Database window, select the Subscribers form, and then click the Design button.

    The form opens in Design view.

2   Scroll down in the form to display the Form Footer section.

3   In the toolbox, click the Command Button tool.

4   Click the form footer just to the right of the Payment History button.

*Command
Button tool*

Click here
to create
the button.

The Command Button Wizard starts, asking what action you want the button to perform.

5   Select Form Operations from the Categories list, select Open Form from the Actions list, and then click Next.

The wizard asks which form you want to open. Because the EnterPayment form is already selected, you don't have to select it.

6   Click Next.

The wizard asks whether you want to display specific information in the form. This time, you'll go with the default option, Open The Form And Show All The Records.

7   Click Next again.

The wizard asks whether you want a picture or text on your button.

8   Select the Open Form text in the Text box, type &**Enter Payment** to replace the text, and then click Next.

The wizard asks what you want to name the button.

9   Type **EnterPayment** and then click Finish.

The wizard creates the button.

Form View button

10   Click the Form View button on the toolbar.

11   Click the Enter Payment button.

The button's Click event procedure runs, opening the EnterPayment form.

Enter Payment	
Subscriber	Paid Through
Date 10/11/96	Payment Method
Yearly Rate $24.00	Check Cash
Years Paid 1	Credit Card
Total Amount $24.00	Card Type
	Number
	Expiration
	Authorization
Save Payment Add New Payment Close	
Record: 1 of 1	

The EnterPayment form is specially designed for entering new payments into the Payments table. For example, the form's DataEntry property is set to Yes, so it opens without any existing payment records displayed, ready for a new payment. It also has the AllowEdits and AllowDeletions properties set to No, so that only new payments can be edited in the form.

Note that the Subscriber field on the form is blank, even though you came from the Subscribers form where you're viewing a specific subscriber. It would be nice if the subscriber record were automatically set when opening this form, so the user wouldn't have to select one. In the next procedure, you'll add code to make this happen.

Features of the EnterPayment Form

The EnterPayment form has several features already implemented in the practice file. Although they aren't directly related to the subject you're learning about in this lesson, you may want to take a look at the Visual Basic code for these features to see how the form works. Here's what you'll find behind the form:

- Three command buttons created using the Command Button Wizard: Save Payment, Add New Payment, and Close.

- Code that enables the credit card text boxes in the PaymentMethod option group when a user selects the Credit Card option. To view this code, open the AfterUpdate event procedure for the PaymentMethod option group.

- Code that runs when the user tries to save a record, in response to the form's BeforeUpdate event. The first half of this procedure checks to make sure the user entered a value for the PaymentMethod field, and cancels the update if its value is 0. If the record is valid, the second half of the procedure updates the PaidThrough field to add the number of months the subscriber paid for. The PaidThrough field is actually stored in the Payments table, but is included in the underlying query of this form to make it easier to update. Here's the code:

```
Private Sub Form_BeforeUpdate(Cancel As Integer)
' Check to make sure a payment method is selected.
' Then update the PaidThrough field (Subscribers table)
' to reflect additional time due to this payment.

    Dim bytMonths As Byte

    If PaymentMethod = 0 Then
        DisplayMessage "You must select a payment method."
        Cancel = True
        Exit Sub
    End If

    bytMonths = YearsPaid * 12

    If IsNull(PaidThrough) Or PaidThrough < Date Then
        ' If this is the first payment, set PaidThrough
        ' from current date.
        PaidThrough = DateSerial(Year(Date), Month(Date) + _
            bytMonths, 1)
```

Features of the EnterPayment Form, *continued*

```
    Else
        ' Otherwise, add additional months to PaidThrough value.
        PaidThrough = DateSerial(Year(PaidThrough), _
            Month(PaidThrough) + bytMonths, 1)
    End If
End Sub
```

The second part of this procedure uses an If...Then statement to check whether the PaidThrough field is already set. If it isn't, or if the subscription has expired, it adds additional months to the PaidThrough value beginning at today's date. If the PaidThrough field is set and the subscription is current, it adds the additional months to the current PaidThrough value.

Both these statements use Microsoft Access date functions to calculate the new PaidThrough date value. Date values are stored as numbers by Microsoft Access, so you can't work with them directly, except to add or subtract days from them. But using date functions as shown in this procedure makes it possible to add *months* to the date value rather than days, and also makes it easy to set the PaidThrough value to the first day of the month. The Year and Month functions, as their names suggest, return the year and month for a given date value; the DateSerial function lets you build a date value from individual date parts. So the second line that includes these functions in effect says, "Create a date where the year is the same as the PaidThrough date, the month is so many months later than the PaidThrough month, and the day is the first of the month—and set the new PaidThrough value to that date."

Add code to set the subscriber automatically

When users click the Enter Payment command button on the Subscribers form, they most likely want to add a payment record for the subscriber they were looking at. In order to help users enter data more easily, you can set the default value for the SubscriberID control on the data entry form.

Design View button

1   Click the Design View button on the toolbar.

2   Click the OnOpen property in the property sheet, and then click the Build button.

3   Double-click Code Builder.

   Microsoft Access opens the Module window and displays the Form_Open event procedure for the EnterPayment form. Whenever a user opens the form, the code in this procedure will run—which makes it a great place to initialize controls on the form such as the SubscriberID combo box.

223

4 Add the following code to the event procedure:

```
Private Sub Form_Open(Cancel As Integer)
' Set the default to the current subscriber
' on the Subscribers form.

    If IsOpen("Subscribers") Then
        SubscriberID.DefaultValue = Forms!Subscribers!SubscriberID
    End If

End Sub
```

This code first checks whether the Subscribers form is open using the IsOpen function, which you used before. Users might open the EnterPayment form by itself, in which case trying to match it up with the Subscriber form would cause an error.

If the Subscribers form is open, the line of code in the middle sets the DefaultValue property of the SubscriberID combo box to the value of the SubscriberID field on the Subscribers form. As you've seen before, you can refer to a field on another open form using the Forms keyword. This line of code says, "Set the default value for the SubscriberID field (on this form) to the current value of the SubscriberID field on the form called Subscribers."

5 Close the Module window.

6 Click the Form View button on the toolbar.

Form View button

Your event procedure runs, using the current subscriber on the Subscribers form as the default value for the field. Note that although the combo box displays the name of the subscriber, your code actually set it to the appropriate SubscriberID value, because this is the field the combo box is actually bound to.

The current subscriber...

...becomes the default for a new payment.

224

Add code to update other open forms after the user enters a payment

When a user enters a payment, the status of that subscriber changes—the PaidThrough field gets changed to reflect the new payment, for example. If you open another form to display data after the change is made, that form will reflect the changes; but forms that are already open don't automatically show the new data. If forms that show changed data are open, you should update them. You can do this by adding code to the AfterUpdate event procedure for the form, which runs whenever a change gets saved in the form.

Design View button

1   Click the Design View button on the toolbar.

2   Click the AfterUpdate property in the property sheet, and then click the Build button.

3   Double-click Code Builder.

Microsoft Access opens the Module window and displays the Form_AfterUpdate event procedure for the EnterPayment form. Whenever a user saves a new payment, this event procedure will run.

4   Add the following code to the event procedure:

```
Private Sub Form_AfterUpdate()
' Update other forms if they are open.

    If IsOpen("Subscribers") Then
        ' Refresh the Subscribers form to show
        ' the PaidThrough value.
        Forms!Subscribers.Refresh
    End If

    If IsOpen("PaymentHistory") Then
        ' Requery the PaymentHistory pop-up form
        ' to show the new payment.
        Forms!PaymentHistory.Requery
    End If

End Sub
```

The first If...Then statement in this procedure checks whether the Subscribers form is open. If it is, the code uses the Refresh method for the form, which tells Microsoft Access to update the data displayed on the form with the current values from the underlying table. Note that using the Refresh method doesn't cause the query to run again, so new records aren't added, deleted records aren't removed, and the sort order remains the same. You don't need to make these types of changes now, because adding a payment doesn't affect the number of subscribers in the database.

The second part of the procedure checks whether the PaymentHistory pop-up form is displayed. If it is, the code uses the Requery method of the form, which tells Microsoft Access to requery records in the form as if you'd closed and reopened it. Unlike refreshing, requerying a form does add new records, which is necessary in this case so that the pop-up form will show the new payment record. Note, however, that this has the sometimes undesirable side effect of resetting the current record—when you requery a form, the first record in the recordset becomes the current one. In an informational pop-up form like this one, you don't mind, because it doesn't matter which record is current.

5   Close the Module window.

6   Close the EnterPayment form, clicking Yes when Microsoft Access asks if you want to save changes.

Try the new features

If the Subscribers form and the PaymentHistory form are open, adding a new payment should now be reflected in these two forms. Let's see if it works.

1   On the Subscribers form, click the Payment History button.

Code behind the button opens the Payment History pop-up form, showing the payments for the current subscriber. Next, you'll enter a new payment for this subscriber.

2   Click the Enter Payment button.

Code behind this button opens the Enter Payment form, ready for you to add a payment for the current subscriber. If the Payment History form is in the way, you may need to move it out of the way.

3   In the Payment Method option group, select Check.

Changing a field in this form adds a new record to the Payments table, and causes it to display the subscriber's current PaidThrough date. You could go on to specify values for other fields, but because the other fields all have default values, you don't have to enter anything in them (assuming you want the default payment of one year at $24).

4   Click the Save Payment button.

Clicking this button saves the payment record. The PaidThrough field is now a year later than before. When the record was saved, your

AfterUpdate event procedure also updated both the Subscribers form and the Payment History form. In the pop-up form, you'll notice the new payment is listed—your code requeried that form.

When you save a payment, your event procedure requeries the pop-up form so it displays the new record.

5   Close the Payment History form.

6   In the Enter Payment form footer, click the Close button.

The PaidThrough field in the Subscribers form shows the new date—your code refreshed it.

Refreshing the form ensures that this field is updated immediately.

It's tough to anticipate when you'll need to refresh or requery the data in a form. When you test your application, look out for changes you make that aren't reflected as you expect. If they aren't, add a line of code that uses the Refresh or Requery method.

TIP You can also use the Requery method on a combo box or list box to update the records that are displayed in the list. For example, if you add a new subscriber in the Subscribers form, the combo box on the EnterPayment form won't automatically include that subscriber (until the next time the form is opened). To take care of this detail, you could requery the list each time a record is saved in the Subscribers form.

Close the form and exit Microsoft Access

1 Close the Subscribers form, clicking Yes when Microsoft Access asks if you want to save changes to the form.

2 On the File menu, click Exit.

Lesson Summary

To	Do this
Make a form stay on top of other forms at all times	Set the form's Popup property to Yes.
Create a button that opens another form and displays only records that are related to the currently displayed record	Use the Command Button Wizard, selecting the Open The Form And Find Specific Data To Display option. Specify the key fields that link data in the two forms.
Keep a form synchronized to display related records as you move between records in a main form	In the Current event procedure for the main form, write code that sets the Filter property of the other form. In the property setting, concatenate the key fields that you want to match in the two forms.
Check whether a form is open before you refer to it in code	Call the IsOpen function, which is included in the Miscellaneous module in the practice database.
Automatically set the value of a field on a form designed to add new records	In the Open event procedure for the form, set the DefaultValue property of the control.
Update data currently displayed on a separate form, showing new values but not adding, deleting, or reordering records	In the AfterUpdate event procedure, use the Refresh method on the form you want to update.
Update all data displayed in a separate form when the user adds or deletes a record	In the AfterUpdate event procedure, use the Requery method on the form you want to update.

For online information about	On the Help menu, click Contents and Index, click the Index tab, and then
Creating pop-up forms	Search for "pop-up forms"
Synchronizing forms to display related data	Search for "synchronizing forms"
Using date functions	Search for "date"
Referring to objects and their properties	Search for "objects"
Using methods	Search for "methods"

For more information on	In *Building Applications with Microsoft Access 97*, see
Creating pop-up forms, or synchronizing forms to display related data	Chapter 3, "Using Forms to Collect, Filter, and Display Information"
Using date functions	Chapter 2, "Introducing Visual Basic"
Referring to objects and their properties, or using methods	Chapter 5, "Working with Objects and Collections"

Preview of the Next Lesson

So far, you've used primarily command buttons to help users tell you what they want to do. But like most Windows applications, yours can allow users to select menu items and click toolbar buttons to access common application commands. In the next lesson, you'll learn to customize the menus and toolbars that are displayed with your application's forms.

Display Custom Menus and Toolbars

In this lesson you will learn how to:

- Create your own menus to run your application's commands.

- Create and customize your application's toolbars.

- Designate a custom menu bar and toolbar for use with a particular form in your application.

When you work in a well-organized kitchen, cooking can be a joy. The cookware and utensils you need are at hand but not in the way; your ingredients are all within easy reach in the cabinets; the counter space is clear and ready for action. If you're like me, on the other hand, you don't always plan ahead for creating your culinary masterpieces—so you end up searching for tools and ingredients, and running out of space. "Next time," you say, "I'll get the kitchen in shape before I start...."

In some ways, using a database application is like working in the kitchen. It's much easier to get your work done if you have all the tools you need within reach—but space on the screen is limited, so you want features to stay hidden away until you're ready to use them. In order to prepare the "data kitchen" for your users, you'll want to organize your application's commands and objects in the cleanest possible way.

In this lesson, you'll learn two important elements of an organized user interface: menus and toolbars. By hiding commands away on menus and using compact toolbar buttons to provide access to forms and reports, you'll keep the Subscription application less cluttered, while at the same time making sure everything users need is easy to find.

Start the lesson

 Start Microsoft Access and open the 10Subscr database in the practice files folder.

Using Menus and Toolbars in Your User Interface

So far, you've used command buttons on forms to make commands available to users—for example, you created three buttons on the Subscribers form that allowed users to jump to a specific record, view payment history, or enter payments. Although some common actions are important enough to warrant a command button on a form, most of the commands users need can be organized on your application's menus and toolbars, where they take less space. Like other Windows applications, your application can include *both* a menu command and a toolbar button to perform a given action, making it even more accessible. In this lesson, you'll create menus and a toolbar for the Subscribers form, replacing the command button strategy you used before.

You can design menus and toolbars to be used with a single form, or to work with several forms. You can even design a global menu or toolbar that's available throughout your application. However, because many commands apply only to certain places in your application, you're likely to need separate menus and toolbars for individual forms. Of course, you can always display the standard Microsoft Access menu or toolbar for some of the forms and reports in your application if they don't need custom commands.

When creating either menus or toolbars, you also have the option of using existing Microsoft Access commands. In most cases, you'll want to make most standard commands available to users, especially if they already know how to use Microsoft Access or other Windows applications. On the other hand, if you want to limit the options users have in your application, you can create menus and toolbars that contain just the commands you want to make available. To plan for your menus and toolbars, take a look at the other Windows applications you use to see how their interfaces are structured. Then, when you've planned your interface, you'll use the techniques shown in this lesson to put it into place.

Open the Subscribers form

1   In the Database window, click the Forms tab.
2   Double-click the Subscribers form.

As you can see, the Subscribers form in the practice database no longer has command buttons in its footer—you're going to replace them with menu commands and toolbar buttons.

Creating a Custom Menu Bar

The menus in Microsoft Access—File, Edit, View, and so on—are grouped into one object called a *menu bar.* You should think of a menu bar as a type of toolbar (although it looks and behaves differently) because you'll use the same techniques to create and edit both. Microsoft Access itself thinks of them as the same type of object; in fact, toolbars and menu bars are both called *command bars* when you refer to them in Visual Basic code. Knowing this, you won't be too surprised to hear that the tool you use to create menus is the Customize Toolbars command. Using it, you can add commands and customize the behavior and appearance of both menus and toolbars.

While you can create all the menus for a new menu bar from scratch, you'll often want to place existing Microsoft Access menus on your menu bar. When a menu's standard set of commands doesn't make sense, on the other hand, you can create a new menu with your own set of commands. On the Subscribers form menu bar, for example, you might want to make most of the built-in Microsoft Access menus available, but also include a special menu with custom commands that help users navigate through the application.

To make these menu commands appear with the Subscribers form, you'll create a new custom menu bar, copy built-in menus and create your own menus with custom menu commands, and then specify that the Subscribers form should use the custom menu bar. Microsoft Access will take it from there, displaying your additional menu commands whenever the Subscribers form is active.

Create a custom menu bar for the Subscribers form

Before you can specify a custom menu bar for a form, you need to create it and add menus and commands to it. In this section, you'll create a custom menu bar called Subscribers Menu Bar and then add built-in menus to make it look similar to the standard Form View menu bar. Then you'll add your own version of the Tools menu, as well as a new menu designed especially for the Subscribers form.

1 On the View menu, point to Toolbars, and then click Customize.

The Customize dialog box appears, listing all the toolbars and menu bars available to your application. At this point, you could begin making changes to the built-in menu bar or toolbar that's shown; however, your changes would apply for all databases. Since you want your changes to apply to the Subscribers form only, you'll begin by creating a new menu bar.

2 Click the New button.

Microsoft Access asks what you want to name the custom toolbar or menu bar.

3 In the Toolbar Name box, type **Subscribers Menu Bar**, and then click OK.

A blank new toolbar (or is it a menu bar?) appears near the middle of your screen, and Subscribers Menu Bar appears at the end of the Toolbars list in the Customize dialog box.

4 Move the blank new menu bar up and to the left, out of the way of the Customize dialog box. (As you work through the lesson, you may also need to move the Customize dialog box out of the way of the menu from time to time.)

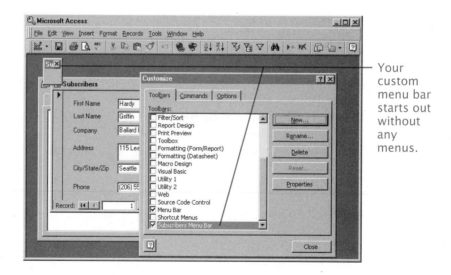

Your custom menu bar starts out without any menus.

5 In the Customize dialog box, click the Properties button.

The Toolbar Properties dialog box appears, where you can set properties that change the behavior of the selected toolbar or menu bar.

6 In the Type box, select Menu Bar.

7 Click the Close button.

For the time being, there are two menu bars. After you add menus to your new menu bar, you'll make sure only one menu bar appears at a time.

Add built-in menus to your custom menu bar

Now that you have a menu bar, you'll add a few built-in Microsoft Access menus. To add menus or commands to a menu bar or toolbar, you use the Commands tab in the Customize dialog box.

1 In the Customize dialog box, click the Commands tab.

In the Categories list, you can see all the categories of Microsoft Access commands that you can put on your menu bars and toolbars. As you click each category, such as File, Edit, and so on, the available commands are shown in the Commands list on the right.

Select a category...

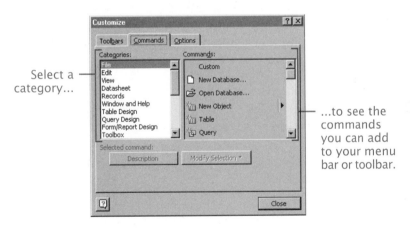

...to see the commands you can add to your menu bar or toolbar.

There are special categories in the list for adding entire built-in menus or creating custom menu commands. You'll use the Built-in Menus category to add several familiar menus.

2 In the Categories list, select Built-in Menus.

3 In the Commands list, click the File menu entry and drag it to your custom menu bar.

Microsoft Access creates a copy of the built-in File menu, complete with all its commands and submenus. (If you want, you can verify that it's all there by clicking the new menu to view its contents.)

Drag from here...

...to here, creating a copy of the File menu.

4 Drag the Edit menu from the Commands list, placing it just to the right of the new File menu on your custom menu bar.

5 Repeat this procedure for the View, Records, Window, and Help menus, dragging each in turn to the right side of your custom menu bar. (You can skip the Insert, Format, and Tools menus, because users don't need the first two of these menus in Form view, and you'll create your own version of the Tools menu.)

Here's what the menu bar should look like.

Add your own version of the Tools menu

There are many commands on the Tools menu that are exclusively for power users and developers—you don't want your users to be messing around with them. Rather than including the built-in Tools menu, you'll now create your own version, copying only the commands you want to make available. This way, you'll make the menu much simpler, and you won't have to worry about users getting themselves into trouble.

1   In the Categories list, click New Menu.

2   In the Commands list, click New Menu, and then drag the text to your
     custom menu bar, placing it between the Records and Window menus.

Drag from
here...

to here.

A menu called New Menu appears on your custom menu bar.

3   With the right mouse button, click New Menu on the menu bar.

     A shortcut menu appears showing options for the menu.

4   Select the existing text in the Name box, type **&Tools**, and then
     press ENTER.

     As with command button captions, you can include an ampersand in a
     menu name to provide an accelerator key for users who prefer the key-
     board. The menu now shows its new name; however, if you click it,
     you'll see that it has no menu commands yet. Next, you'll copy three
     commands from the built-in Tools menu. To copy a menu or toolbar
     command, you drag it from one menu bar or toolbar to another while
     holding down the CTRL key (if you don't hold down the CTRL key, you
     move the command rather than copy it).

5   On the built-in menu bar at the top of the Microsoft Access window,
     click the Tools menu.

     Of the commands you see on this menu, you want to include only three
     on your custom Tools menu: Spelling, AutoCorrect, and Options.

6   Holding down the CTRL key, click the Spelling command, drag it down
     to the Tools menu on your custom menu bar until the menu drops

237

down, and then (still holding down the CTRL key) drag it on to the blank menu and place it there.

Drag the Spelling command from the standard Tools menu...

...to here...

...and then to here.

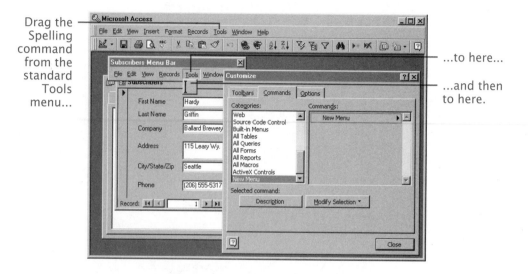

The Spelling command appears on the menu.

7 Repeat this technique to copy the AutoCorrect command and the Options command from the built-in Tools menu, placing them below the Spelling command on your custom menu.

Now your custom Tools menu includes only the three commands that users need. Your last step is to add a dividing line just above the Options menu command—as with standard menu bars, you can group menu commands on your custom menus.

8 With the right mouse button, click the Options command at the bottom of your custom menu bar, and then click Begin A Group on the shortcut menu.

The custom Tools menu is complete.

NOTE If you inadvertantly made changes to the built-in menu bar—for example, if you deleted a command from it—it's easy to revert to its standard menus. In the Customize dialog box, select Menu Bar from the list and then click the Reset button.

Add another menu to your custom menu bar

Next, you'll add another new menu to the Subscribers menu bar. Because the menu will contain only commands that are specific to the Subscribers application, you'll name the menu Subscribers.

1 In the Categories list, click New Menu.

2 In the Commands list, click New Menu, and then drag the text to your custom menu bar, placing it between the Tools and Window menus.

3 With the right mouse button, click New Menu on the menu bar.

A shortcut menu appears showing options for the menu.

4 Select the existing text in the Name box, type **&Subscribers**, and then press ENTER.

The new menu is ready for your custom commands.

Add custom menu commands to open forms in your application

Users want to perform two primary tasks in the Subscribers application: locating subscribers and printing mailing labels. In Lesson 8, you created the GoToRecordDialog form, which provides a better way for users to find records in the Subscribers form, and the MailingLabelsDialog form, which helps users print a report. Now you'll add custom menu commands that open these forms automatically. There is a special category in the Customize dialog box, called All Forms, that makes it easy to add a command to open an existing form.

1 In the Customize dialog box, click the Commands tab.

2 Select All Forms from the Categories list.

The Commands list displays all the forms in the Subscribers database. To add a command to a menu, you drag it from the Commands list to the desired menu.

3 In the Commands list, click the GoToRecordDialog entry, drag it up to the Subscribers menu until the menu drops down, and then drag it down onto the blank menu.

The GoToRecordDialog command appears on the menu.

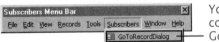

Your custom menu command will open the GoToRecordDialog form.

To match other menu commands, you'll want to change the text shown on this command.

4 With the right mouse button, click the GoToRecordDialog command.

239

5   Select the existing text in the Name box, type **&Find Record...**, and then press ENTER.

Once again, you include an ampersand in the name of the menu command to provide an accelerator key. Also, it's customary to include an ellipsis (three dots) after any menu command that displays a dialog box rather than immediately carrying out an action.

Next, you'll copy an appropriate icon—the binoculars icon from the Find command—to the new menu command. The icon is displayed on a button on the current toolbar.

6   With the right mouse button, click the Find button on the toolbar (it's the sixth button from the right), and then click Copy Button Image on the shortcut menu.

7   Click the Subscribers menu.

8   With the right mouse button, click the Find Record menu command, and then click Paste Button Image on the shortcut menu.

In two easy steps, you've managed to steal the standard image for your new command—a handy technique that you may want to use with other custom menus and toolbars down the road. Now you're ready to add a second command to the menu.

9   In the Customize dialog box, click the MailingLabelsDialog entry in the Commands list, drag it up to the Subscribers menu until the menu drops down, and then drag it down onto the menu just below the existing menu command.

Another new command, MailingLabelsDialog, appears on the menu.

10   With the right mouse button, click the new menu command.

11   Select the existing text in the Name box, type **&Print Mailing Labels...**, and then press ENTER.

For this menu command, you'll copy the printer icon from the Print button on the toolbar.

12   With the right mouse button, click the Print button on the toolbar (it's the third button from the left), and then click Copy Button Image on the shortcut menu.

13   Click the Subscribers menu.

14   With the right mouse button, click the Print Mailing Labels menu command, and then click Paste Button Image on the shortcut menu.

Your new menu is complete.

Tell the Subscribers form to use the custom menu bar

Now that you have a custom menu bar, you can make the Subscribers form use this one instead of the standard menu bar by setting the form's MenuBar property.

1 Drag the menu bar up to the top of the Microsoft Access window—between the standard menu bar and the toolbar—to "dock" it there. (Docking a menu bar or toolbar refers to sticking it against the top or side of the screen, rather than letting it float in the middle.)

Dock your custom menu bar just below the standard menu bar.

Next, you'll make sure Microsoft Access displays only one menu bar at a time.

2 In the Customize dialog box, click the Toolbars tab.

3 In the Toolbars list, clear the check box next to Subscribers Menu Bar.

The custom menu bar disappears, and will no longer show unless the Subscribers form is active. However, you still need to designate it as the menu bar for the Subscribers form.

4 In the Customize dialog box, click the Close button.

5 Click the Design View button on the toolbar.

Design View button

6 If the property sheet isn't displayed, click the Properties button on the toolbar.

7 Click the Other tab in the property sheet.

Properties button

8 Set the MenuBar property to Subscribers Menu Bar.

Setting this property tells Microsoft Access that whenever the Subscribers form is active, it should display your custom menu bar instead of the standard one.

Form View button

9   Click the Form View button on the toolbar.

Your custom menu bar is shown. You can tell it isn't the standard menu bar, because it has your special Subscribers menu on it.

Try your custom menu bar

You're ready to test your custom menu bar.

1   On the Subscribers menu, click Find Record.

Your custom command opens the dialog box, which you created in Lesson 8.

2   Double-click an entry in the list box.

You jump to the specified record in the Subscribers form. Now, try out the other command you added.

3   On the Subscribers menu, click Print Mailing Labels.

The Print Mailing Labels dialog box appears.

4   Click Cancel.

Finally, you might as well check the Tools menu to make sure your changes are there.

5   Click the Tools menu.

There are only three commands on the menu—the rest of the commands usually found on the Tools menu aren't there. Of course, they still exist on the built-in menu bar, which you can return to by switching to a window other than the Subscribers form.

Database Window button

6   Click the Database Window button on the toolbar.

7   Click the Tools menu again.

All the standard commands have returned.

As you can see, your custom menu bar appears only when the Subscribers form is active—that's the form you created it for. However, if you create a menu bar that's appropriate for more than one form, the forms can share it: just set the MenuBar property in each form to the same menu name. You can also create a single menu bar that applies to all forms in your application (unless they each have their own menu bar). To specify a "global" menu, you set the Menu Bar option using the Startup command on the Tools menu.

Creating Custom Shortcut Menus

When you click the right mouse button nearly anywhere in Windows 95 or Microsoft Access, a shortcut menu appears with commands that are appropriate to the current context you're in or the place you've just clicked. For example, when you click a field on a form with the right mouse button, a shortcut menu appears with options for filtering, copying, and pasting. By default, these shortcut menus appear in your application just as any other menu does.

In most cases, the default shortcut menus will work fine for your applications. If you want, however, you can replace shortcut menus with your own—using steps similar to those for regular menu bars. To replace the shortcut menu bar for a form, create a custom menu bar, setting its Type property to Popup (rather than Menu Bar or Toolbar). Then, set the form's ShortcutMenuBar property to the name of the custom menu bar. You can also specify different shortcut menus for individual controls on your forms by setting the ShortcutMenuBar property for each control (regular menu bars don't allow this).

As with a menu bar, you can add commands to a shortcut menu that perform Microsoft Access menu commands, open existing objects such as forms or reports, or run Visual Basic functions.

Customizing Toolbars

For better or worse, software today uses graphical interface elements more and more to interact with users. In your Microsoft Access applications, one way you can follow this graphical trend is by making use of toolbars. Toolbars are a handy way to make commands available to users. Many buttons can fit on a toolbar, and once users learn what they are, the commands they need are always just a click away. When you want to add new buttons to a toolbar, Microsoft Access provides many icons to choose from; if you're an aspiring artist, you can create your own.

As with menu bars, there are several basic strategies for creating toolbars. The simplest strategy is to customize an existing toolbar, such as the Form View toolbar, adding and deleting buttons as desired. However, the standard toolbars are stored with your Microsoft Access installation, so other users who open your databases won't see your toolbar changes.

To make special toolbars available on other computers, you'll want to create your own custom toolbars, either supplementing or replacing the standard ones. Just like custom menu bars, custom toolbars are stored with your application's database, so they're available to all users. When you customize toolbars, you choose which buttons they have and whether the buttons have icons or text on them. You can even customize the ToolTip text (also called ScreenTip text) that appears when users hold the mouse pointer over a button.

In this section, you'll create a simple toolbar designed to replace the standard toolbar. Because users won't see the standard toolbar when the Subscribers form is active, you'll want to include some of the buttons users are accustomed to seeing there (such as the Cut, Copy, and Paste buttons) and then add your own selection of buttons in place of those you don't expect users to need.

Creating a Custom Toolbar for the Subscribers Form

The toolbar you'll create will help users of the Subscribers form to open other forms quickly and easily. Fortunately, as you saw when customizing menus, the easiest type of toolbar button (or menu command) to create is one that opens a form or report in your database. You'll start by creating a new, empty toolbar, and then you'll add several buttons to it.

Create a new toolbar for the Subscribers form

1 Switch back to the Subscribers form.

2 On the View menu, point to Toolbars, and then click Customize.

It's your old friend the Customize dialog box.

3 Click the New button.

Microsoft Access displays the New Toolbar dialog box.

4 In the Toolbar Name box, type **Subscribers**, and then click OK.

An empty floating toolbar appears near the center of the screen.

5 In the Customize dialog box, click the Close button.

6 Drag the empty toolbar up to the top of the screen—between the menu bar and the existing toolbar—to dock it. (Make sure you dock the toolbar at the far left of the window, lined up with the left side of the menu bar.)

Your custom toolbar will soon replace the standard Form View toolbar for the Subscribers form.

7 With the right mouse button, click one of the toolbars, and then click Subscribers on the shortcut menu.

Your custom toolbar disappears for the moment.

Design View button

8 Click the Design View button on the toolbar.

9 Set the Toolbar property to Subscribers.

Setting this property tells Microsoft Access that whenever the Subscribers form is active, it should display your custom toolbar instead of the standard one.

10 Click the Form View button on the toolbar.

Form View button

Your custom toolbar is shown, although so far it's just a blank box, without any buttons to click.

Add standard buttons to the toolbar

On any toolbar you create, you can add as many standard buttons as you like, and they work just as they do on the built-in Microsoft Access toolbars. Here you want to include a few of the Edit commands users are accustomed to seeing: Cut, Copy, Paste, and Undo.

1 With the right mouse button, click the empty toolbar, and then click Customize on the shortcut menu.

2 In the Customize dialog box, click the Commands tab.

3 Select Edit from the Categories list.

The standard Edit commands are shown in the Commands list.

4 Select Cut from the Commands list, and then drag the text up to the toolbar.

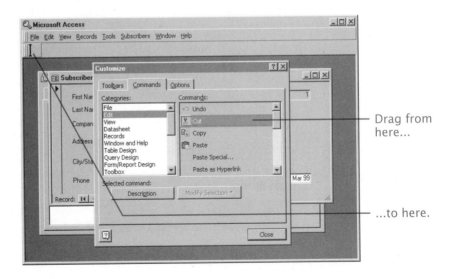

The Cut button appears on your toolbar.

245

5 Using the same technique, add the Copy, Paste, and Undo buttons to the right of the Cut button.

Just like standard toolbars, your custom toolbars can include dividing lines for grouping buttons. Because the Cut, Copy, and Paste buttons are a logical group, you want to include a dividing line before the Undo button.

6 With the right mouse button, click the Undo button, and then click Begin A Group on the shortcut menu.

A dividing line appears between the Paste and Undo buttons.

Add three custom buttons

Now you'll add three custom buttons—one to open the GoToRecordDialog form, one to open the MailingLabelsDialog form, and one to open the EnterPayment form. For the GoToRecord and PrintMailingLabels buttons, you'll just copy the commands you created for your custom menu, because this is exactly what you want to show on the toolbar.

1 Click the Subscribers menu to drop it down.

2 Holding down the CTRL key, drag the Find Record command from the Subscribers menu to the toolbar and place it just to the right of the existing buttons.

The new button appears on the toolbar. As you can see, menus and toolbars are just two different views of the same thing—a place to put commands—and you can therefore share and copy commands between them. Next, you'll set properties for the button.

3 With the right mouse button, click the new button, and then click Properties on the shortcut menu.

4 Select the existing text in the ToolTip box, and then type **Find Record**.

This text will display in a ToolTip when users point at your custom button.

5 Select the Begin A Group box, and then click Close.

Next, you'll copy the Print Mailing Labels menu command to your toolbar.

6 Click the Subscribers menu again.

7 Holding down the CTRL key, drag the Print Mailing Labels command from the Subscribers menu to the toolbar and place it just to the right of the existing buttons.

8   With the right mouse button, click the new button, and then click Properties on the shortcut menu.

9   Select the existing text in the ToolTip box, type **Print Mailing Labels**, and then click Close.

Next, you'll add another button to open the EnterPayment form.

10   In the Customize dialog box, select All Forms from the Categories list.

11   Select EnterPayment from the Commands list and drag it to the toolbar.

12   With the right mouse button, click the EnterPayment button, and then click Properties on the shortcut menu.

13   Select the existing text in the ToolTip box, type **Enter Payment**, and then click Close.

Your toolbar now has seven buttons ready for action! If you want, you can add other standard buttons, or rearrange buttons by dragging them around on the toolbar.

Each of your custom buttons opens a different form.

14   In the Customize Toolbars dialog box, click Close.

Try out the new toolbar

It's time to take your new toolbar for a spin! Try hovering over each of the buttons to view the ToolTip. Then follow these steps to see the toolbar buttons in action.

1   Click the Find Record button on the toolbar.

The button opens the Go To Record dialog box.

2   Double-click a subscriber in the list.

3   Click the Print Mailing Labels button on the toolbar.

The button opens the Print Mailing Labels dialog box.

4   Click Cancel.

5   Click the Enter Payment button on the toolbar.

The button opens the Enter Payment form.

6   Click Close.

Next, you'll add one more button to the toolbar before calling it complete—a button that lets users view payment histories. When you're finished, you will have replaced all the command buttons that used to be in the Subscribers form footer.

Creating Toolbar
Buttons to Run Visual Basic Code

The toolbar buttons you've created so far have simply opened forms—they haven't done anything special beyond this. If opening an object is all you want to do, this technique is very straightforward. But you may want a toolbar button to do more—for example, you may want to run a Visual Basic procedure when users click the button. To do this, you set a property of the button to the name of a Visual Basic function you want it to run.

In this section, you'll create a toolbar button that runs a Visual Basic function. In this case, you want the button to open the PaymentHistory pop-up form, which shows a subscriber's payment history. However, you don't just want to open the form—you also need to set a filter so that the form displays only payments for the current subscriber. Although a toolbar button can't do this by itself, you can write a simple function that does the job.

Write a Visual Basic function
to open the PaymentHistory form

1 On the Window menu, click 10Subscr : Database.

2 In the Database window, click the Modules tab.

3 Double-click the Miscellaneous module.

   The Module window opens and shows the module's code.

4 On the Insert menu, click Procedure.

5 In the Name box, type **ViewPaymentHistory**, and then click OK.

   Microsoft Access creates the function at the end of the module, entering the Function and End Function statements for you.

6 Enter the following code for the procedure:

```
' Open the PaymentHistory form and set its filter.

   DoCmd.OpenForm "PaymentHistory", , , "SubscriberID = " _
      & Forms!Subscribers!SubscriberID
```

   This code uses the OpenForm method of the DoCmd object to open the PaymentHistory form. It uses the WhereCondition argument—a technique you learned in the previous lesson—to specify a filter for the form. When the form opens, it will display only records whose SubscriberID field matches the record currently displayed in the Subscribers form.

7 Close the Module window, clicking Yes when Microsoft Access asks if you want to save changes.

Add a toolbar button that runs the function

The last button you'll add to the toolbar will use the ViewPaymentHistory function. Of course, you could run a much more complex function when a toolbar button is clicked; in this case, however, all you need to do is open the form.

1 Switch back to the Subscribers form.

Your custom menu bar and toolbar appear.

2 With the right mouse button, click the toolbar, and then click Customize on the shortcut menu.

When you plan to provide a Visual Basic function for a button to run, it doesn't matter which command or category you choose—the button will run your code instead of performing its usual action. For this reason, it makes the most sense to select a command with an icon you want the button to have. You'll use the Table icon to represent the View Payment History command.

3 Select File from the Categories list.

4 Select Table from the Commands list and drag the text up to the new toolbar, placing it just to the right of the Enter Payment button.

As it stands, clicking this button would create a new table. Of course, you have other plans for the button.

5 With the right mouse button, click the new toolbar button, and then click Properties on the shortcut menu.

6 Select the existing text in the ToolTip box and then type **View Payment History**.

7 In the On Action box, type **=ViewPaymentHistory()**.

Setting the OnAction property tells Microsoft Access to run the function when the button is clicked.

249

When you use a function with the OnAction property, always be sure to precede the function name with an equal sign, and follow it with parentheses (including arguments if the function requires them).

8 In the Subscribers Control Properties dialog box, click Close.

9 In the Customize Toolbars dialog box, click Close.

Test the toolbar once again

You'r ready to try out the final toolbar button.

1 Click the View Payment History button on the toolbar.

The toolbar button runs the ViewPaymentHistory function, which in turn opens the PaymentHistory pop-up form and sets its filter.

2 Close the Payment History form.

Your custom toolbar is complete!

Working with Command Bars in Visual Basic

In this lesson, you've customized menus and toolbars using the tools available in Microsoft Access. However, if you need additional power—for example, if you want to change menus or toolbars in response to actions users take in your application—you can work directly with menus and toolbars in Visual Basic code. In Visual Basic, menu bars and toolbars are collectively known as *command bars*. They have a complete set of objects, properties, and methods you can use when working with them.

There are many reasons you might want to manipulate command bars, but here are some common possibilities:

- To add or hide menu commands or toolbar buttons in response to events in your application.

- To disable custom menu commands or toolbar buttons when they don't apply.

- To create and manipulate special command bar controls, such as combo boxes, that aren't available through the standard Microsoft Access tools.

Working with Command Bars in Visual Basic, *continued*

> Before you can work with command bars in code, you need to alert Microsoft Access by choosing the References command (Tools menu) and selecting the Microsoft Office 8.0 Object Library. Then, you use the CommandBar and CommandBarControl objects to access menus and toolbars. You'll learn more about using objects in Lesson 12. For information and examples specifically on programming with command bars, search the Help index for "CommandBar object."

Close the form and exit Microsoft Access

1 Close the Subscribers form, clicking Yes when Microsoft Access asks if you want to save changes.

2 On the File menu, click Exit.

Lesson Summary

To	Do this
Create a custom menu bar or toolbar	On the View menu, point to Toolbars, and then click Customize. Click the New button and type a name for the menu bar or toolbar.
Copy commands or buttons from one menu or toolbar to another	While the Customize dialog box is open, hold down the CTRL key and drag the menu command or button to the menu or toolbar you want to copy it to.
Create menu commands or buttons that run standard commands or open existing forms and reports	In the Customize dialog box, select the category of command you want the menu command or button to run, and then drag the text of the command to a menu or toolbar. For buttons that open database objects, use the All Forms or All Reports category and drag the name of the form or report.
Create menu commands or toolbar buttons that run a Visual Basic function	Set the OnAction property for the menu command or toolbar button to an equal sign followed by the name of the function.

For online information about	On the Help menu, click Contents and Index, click the Index tab, and then
Creating custom menu bars and menu commands	Search for "menus"
Creating custom toolbars	Search for "toolbars"
Working with command bars in Visual Basic code	Search for "CommandBar object"
Using methods of the DoCmd object	Search for "DoCmd" or the method name (such as "OpenForm")

For more information on	In *Building Applications with Microsoft Access 97*, see
Creating custom menu bars, menus, and toolbars	Chapter 1, "Creating an Application"
Programming with Microsoft Office objects, such as command bars	Chapter 5, "Working with Objects and Collections"
Using methods of the DoCmd object	Chapter 2, "Introducing Visual Basic"

Preview of the Next Lesson

Now that you've created dialog boxes, menus, and toolbars, you know how to create almost every part of a custom user interface. All that's left is to package all the parts of your application into a coherent whole. In the next lesson, you'll learn ways to customize your application's general appearance and behavior, such as giving it its own title bar and icon. What's more, you'll learn how to control what happens when your application starts—and how to provide a startup form that leads users through their tasks.

Put Final Touches on an Application

In this lesson you will learn how to:

- Create an application startup form.
- Control how your application starts.
- Customize the title bar and appearance of your application.
- Separate your application's data from its other objects.

The first impression is the most important, goes the common wisdom. Of course, it's important that when you order a fancy cake it tastes good, but it's the "icing on the cake" that catches people's attention—and their first look at that delicious cake will affect their overall opinion more than any other factor. As in other areas of life, this maxim holds true for computer software: the appearance and first impression of a product is as important as its capabilities. As Microsoft itself has learned, a polished, graphical product inspires excitement that might cause users to excuse a missing feature or two.

In previous lessons, you've learned how to put most of the substance into your applications, creating and customizing forms, adding menus and toolbars, linking everything together in a logical way. Before your application is ready for public consumption, however, it needs a few final touches—the icing on the cake. After all, the application will represent *you* to the users who start it up, and you want their first experience with your application to be a good one.

In this lesson, you'll learn techniques for making your applications look professional and polished. You'll work with the Subscription application, making it easier for users to get started—and helping the application make a great first impression. Finally, you'll learn tips and tricks for distributing an application to users so that it will be easier to maintain down the road.

Start the lesson

 Start Microsoft Access and open the 11Subscr database in the practice files folder.

Controlling How Your Application Starts

After you've created the tables, forms, and reports for your application and added all the code to make them work together well, it's time to prepare your application for delivery. You want to make your application look like a unique, finished product rather than simply a Microsoft Access database with a few frills. Additionally, if users are to have a good experience with the application, you'll need to make sure it's easy for them to get started.

Here are some of the final preparations you'll want to consider:

Designate a startup form.   You can select a form in your database that Microsoft Access opens automatically each time a user starts the application. For example, you might want to jump directly to your application's main data entry or display form, such as the Subscribers form you've been working with. Or, in many applications, you'll want to provide a switchboard-type form—similar to the Switchboard form the Database Wizard creates—that acts as a main menu for users' tasks. In either case, you'll most likely want to hide the standard Database window, because your forms will provide users with easy access to all your application's capabilities.

Customize the startup appearance of your application.   In addition to providing a startup form, you can customize several other startup details, such as what the title bar displays. And if you create general application menu bars, shortcut menus, and toolbars, you'll want them to be hooked up when your application starts.

Prepare your application for network use and easy maintenance. Before you deliver your application, you should consider how it will be used and maintained. To make things easier down the road, you may want to split your application into two separate files: one for tables, and another for other objects. Additionally, you'll decide whether the application will be located on a network, and whether you need to protect your data by setting a password.

Test, test, test!   Of course, the final step before you distribute your application is to make sure everything is foolproof. Try all the possible paths through the forms and reports, and make any necessary fixes before you deliver it. The work you put in up front will pay off in reducing the updates you'll need to provide down the road!

In this lesson, you'll use several of these techniques to customize the Subscription application. When you're finished, the Subscription application will be ready to deliver—making its debut to users as a stand-alone product rather than just another database, and helping users get started with their work right away.

Providing a Startup Form for Your Application

Any form in your application can act as the startup form, opening automatically for users. However, the most common strategy for starting an application—and the one you'll use with the Subscription application—is to provide a separate startup form that acts as a main menu for users. The Subscription practice database already includes a preliminary version of such a startup form, designed to introduce the application to users at an imaginary publication called *Dance Journal*.

In this section you'll add the final elements to the design of the Switchboard form. In the practice database, the form already contains the picture, text in several labels, and two simple buttons created using the Command Button Wizard. You'll add the third button, and then get the form ready for use as the application's startup form. In your own database, you would create a switchboard form from scratch, adding whatever text, pictures, and buttons you'd like. A startup form is a great place to show your creativity and put your personal touch on your application.

Completing the Switchboard Form for the Subscription Database

To finish up the Switchboard form in the practice database, you'll open it in Design view, add a command button using the Command Button Wizard, and then add a label for the button. You'll also set several form properties that make the form look like a switchboard—similar to properties you set for dialog boxes and pop-up forms in previous lessons.

255

Add a command button

1   In the Database window, click the Forms tab.

2   Select the Switchboard form, and then click Design.

The Switchboard form opens in Design view. The two command buttons on this form open the Subscribers form and the PrintMailingLabelsDialog form. You'll create one additional button at the bottom of the form, providing an easy way for users to exit the Subscription application when they're finished with their work.

3   Scroll down a bit in the form to display the blank area underneath the two buttons.

Control Wizards tool

4   In the toolbox, make sure the Control Wizards tool is selected, and then click the Command Button tool.

Command Button tool

5   Click to create the new button just underneath the left side of the OpenMailingDialog button (the one that has an envelope icon on it).

Switchboard : Form

Subscription Database Application

What do you want to do?

View and enter subscriber information

Preview or print subscriber mailing labels

Click here to create the command button.

The Command Button Wizard starts, asking what action you want the button to perform.

6   Select Application from the Categories list.

Quit Application is already selected in the Actions list, so you can continue.

7   Click Next.

The wizard asks whether you want a picture or text on your button. Unlike the command buttons you've created in earlier lessons, for which you typed text, you'll put a picture on this button. The Stop Sign picture, already selected, will do the trick.

8   Click Next.

The wizard asks what you want to name the button.

9 Type **QuitApplication** and then click Finish.

The wizard creates the button, including an event procedure that automatically closes your application—and Microsoft Access—whenever the button is clicked.

Label the command button

Next, you'll add text next to the button to clarify what the button is for.

Label tool

1 In the toolbox, click the Label tool.

2 Click just to the right of the new button.

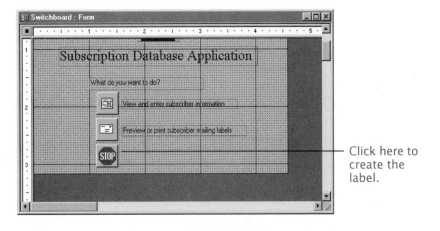

Click here to create the label.

An empty label appears on the form, ready for you to enter the text you want to display. You could use this same technique to add other text to the form, just like the labels that display the title of the application at the top of this form.

3 Type **Exit the Subscription application**.

Set the Switchboard form's properties

To make the form look and work like a switchboard, all that's left is to set form properties.

Properties button

1 On the Edit menu, click Select Form.

2 If the property sheet isn't displayed, click the Properties button on the toolbar.

3 Click the Format tab in the property sheet.

4 Set the following properties to the values shown:

257

Property	Value
Caption	Switchboard
ViewsAllowed	Form
ScrollBars	Neither
RecordSelectors	No
NavigationButtons	No
AutoCenter	Yes
BorderStyle	Thin

These settings will make the Switchboard form look much like a dialog box, with a thin border and no extra navigation tools.

5 Close the Switchboard form, clicking Yes when Microsoft Access asks whether you want to save changes to the form.

Try out the Switchboard form

The Switchboard form will act as the control center of your application—users will think of it as their "home base," from which they'll navigate to their various tasks. Let's try it out.

1 In the Database window, double-click the Switchboard form.

The form appears in the center of the screen, announcing your application and showing the three buttons available for navigation.

2 Click the first button, View And Enter Subscriber Information.

The button's event procedure opens the Subscribers form. The toolbar and menus you created in Lesson 10 appear as well, providing a way to navigate through the other parts of your application. When you close the Subscribers form, you'll return to the application's switchboard.

3 Close the Subscribers form.

When users finish working in the Subscription application, they would normally click your new button to exit Microsoft Access. However, we have some more work to do, so you should just close the form.

4 Close the Switchboard form.

 TIP When you deliver your application to users, you may not want to allow them to close the Switchboard form without closing the whole application. To prevent the application from staying open, you could add a simple line of code to the form's Close event procedure that either closes the application or exits Microsoft Access. Use the CloseCurrentDatabase method to close the application; to exit Microsoft Access, use the Quit method of the DoCmd object.

Make your switchboard form open automatically

Now that the switchboard form is ready to go, the next step is to tell Microsoft Access to open the form automatically when users start your application, making it the startup form for the application. You do this with the Startup command.

1   On the Tools menu, click Startup.

    Microsoft Access displays the Startup dialog box, where you can specify options for how your application starts.

2   In the Display Form box, click the drop-down arrow, and then select Switchboard from the list of forms.

— Select the form you want to open when your application starts.

    Next time you open the database, the Switchboard form will open automatically.

Customizing Your Application's Appearance

While you're in the Startup dialog box, you can set other options for your application. One nice detail to customize is the application's title bar. Instead of "Microsoft Access" you can specify the title of your application. Additionally, now is the time to tell Microsoft Access to hide the standard Database window from users, and to make sure users don't change the toolbars you've provided in your application.

Set startup options to control how your application looks

1   In the Startup dialog box, click the Application Title box, and then type **Subscription Database Application**.

    This text will appear in the title bar of the application window in place of "Microsoft Access," making your custom application look less like a Microsoft Access database and more like your own creation.

2   Clear the Display Database Window check box.

Now, when users open the Subscription database, the Database window won't appear. They won't need it—your switchboard form replaces it as the navigation tool for the application.

3   Clear the Allow Toolbar/Menu Changes check box.

Clearing this option ensures that users can't change your custom Subscribers toolbar or menu—or the built-in ones—so they'll always be available.

Complete startup settings for the Subscription application

4   Click OK.

Although the Subscription database doesn't require any other startup options, you may want to use some of the other options in your own applications. Here are some additional changes you can make by setting options with the Startup command:

Provide your own application icon.   By setting the Application Icon option to an icon or bitmap image file, you can change the icon that's displayed in the upper left corner of the title bar (and in the taskbar button when your application is minimized).

Hide the status bar.   If you clear the Display Status Bar check box, the status bar won't appear at the bottom of the application window.

Change standard menus.   In Lesson 10, you learned how to change menus on a single form. However, you can also specify menu behavior for your entire application by setting startup options. To display a menu bar for forms and reports that don't have their own custom menu bar, set the Menu Bar and Shortcut Menu Bar options. To make built-in menus unavailable, clear the Allow Full Menus and Allow Default Shortcut Menus check boxes.

Hide built-in toolbars.   By clearing the Allow Built-in Toolbars check box, you can tell Microsoft Access not to display the toolbars that are normally available, so that only your custom toolbars appear.

Secure your application from tampering.   If you click the Advanced button in the Startup dialog box, you'll see two more options: Allow Viewing Code After Error and Use Access Special Keys. By clearing these check boxes, you can make it impossible for users to break into your application's code. Be careful, though—you'll be locking *yourself* out as well.

NOTE After you've set startup options, they take effect the next time you open your application. Having these options in effect is great for your users—but while your application is still under development, you may not want the startup options to apply. For example, you'll probably want to open the Database window rather than the startup form, so you'll have access to all objects in the application.

To bypass the startup options for an application, hold down the SHIFT key when you open the database, either as you double-click the database file's icon or as you click the Open button. Microsoft Access will ignore all options you've set using the Startup command.

Replacing the Microsoft Access Splash Screen

Each time you start Microsoft Access, it displays a *splash screen*, a bitmap that announces the name and version number of Microsoft Access. For your applications, you may want to replace this screen with your own, so that opening your application will display your application's name.

To replace the standard splash screen, all you have to do is place a bitmap image (.bmp) file in the same folder as your application's database (.mdb) file, giving it the same name as the database file. To create a custom splash screen, you can use the Windows Paint application or any other application that creates bitmap image files.

Rename the splash screen file so Microsoft Access will display it

The practice files folder includes a bitmap file called 11Splash, which provides the splash screen bitmap for the Subscription database. To cause Microsoft Access to display this bitmap, you'll simply rename it to match the name of the Subscription database.

1 Minimize Microsoft Access (and any other open applications).

2 On the Windows desktop, double-click the shortcut icon for the practice files folder. (Or, if the practice files folder isn't there, locate it in Windows Explorer.)

3 Select the 11Splash file, and then click its name to select the text.

4 Type **11Subscr** to rename the file, and then press ENTER.

Microsoft Access will automatically use this bitmap file as the splash screen whenever you start your application by double-clicking its Windows icon. Note, however, that the splash screen doesn't appear if you open the application from within Microsoft Access.

5 Click the Subscription Database Application button on the taskbar to restore Microsoft Access.

Soon, you'll try out your application with its new startup options and splash screen. First, however, there are a few more details to take care of.

Protecting Your Application by Setting a Password

Many databases contain sensitive or confidential information, which you may want to protect by requiring that users enter a password before they begin working in the application. The simplest way to do this is by setting a password for the database. To do this, on the Tools menu point to Security, and then click Set Database Password. Each time the database opens, Microsoft Access will ask for the password.

Although setting a database password is a simple method of securing your database, it isn't very flexible. For example, what if you want to provide access only to certain objects, or data in your application only to specific users and not to others? Or what if you want to provide various levels of access, such as allowing users to view data, but not to change it? You can customize access to your application in these ways by setting up user and group security. And if you do create this more advanced type of security, you can protect your application itself from any design changes—making yourself the only user who has permission to view code and change objects.

To set up advanced security, you start by running the User-Level Security Wizard. You then use the other Security commands on the Tools menu to create user and group accounts, and to grant permissions to each account for the various objects in your application. Beware, however: advanced security is not for the faint of heart. Although Microsoft Access provides all the tools you need for setting up security, it is a time-consuming and challenging process. If a single password for your application will suffice, consider sticking with the database password strategy.

Preparing to Distribute Your Application to Users

Your application is ready to go to work—all you need to do is make it available to users. In the simplest case, this just involves copying the database application file to the user's system or to a network location where users can access it. However, before you send out your application, it's a good idea to give some thought to how you'll distribute and maintain it. How will you distribute updates to the application? How will users back up and compact the database? Are there any additional files you need to deliver along with your application?

If your application is designed for many users or for users on a network, or if it's a large application, these questions will become important to you. Here are some ideas for addressing the challenges of distributing and maintaining a Microsoft Access application:

Split your application into two database files. By default, all the data and objects for an application are stored in a single database file. This file can become very large and difficult to handle. With a large application, it's a good idea to have one Microsoft Access file for the queries, forms, and other objects that make your application work, and a separate file for its tables. The main application file is often referred to as the *front-end* database, because this is what users open and use; the data file containing your tables is referred to as the *back-end* database.

Place your application or its data file on a network drive. Microsoft Access is a *multiuser* database system, which means that more than one user can view and change data in the same database at the same time. To make your application available to multiple users, you can simply place the file on a network. Or, if you split the application into two separate databases, you can place only the data file on a network drive, while distributing copies of the application file to each user—which may make your application run faster.

Create Windows shortcuts to run your application or perform other tasks. In Windows 95, you can provide shortcut icons that make your application easier to run, especially if it's located on a network or stored in a folder along with many other files. You may want to provide other miscellaneous shortcuts for users as well—for example, you might create a shortcut for compacting or backing up a database file. For information on creating shortcuts, see your Windows documentation or search Help for "shortcuts."

Make sure users have all the files they need. Most everything your application needs is included in your database file or installed with Microsoft Access. If your application uses more than one file, be sure to distribute all the files users need. For example, if you split your application into two files, users must have access to both. If your application has a splash screen or other external files, these files must be available as well. Finally, if your application uses special features of Microsoft Access, such as data access drivers or custom controls, users must have installed them with Microsoft Access.

In this section, you'll implement the first of these strategies for the Subscription application, splitting it into two separate database files for easier maintenance.

Split the Subscription database into two files

As you'll see, splitting an application into two database files is easy: you just run the Database Splitter.

1 On the Tools menu, point to Add-Ins, and then click Database Splitter.

The Database Splitter starts.

2 Click the Split Database button.

The Database Splitter displays the Create Back-End Database dialog box, where you specify the name and location of the database file that will contain your application's tables.

3 In the dialog box, move to the practice files folder on your computer's hard disk (if you're not already there).

Note that if you were planning to make this data available to users on a network, you would move instead to a folder on a network drive. That way, the Database Splitter would put the data on the network for you. For your current purpose, however, having both databases on your hard disk is fine.

4 Click the Split button.

The Database Splitter creates a new database file called 11Subscr_be (the "be" stands for "back end"), exports the two tables in the Subscription database to the new file, creates linked tables to them in the current database, and then displays a message saying that the database was successfully split.

5 Click OK.

6 On the File menu, click Exit.

When Microsoft Access closes, you can see files in the practice folder, which is still displayed on your desktop. The folder now contains three files belonging to the Subscription database for this lesson: the application itself, the data file, and the splash screen bitmap file.

Even though you've split it into two database files, your application will work exactly as before. Now, however, the database is much more flexible. First, you can back up the data file—a very important task—without backing up the entire application, which doesn't often change. What's more, you can replace the application file (to update forms and reports, for example) without any effect on the existing data. Finally, if users work on a network, they can run your application from their individual systems while accessing the data on a network drive.

 NOTE After you've split a database, the linked tables in the application file refer to the folder they're in on your computer's hard disk at the time you perform the split. If you rename folders or move the data file to another location—for example, if you place it on a network drive—you'll have to refresh the linked tables, or else Microsoft Access won't be able to find them.

To refresh linked tables easily, use the Linked Table Manager (on the Add-Ins submenu of the Tools menu). The Linked Table Manager locates the data file—wherever it has been moved to—and relinks the tables so the database works again.

Try out the final Subscription application

1 In the practice files folder on the Windows desktop, double-click the 11Subscr database file (be sure to double-click the Microsoft Access database file, not the bitmap image file).

Microsoft Access starts up behind the scenes. What you see, however, is a custom splash screen announcing the Subscription Database Application—the bitmap you renamed earlier in the lesson. After a few seconds, the splash screen disappears, and Microsoft Access displays your startup form: the Switchboard form.

Your application name is displayed in the title bar.

Your startup form appears instead of the Database window.

The Subscription database is now a complete, stand-alone application— it has its own splash screen, its own title bar, and a customized user interface to help users navigate while performing their work. And when they're finished, it even has a custom way for them to quit!

2 On the Switchboard form, click the Exit The Subscription Application button.

The button's event procedure runs the Quit method of the DoCmd object, and Microsoft Access shuts down.

Additional Tools in the Microsoft Office Developer Edition

In order to run your Microsoft Access application, users must have Microsoft Access installed on their computers. However, now that you've customized an application so it looks like it could stand on its own, you may be wondering if there's a way to distribute it to users who *don't* have Microsoft Access. You can do this—if you have Microsoft Office 97, Developer Edition. This add-on product contains several tools for Microsoft Office developers, including the *run-time* version of Microsoft Access, a version that runs applications but doesn't allow you to change or create them. You can distribute the run-time version of Microsoft Access to an

Additional Tools in the Microsoft Office Developer Edition, *continued*

unlimited number of users, so they can run your application regardless of whether they have Microsoft Access.

One other important tool in the Developer Edition is the Setup Wizard, which allows you to create a full-featured custom Setup program for your application. In addition to installing your application's files on users' systems, the Setup program can install the Microsoft Access run-time files, create Windows shortcuts, and customize users' systems in other ways.

If you're distributing applications to many different users, you'd probably benefit from purchasing this product. In addition to these tools, the Developer Edition includes a CD full of developer software and several programming-related books, one of which is *Building Applications with Microsoft Access 97*.

Lesson Summary

To	Do this
Create a custom switchboard form	Create a new blank form, add text and pictures that introduce your application, and then add command buttons that navigate to common user tasks. Set Format properties to make the form look like a switchboard.
Cause a form to open automatically when your application starts	On the Tools menu, click Startup, and then select the form in the Display Form box. Set other startup options as desired, and then click OK.
Ignore startup options for an application	Hold down the SHIFT key as you open the application.
Provide a custom splash screen that appears when you start an application from Windows	Create a bitmap image file of the screen you want to display, giving the file the same name as your application file and placing it in the same directory.
Split an application into two database files for easier maintenance	On the Tools menu, point to Add-ins, and then click Database Splitter.
Protect data by setting a password	Using commands on the Security submenu of the Tools menu, specify a database password or set up user and group security.

For online information about	On the Help menu, click Contents and Index, click the Index tab, and then
Creating a startup form or setting startup options	Search for "startup options, setting"
Splitting an application into two database files	Search for "Database Splitter"
Using security features to protect your databases	Search for "security"
Creating multiuser applications	Search for "multiuser environment"

For more information on	In *Building Applications with Microsoft Access 97*, see
Creating a startup form or setting startup options	Chapter 1, "Creating an Application"
Using security features to protect your databases	Chapter 14, "Securing Your Application"
Creating multiuser applications	Chapter 10, "Creating Multiuser Applications"

Preview of the Next Lesson

Throughout Part 3, you've learned the key techniques for customizing the user interface of an application. In the final part of the book, you'll delve into more advanced Visual Basic programming topics, learning to work directly with data and objects in powerful new ways. In Lesson 12, you'll learn more about manipulating Microsoft Access objects in Visual Basic code—and how you can achieve impressive results in your forms, subforms, and reports by working directly with objects.

Working with Data and Objects

Explore Objects and Collections

In this lesson you will learn how to:

- Understand object references in Visual Basic code.
- Perform the same action on all objects in a collection.
- Create a list box that allows users to select multiple items from the list.
- Open a Recordset object and change data in selected records.
- Create a QueryDef object in code that runs an action query and changes data.

Estimated time
45 min.

Looking at the packaging, I see that the noodles I'm planning to cook for dinner tonight are made from semolina flour—the only ingredient. Modern science tells me that this flour is itself made up of many distinct bits called molecules. The molecules, in turn, are composed of atoms, and those in turn of still smaller particles. Fortunately, I don't need to understand any of this in order to cook my pasta! On the other hand, if I worked in a food-testing laboratory and wanted to understand precisely how the noodles would behave when cooked, I would need to know what was happening below the surface. I imagine I'd need to consult my chemistry books pretty thoroughly before I could predict how the molecules and atoms would work together.

Like chemistry, Microsoft Access admits of many different levels of understanding. As a Microsoft Access user editing data, for example, you don't usually need to know what's going on behind the scenes. But as an application developer, you'll need a better grasp of the underlying mechanism that makes

Microsoft Access tick. Like a periodic table of chemical elements, the object model of Microsoft Access is a complex framework of objects that make it all work—and as you increase your understanding of this foundation, you'll be able to create more powerful applications.

In this lesson, you'll discover the framework of objects and collections underlying every Microsoft Access application. You'll learn how to use objects to control forms and data in powerful new ways—and along the way, you'll uncover many of the fundamental principles on which Microsoft Access is built. Although we'll only scratch the surface of the complexities underlying Microsoft Access, the understanding you'll gain should lay the foundation for any further exploration you do on your own.

Start the lesson

 Start Microsoft Access and open the 12Issues database in the practice files folder.

A dialog box appears, introducing the Issues database application, which you'll work with throughout Part 4 of this book.

Introducing the Issues Application

The practice database file you've opened is a useful Microsoft Access application for tracking issues in a workgroup. The fact that several users can open a database at one time over a network makes Microsoft Access an ideal environment for creating *workgroup applications*—systems designed to help people work together better in a networked office environment. The Issues application is an example of such a system: it allows users to keep track of open business issues interactively, assigning them to the appropriate employees and querying the database to find out which issues need to be followed up on.

Sign in to the Issues application

When you first open the Issues application, a dialog box appears asking you to enter your name. This dialog box is a startup form created using the same technique you used in Lesson 11 for the Subscription application.

![Enter Employee Name dialog box with title "Welcome to the Issue Tracking Application", a prompt "Please enter your name or select it from the list:", a dropdown box, and two buttons: "Show All Issues" and "Show My Issues".]

The dialog box requires you to "log in" to the Issues application (saving your name for later use), and then opens another form that shows open business issues stored in the database. As the user of the Issues application, your first step is to sign in.

1   In the combo box, select Bonnie Christensen.

The dialog box has two command buttons, both of which open a form called Issues. One of them displays issues for all employees; the other filters issues for employees who want to see only the issues currently assigned to them.

2   Click the Show All Issues button.

The button's Click event procedure opens the Issues form, which displays the first issue in the database. Here, you can browse through current issues, assign them to other employees, or make comments concerning them.

The Issues form lets users track the status of business issues...

...assign issues to other employees...

	Issues

| Issue ID | 1 | Entered By | Charles Willmes | Date | 9/6/96 |

Title   Problem with product name

Description   The name of our product conflicts with another company's copyright.

Status   Open   Date Resolved

Assigned To   David Hunting   Resolved By

Priority   Medium   Resolution

Comments

Employee	Date	Status	Comment
Janée Baugher	9/6/96	Open	Checked with our general counsel. We must fix this problem before releasing the product.
Bonnie Christensen	9/9/96	Open	Dave, can you set up a meeting to discuss?
*			

Record: 14 4   1 ▶ ▶I ▶* of 11

...and make comments on the progress of an issue.

The Issues form is nearly complete as it stands—you won't have to add much to it. The form already has several event procedures that make it an effective tool for tracking business problems and items that employees need to act on. In this lesson and the remaining lessons of the book, you'll explore some of these features, and add some of your own capabilities to this custom application.

TIP   On your own, you may want to browse the Visual Basic code that makes up the application—it uses many of the techniques you've already learned in previous lessons, combining them in new ways. To do this, open the Issues form in Design view and then explore its form module.

273

Open the Miscellaneous module

Although you'll be seeing more of the Issues form, you'll put it aside for now to explore some general principles of Microsoft Access. Before getting started, you'll need to open a standard module stored in the Issues database.

*Database
Window button*

1   Click the Database Window button on the toolbar.

2   Click the Modules tab.

3   Double-click the Miscellaneous module.

The module opens and displays its Declarations section and two procedures.

A **NOTE**   You'll notice one Dim statement in the Declarations section of the module—it declares a variable called lngCurrentEmpID. Remember the dialog box that asked for your name in the previous procedure? This variable stores the ID number of the employee name entered in the opening dialog, and because the variable is declared as Public, it is available throughout the application, whenever you need to know who the current user is.

Understanding Objects and Collections

Believe it or not, all the Visual Basic code you've written to this point fits into a logical framework called an *object model*. The object model is a hierarchy of all the items you use in an application—forms and their controls, tables and their fields, controls and their properties. Here, for example, is the graphical representation of the Microsoft Access object model provided in online Help.

Many of the objects in Microsoft Access contain collections of other objects, creating a complex hierarchy.

Application
Forms
Controls
Reports
Controls
Modules
Screen
DoCmd

Legend	
	Object and collection
	Object only

In this section, you'll explore parts of the object model and write some simple Visual Basic code that demonstrates how it works. Then, as the lesson continues, you'll explore some practical uses for powerful objects that you haven't yet worked with.

Try out the Object Browser

So far, you've tried out several of the Module window tools at your disposal. But there's one more handy tool you've yet to try—the Object Browser. The Object Browser is a dialog box that lists all the objects available to your application, shows you how they're related, and allows you to consult online Help about each of them.

Object Browser button

1 Click the Object Browser button on the toolbar.

The Object Browser appears.

2 Drag the lower-right corner of the Object Browser window to make it a bit larger.

3 Click the drop-down arrow next to the Project/Library combo box (the one that contains the text "<All Libraries>") to display the list.

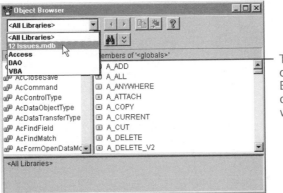

To shorten the list of objects in the Object Browser, select the object library you want to browse.

This list includes the object libraries and databases that Microsoft Access is aware of. Just about everything you type in code or refer to in an expression—objects, fields, methods, properties, functions, and other items—belongs to one or another of these groups. The following list describes the four object libraries you'll need to know about:

12Issues.mdb Your application itself is an object library. It contains the forms, reports, and modules of the database, along with their controls, properties, and any procedures they contain. Because Microsoft Access keeps track of your application's objects in the same way it does for its built-in objects, you can refer to them in code—use a function in a module, for example—just as you would refer to those belonging to the Access or VBA libraries.

Access   The Microsoft Access object library contains the objects, methods, and constants you use to control the user interface of your application, such as forms, reports, and controls. This library also includes the familiar DoCmd object and its methods.

DAO   The Microsoft Data Access Objects (DAO) library contains the objects, methods, and constants you use to work directly with database files, and the data stored in them.

VBA   The Visual Basic for Applications (VBA) object library contains all the Visual Basic functions and constants you're used to seeing, such as the MsgBox function.

Using the Object Browser, you can explore each of these object libraries. In this lesson, you'll learn to work with a few important objects in the Access and DAO libraries; most of these techniques will apply to other types of objects as well.

4   In the list, click 12Issues.mdb.

In the Classes list on the left, the Object Browser displays the forms, reports, and modules contained in the Issues application. The Classes list also includes an entry for *globals*, items that are available throughout your application.

5   Select Messages from the Classes list.

When you click an entry, the members of that class—its properties, methods (Sub and Function procedures), and constants—are displayed in the Members list on the right. Each type of member has a different icon, so you can more easily distinguish between them.

<table>
<tr>
<td>Select a class, such as this module in the Issues application...</td>
<td>

Object Browser

12 Issues.mdb

Classes	Members of 'Messages'
⦿ <globals>	▣ conAppName
Form_CommentsSubf	Confirm
Form_EmployeeNameD	DisplayMessage
Form_Issues	
Form_Reassigner	
Messages	
Miscellaneous	
Report_Issues	

Module **Messages**
Member of **12 Issues.mdb**

</td>
<td>...to display its members, such as the constants and procedures contained in the module.</td>
</tr>
</table>

As you can see, the Messages module has as its members one constant, conAppName, and two procedures, Confirm and DisplayMessage. You may recognize these names as the procedures you created in Lesson 5, which have been copied to the Issues application.

6   Select Confirm from the Members list.

The bottom pane of the Object Browser displays information about the Confirm function, such as its arguments and the type of data it returns.

> **TIP**   If you see a procedure or constant you're interested in, double-click its name in the Object Browser. Microsoft Access opens the Module window and jumps directly to the code that defines that object.

Switch to the Microsoft Access object model

If your applications have many modules and procedures, you may find that the Object Browser provides a easy way to take an inventory of their contents. But you'll probably find it most useful for exploring the large object models of Access, DAO, and VBA.

1   In the Project/Library combo box, select Access.

The Object Browser displays the object classes that belong to Microsoft Access. The "<globals>" entry, which is selected by default, is an interesting place to start. Most of the members of this group are constants, some of which you've used in previous lessons to specify arguments in code. However, if you scroll down far enough, near the end you'll begin to see methods, such as RunCommand and SetOption, and properties, such as MenuBar and Visible.

2   Scroll down in the Classes list and select DoCmd.

This part of the Classes list contains more familiar objects in Microsoft Access. Here you can see ComboBox, CommandButton, and Form, all objects you've used quite a bit. With DoCmd selected, the Members list displays all the methods of the DoCmd object, many of which you've seen in previous lessons.

3   Select Close from the Members list.

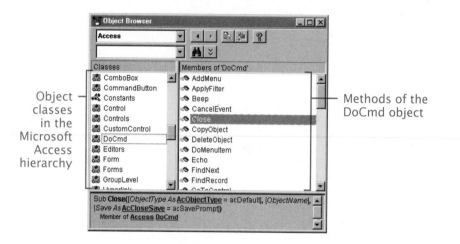

Object classes in the Microsoft Access hierarchy

Methods of the DoCmd object

Just as when you viewed items in the Issues application, the bottom pane of the Object Browser displays information about the item you select. In this case, the Object Browser displays the arguments you use with the Close method. Some object libraries—the DAO library, for example—provide an additional line of text for each item you select telling you what the item is for or what it applies to. (The Access object library doesn't provide this line.)

Use the Object Browser to get online Help

Next, you'll take a look at the Form class, one of the most fundamental classes in the Microsoft Access hierarchy. You'll then jump directly from the Object Browser to online Help about the object you're viewing.

1   In the Classes list box, select Form.

The Members list on the right displays properties and events belonging to forms—you'll recognize the AfterUpdate event and the AllowEdits property, among others. If you scroll down in the list, you'll see some form methods you've used in previous lessons, such as GoToPage, Refresh, and Requery.

2   In the Members list, select Controls.

Controls is the name of a collection of objects. Every form has this collection, and it contains—you guessed it—the controls included on that form.

The Help button in the upper portion of the window (the one with a question mark icon) gives you a handy way to get online Help about the selected item. For Microsoft Access objects, as you'll see, using online Help is one of the best ways to explore the object model.

3   Click the Help button in the Object Browser.

The Help topic for the Controls collection appears in a separate window. It provides lots of information about how you can use the collection, and includes a jump to a Visual Basic code example. The topic also displays a graphical representation of the portion of the object model that the collection belongs to, which you can use to navigate to other Help topics.

Object model graphic

As the object model graphic shows, the Application object has a Forms collection and a Reports collection, which contain individual Form and Report objects. Each form and report in turn has a Controls collection containing individual Control objects.

4   Close the Help window.

5   In the Object Browser, click the Close button.

Other Handy Features of the Object Browser

In addition to showing you available objects and allowing you to jump to online Help, the Object Browser has the following features you might want to use:

■ If you see text in the Object Browser that you'd like to paste into your Visual Basic code—a method or constant name, for example—you can copy it to the Clipboard using the Object Browser's Copy button. You can even select text that's in the bottom pane of the window, such as the syntax line you see when you select a method in the Members list. After you copy the text, switch to the Module window and choose the Paste command.

■ You can search for text in an entire object library, or in all available libraries. This is useful if you can't remember where a keyword fits into the object model. Type any part of the name you're looking for in the Search Text box (just underneath the Library/Project box at the top of the Object Browser), and then click the Search button (the one with binoculars).

■ All three of the standard object libraries—VBA, Access, and DAO—have a Constants class, which includes all the built-in constants available in that object library. Some libraries also have constants grouped into special classes, called *Enum* classes. Because you often use constant values in your code, the Object Browser is a handy place to find out which ones are available, and is especially useful if you can't remember how to spell a constant name.

Referring to Objects and Collections

In earlier lessons, you used plenty of objects—and you learned how to refer to them in your code. For example, you referred to the Contacts form in Part 1 using the expression *Forms!Contacts*, and to the ContactID control on that form using the expression *Forms!Contacts!ContactID*. In fact, most of the object references you'll use in your code will be fairly simple ones like these. Still, because you use them so often, it's important for you to understand more completely how object references work. And as you'll see later in this lesson, not all expressions that include objects are as simple as those you've used up to this point.

When referring to objects in a collection, such as the Forms collection, you can use several alternative forms of reference. One way is to refer to objects by number. Objects in any collection are numbered consecutively starting with zero, so you can refer to an object by placing this number in parentheses. For example, the first form object in the Forms collection is Forms(0), the second is Forms(1), and so on. But there are several other ways to refer to a member of a collection—by name, for example, or by using the exclamation point (!) operator. Each of these methods follows slightly different rules.

Rather than reading about them, perhaps the best way to understand these types of references is to try them out. In this section, you'll experiment with several types of object references using the Debug window.

Make the Debug window stay on top

The Debug window normally moves behind other windows when you switch to them. In this lesson, you'll need it to stay on top of other windows so it's always available. Fortunately, Microsoft Access provides this option.

1 On the Tools menu, click Options.

2 Microsoft Access displays the Options dialog box.

3 Click the Module tab.

4 Select the Debug Window On Top check box.

5 Click OK.

Try out object references in the Debug window

Debug Window button

1 Click the Debug Window button on the toolbar.

2 In the Immediate pane, type **?Forms.Count**, and press ENTER.

The Debug window displays 1, the number of forms in the Forms collection. The one form that's open is the Issues form.

The first object in a collection is object number 0, and you can refer to it that way. Let's see what the name of the form is by referring to the Name property.

3 Replace the top line in the Debug window with **?Forms(0).Name** and press ENTER. (You don't have to retype the entire line, just edit the existing line of text.)

The Debug window displays Issues, the name of the first form in the Forms collection.

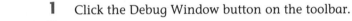

To refer to a member of a collection by name, you can substitute a string value for the object's number—for example, you can use *Forms("Issues")* to refer to the Issues form. Let's use the ActiveControl property of the Forms collection to see which control on the Issues form is currently active.

4 Replace the top line with **?Forms("Issues").ActiveControl.Name** and press ENTER.

The Debug window displays Title, the name of the field that got the focus when you first opened the Issues form.

Note that the technique of placing a string in parentheses after a collection has another important use: if you've stored an object's name in a string variable, you can use this same syntax to refer to it. For example, if the name of the form you wanted to use above had been stored in a variable called *strFormName*, you could use the expression *Forms(strFormName).ActiveControl.Name* to refer to the active control on that form.

Of course, if you know the name of a form, you can just put it after the exclamation point operator as you've done in the past. Next, let's try a reference to the Controls collection, a collection that every form and report object has. To refer to any collection, follow the object that it belongs to—its *parent* object—with a period, and then type the name of the collection. In the next example, *Forms!Issues* is the parent object, while *Controls* is the collection that belongs to it.

5 Replace the top line with **?Forms!Issues.Controls.Count** and press ENTER.

The Debug window displays 24, the number of controls on the Issues form.

Next, you'll refer to the value of the first object in the Controls collection, the IssueID control.

6 Replace the top line with **?Forms!Issues.Controls(0)** and press ENTER.

The Debug window displays 1, the ID number of the issue currently displayed on the Issues form. The reference you used is equivalent to saying *Forms!Issues.Controls("IssueID")*. It's also equivalent to saying *Forms!Issues!IssueID*, the method of reference you're most familiar with. That's because Controls is the default collection for any form object. When you use the exclamation point, Microsoft Access assumes that what follows is a member of the default Controls collection.

Next, you'll refer to the subform on the Issues form. To do this, you refer to the subform control, *Forms!Issues!Comments*. Because you want to refer to properties of the subform that the Issues form is displaying, rather than to the subform control itself, you'll follow the control reference with the Form property—and then follow that with the property whose value you want.

7   Replace the top line with **?Forms!Issues!Comments.Form.Name** and press ENTER.

The Debug window displays CommentsSubform, the name of the actual form stored in the Issues database.

There's one exception to the rule that for subforms you must use the Form property to refer to the form. If you want to refer to a control on a subform, you can leave out the Form keyword—it makes the reference a bit shorter.

8   Replace the top line with **?Forms!Issues!Comments!Comment** and press ENTER.

The Debug window displays the text of the first comment shown in the subform. This expression says, "In the Comments control on the Issues form, what is the value of the Comment field?"

9   Close the Debug window.

Referring to objects and their properties requires some experimentation. Before you write code that uses a new type of expression, it's a good idea to use the Debug window to test your syntax. If you don't get the value you want, or if Microsoft Access displays an error when you enter the reference, consult online Help for examples of expressions that use the type of object you're interested in.

Now that you've discovered some of the ways you can refer to collections and the objects they contain, you're ready to write some code that uses them. In the next section, you'll see object references in action and learn techniques for storing objects in variables so you can perform actions using the objects.

Using the For Each Statement with a Collection

The objects in a collection share many properties and characteristics, so you'll commonly want to perform the same actions on each object in a collection. For example, you might want to change a specific property, such as the color of text, for every control on a form. When you want to run the same block of code for every object in a collection, you surround the block of code with the For Each and Next statements.

Write a procedure that sets control properties

To see how the For Each statement works, you'll write a procedure that changes the ForeColor property—the color of the text—for every label on the Issues form. You'll create the new procedure, called ChangeLabelColor, in the Miscellaneous module. The Module window still shows the Declarations section, which already contains three lines of code. You'll begin entering code for the new procedure underneath the existing Dim statement.

1 In the Module window, scroll down to the end of the Miscellaneous module and click underneath the final End Function statement to position the insertion point.

2 Enter the following code, including the Sub header line. (When you enter the Sub statement, Microsoft Access enters the End Sub line for you automatically.)

```
Sub ChangeLabelColor(lngColorCode As Long)
' Change the color of labels on the Issues form.

    Dim ctl As Control

    For Each ctl In Forms!Issues.Controls
        If TypeOf ctl Is Label Then
            ctl.ForeColor = lngColorCode
        End If
    Next ctl
End Sub
```

Here's what this code does:

■ The Sub procedure head declares an argument, lngColorCode, which stores the code number for the color you want to change labels to. The argument uses the long integer data type, because the ForeColor property accepts this type of value.

■ The Dim line in the procedure declares an object variable. When you want to perform actions on objects, such as tables, forms, or controls, you can store references to them, just as you would store another type of value in a variable. This variable has the data type Control, which can store only a control-type object.

■ The next statement begins a *loop*, a mechanism for repeating a section of code several times. This loop uses the For Each and Next statements—one of several types of loop in Visual Basic—which allow the procedure to perform the same set of actions for every control on the form. At the end of any For Each statement, after the In keyword, is the name of a collection that you want to step through, in this case, the Controls collection on the Issues form. The In keyword is always preceded by a variable, in this case *ctl*, that stores each object in the collection as the code steps through it.

The block of code between the For Each and Next statements will run 24 times, once for each control on the form. Each time it runs, the variable *ctl* will represent a different control on the Issues form.

- The If...Then block inside the loop checks to see whether the current control is a label. To do this, it uses the special *TypeOf* keyword, which allows you to check the type of control stored in a variable. If the control isn't a label, the code continues on to the Next statement, doing nothing.

- If the current control is a label, the line in the middle runs, setting the ForeColor property of the control to the value you passed to the procedure by the lngColorCode argument.

- The Next statement includes *ctl*, the variable that gets incremented each time through the loop. You can think of this statement as saying, "We're finished with that control, move on to the next one please." When Microsoft Access finishes running the block of code for every control in the collection, the procedure ends.

Save button

3 Click the Save button on the toolbar.

Run the procedure from the Debug window

Now you can see your procedure in action, by bringing the Issues form to the front and running your procedure from the Debug window.

Debug Window button

1 Click the Debug Window button on the toolbar.

2 Switch to the Issues form.

The Debug window stays on top of the form.

3 Click the title bar of the Debug window and drag it toward the bottom right corner of the screen (so you can see most of the Issues form behind it).

4 On a new line in the Debug window, type **ChangeLabelColor(vbBlue)**, and press ENTER.

Your procedure runs, changing the foreground color of each label control on the form to blue (the intrinsic constant vbBlue provides the correct color code for blue, so you don't have to know it).

5 Replace the second line in the Debug window with **ChangeLabelColor(vbBlack)** and press ENTER.

The labels become black again.

This type of procedure is useful for giving users the capability of customizing forms while your application is running. In the next section, you'll use some of these same tools—object variables and the For Each statement—to add powerful features to the Issues application.

Using a Multiple-Selection List Box

So far, you've used list boxes that allow users to select a single item. As you'll see, you can also create a list box that allows more than one item to be selected at a time. The practice database already includes a form that has a multiple-selection list box. The form, called Reassigner, is a dialog box form designed to allow users to reassign one or more issues to another employee. Unlike a normal list box, a multiple-selection list box requires you to write some extra code to access the selected items. In the rest of this lesson, you'll add code to the Reassigner form to make it work.

To cause a list box to allow multiple selections, you set its MultiSelect property. The property has three settings: None, Simple, and Extended. If the property is set to None, users can select only one item at a time; if Simple, users can select multiple items by clicking them; if Extended, users can select multiple items by holding down the SHIFT and CTRL keys while clicking items. The list box you'll work with on the Reassigner form has its MultiSelect property set to Simple.

Open the Reassigner form

Before you add any code to the Reassigner form, let's see how it works so far. To open it, you'll use a menu command located on the Issues form's custom menu bar.

1   Switch to the Issues form. (Leave the Debug window open—you'll use it again in just a minute.)

2   On the Tools menu, click Reassign Issues.

    The Reassigner form opens.

3   In the Show Issues Assigned To combo box, select Bonnie Christensen.

    The list box on the form shows the four issues currently assigned to that employee.

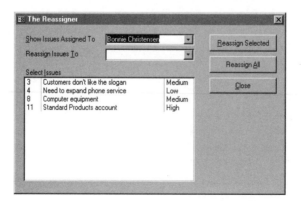

Try out the multiple-selection list box

With any list box you've used before in this book, each time you click an item, the previous item is deselected—the list box has just one value at a time. In this list box, however, you can select more than one value.

1 Click issue number 4 in the list (the second item), and then click issue number 8 (the third item).

When a list box has just one value, you can just refer to the list box itself to access the value—for example, because the list box control is named IssueList, the expression *Forms!Reassigner!IssueList* would return the ID number of the selected issue. When using a multiple-selection list box, by contrast, you find out which items are selected by referring to a special collection called ItemsSelected. You can see how this works in the Debug window.

2 Switch to the Debug window. (In this case, you must click the title bar at the top of the Debug window to bring it to the front, because the Reassigner form—a modal pop-up dialog box—also wants to stay on top of other forms.)

To refer to the items in the list, you'll have to use a pretty complex expression. Don't worry, though, it's really quite similar to references you're already accustomed to.

3 On a new line in the Immediate pane of the Debug window, type **?Forms!Reassigner!IssueList.ItemsSelected.Count**, and press ENTER.

To follow the expression, read it from right to left—it asks for the number of items in the ItemSelected collection of the IssueList control on the Reassigner form. The Debug window displays 2, the number of items you selected in the list box.

Next, you'll try out expressions that tell you what the selected items are. The ItemsSelected collection actually stores numbers corresponding to the position of the selected item in the list. Like items in the collection, the positions in the list are numbered starting with zero, so the first item has position 0, the second position 1, and so on. Therefore, the first item number is stored in ItemsSelected(0), the second item number in ItemsSelected(1), and so on.

4 Replace the line with **?Forms!Reassigner!IssueList.ItemsSelected(0)** and press ENTER.

The Debug window displays 1, the position of the first item you selected. (You selected the second item in the list, which is position number 1.) You might expect the ItemsSelected collection to contain the actual values of the selected items, but it doesn't—it contains only their positions in the list. To find out the value of each selected item, in this case, the IssueID for each issue, you have to use the ItemData method, supplying the item position number you just found out.

5 Replace the line with **?Forms!Reassigner!IssueList.ItemData(1)** and press ENTER.

The Debug window displays 4, which is, at long last, the IssueID of the first issue you selected.

6 Close the Debug window.

7 In the Reassigner dialog box, click the Close button.

Although the process of finding out what's selected in a list box is complicated, it's worth the effort to tap into the power of a multiple-selection list box. In the next section, you'll add code that makes this list box work, using the list box concepts you just learned to change data in the issues the user has selected.

 NOTE If you want the Debug window to behave as you're accustomed to, you may want to choose the Options command (Tools menu) again and clear the Debug Window On Top option. While it is often convenient to have the Debug window on top, it can also get in the way of your work.

Working with Data Access Objects

When users change data in a form that's bound to a query or table—the Issues form, for example—Microsoft Access automatically makes the changes in the underlying tables. So far, you've allowed Microsoft Access to do most of this work behind the scenes. However, when you need to take more control over what gets changed in your database, you can work directly with data by writing code that uses data access objects (DAO). In this section, you'll learn two powerful techniques for changing data using DAO code. You'll use these techniques to make the Reassigner form do its work.

The Reassigner form has two command buttons whose event procedures aren't yet complete: Reassign Selected and Reassign All. When a user clicks the Reassign Selected button, you want to open the Issues table and update only the records the user has selected in the list box. To do this, you'll use a Recordset object. When a user clicks the Reassign All button, you want to update every record in the Issues table that has a certain AssignedTo value. To do this you'll run an action query. To perform these two operations in code, you'll need to learn new techniques for working with objects.

What Do Data Access Objects Look Like?

The Data Access Objects library has a complex hierarchy (some might even call it ugly) containing many more objects and collections than even the Microsoft Access hierarchy has. And unlike Microsoft Access objects, which you're used to seeing on your screen, objects in the DAO hierarchy are difficult to visualize—they're really no more than a bunch of abstract structures for storing information.

The DAO hierarchy's huge first layer starts with the DBEngine object, which represents the underlying Microsoft Access database engine (also known as the "Jet" database engine). The DBEngine object has a Workspaces collection, which in turn has a Databases collection, which has many other collections, and so on down the line. Here's a graphical representation of part of the DAO object model—it shows the three object collections you'll work with in the rest of this lesson: Databases, Recordsets, and QueryDefs.

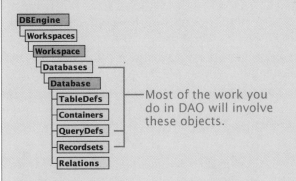

After you become familiar with DAO basics, you may want to delve deeper—especially if you want a finer degree of control over the way your applications handle databases. As with Microsoft Access objects, you can use the Object Browser in combination with online Help to learn more about DAO objects and the capabilities they provide.

Finding and Changing Data in a Recordset

Your first task is to add code for the Reassign Selected button. Whenever a user clicks this button, you need to open the Issues table, move to each selected record, and change the value of the AssignedTo field for that issue to another employee's ID number: the one the user chooses in the NewAssignee combo box.

When you want to change a record in a table directly, you first open a Recordset object. Next, you move to the record you want to change. If the recordset is based on a table in a Microsoft Access database, such as the Issues table, the fastest way to do this is to use the Seek method. Then you actually make the change, using the Edit and Update methods to set the values of the fields you want to change. In this section, you'll add code that will go through this process for each record the user selects in the IssueList list box.

Edit the Click event procedure
for the Reassign Selected button

The Reassign Selected button already has an event procedure—it's just missing the code that actually reassigns the issues to other employees. To open the event procedure, you'll first need to open the form in Design view.

*Database
Window button*

1   Click the Database Window button on the toolbar.

2   Click the Forms tab.

3   Click the Reassigner form, and then click the Design button.

   As you saw before, the Reassigner form is nearly complete. It even has code that keeps the IssuesList control synchronized with the currently selected employee. Now it's time to add the final touches to the Click event procedure for the Reassign Selected button.

4   With the right mouse button, click the Reassign Selected button, and then click Build Event on the shortcut menu.

   The Module window appears, displaying the ReassignSelected_Click procedure. As you can see, the procedure already contains several lines of code.

```
Form_Reassigner : Class Module                        _ □ ×
ReassignSelected                    ▼   Click                    ▼
  Private Sub ReassignSelected_Click()                          ▲
  ' Open a recordset and reassign selected issues.

      Dim strMessage As String


      ' Make sure NewAssignee has a value selected.
      If IsNull(NewAssignee) Then
          DisplayMessage "You must select an employee to assign is
          Exit Sub
      End If

      ' Make sure one or more issues are selected.
      If IssueList.ItemsSelected.Count = 0 Then
          DisplayMessage "You must select issues to reassign."
          Exit Sub
      End If
                                                                ▼
```

The code that's already present does several things:

- The Dim statement declares a variable used later in the procedure to store the text of a message.

- The first block of code checks that the NewAssignee combo box has a value in it—otherwise, you wouldn't know which user to reassign issues to. If the combo box is blank, the procedure displays a message and exits.

- The second block of code makes sure that at least one issue is selected in the list—to do this, it checks the Count property of the ItemsSelected collection for the list box, just as you did earlier in the lesson.

- Next, the procedure confirms that the user wants to reassign the selected issues. To do this, the procedure calls the Confirm function you wrote in Lesson 5—that function is included in this database as well.

- If the user does confirm the operation, the next line of code uses the Hourglass method of the DoCmd object to display the hourglass cursor while your code changes records. Whenever you run code that might cause a delay, you can use this technique to let the user know your code is working.

- The last block of code is designed to run after your code finishes reassigning issues, to update what's displayed in the dialog box before the procedure ends. For example, the first line sets the value of the AssignedTo combo box to the ID of the employee you just assigned issues to, and the third line requeries the list box to show the new set of issues. This way, the user can easily see that all changes have taken place.

To complete the procedure, you'll add code in two places: near the top of the procedure you'll declare three variables that your code will use, and near the bottom you'll add the code that changes selected records.

5 Click underneath the Dim statement in the procedure, and then enter the following lines of code:

```
Dim dbs As Database, rstIssues As Recordset
Dim varPosition As Variant
```

These Dim statements declare three variables:

- The dbs variable will represent the current database.

- The rstIssues variable will store a reference to the Issues table so that you can change data in it.

- The varPosition variable will store the position of each item selected in the list, so you can get hold of the actual ID value for each selected issue. This variable has the Variant data type, because this is the type of value used to store the position number in the ItemsSelected collection.

6 Scroll down in the window, click the blank area underneath the *DoCmd.Hourglass True* statement, and then enter the following code:

```
' Open a recordset object in the current database.
Set dbs = CurrentDb()
Set rstIssues = dbs.OpenRecordset("Issues", dbOpenTable)

' Begin a transaction before changing data.
DBEngine.BeginTrans

' Set the Index property to search on the primary key.
rstIssues.Index = "IssueID"

' Loop through each issue selected in the list.
For Each varPosition In IssueList.ItemsSelected

    ' Find the record in the Issues table.
    rstIssues.Seek "=", IssueList.ItemData(varPosition)

    ' Change the AssignedTo value in the table.
    rstIssues.Edit
    rstIssues!AssignedTo = NewAssignee
    rstIssues.Update

Next varPosition

' Save all changes for this transaction.
DBEngine.CommitTrans
```

Let's walk through this code line by line—it introduces several new concepts:

- The first line of code uses the CurrentDb function to store a reference to the current database, which is required in order to open a table in code. Remember, whenever you set the value of an object variable—as opposed to an ordinary variable, such as a string—you must use the Set statement.

- The second line uses the OpenRecordset method of the database to open the Issues table, and stores the recordset in the variable rstIssues. Providing the dbOpenTable constant as the second argument to OpenRecordset tells Microsoft Access that you want a table-type recordset. It's important that you open a table-type recordset, because later code in the procedure uses the Seek method, which is allowed only on tables.

- The next line uses the BeginTrans method of the DBEngine object to open a *transaction*. A transaction is a group of changes that you want Microsoft Access to treat as a single operation. Opening a transaction tells Microsoft Access to keep track of changes you make, but to wait until you close the transaction to save them on disk. You use this method with the DBEngine object, a special object representing the underlying database engine for Microsoft Access. Later, you'll close the transaction using the CommitTrans method.

  Using a transaction for multiple changes to data has two advantages: first, it speeds up your code, because you access the disk drive or network only once, rather than each time you change a record; second, you'll never end up with partially changed records—if an error occurs before all the changes have been made, you don't have to save the transaction. (To cancel changes made in a transaction, you use the Rollback method.)

- Before you can use the Seek method to locate records in a table, you have to set the Index property for the recordset, which tells Microsoft Access which field you want to search. The next line sets the Index property to the IssueID field, the primary key of the Issues table. The field or fields you designate for searching must either be the primary key of the table or else have an index. Because the field has an index, the search will be very fast.

- The next line uses the For Each statement you learned about in the previous section. In this procedure, you want to update every issue that's selected in the list. Because you'll locate and change records one at a time, you need to run the block of code once for each item in the ItemsSelected collection of the list box. This statement says, "Run the following block of code once for each item in the

ItemsSelected collection of the IssueList control, each time storing the position of the selected item in the varPosition variable."

■ The four lines of code you'll loop through for each selected issue must locate the issue in the recordset and then change its AssignedTo value. The first of these lines uses the Seek method to move to the selected record.

■ The Seek method takes two arguments. The first is an operator string, which tells Microsoft Access what type of search you want. Because you want to find only the one record that exactly matches the IssueID value selected in the list, you've used the "=" operator. The second argument tells Microsoft Access what value to look for. As you saw earlier in this lesson, the way to refer to the value of the selected item in a list is to use the ItemData method of the list box control. This argument tells Microsoft Access to search for the IssueID value that's at the current position—stored in the varPosition variable—in the IssueList control. After this line of code runs, the current record in the rstIssues recordset will be the record for one of the issues selected in the list.

■ The next three lines actually reassign the issue by replacing the value in the record's AssignedTo field with the value of the NewAssignee combo box on the form. Before you change data in an existing record, you must use the Edit method of the Recordset object to tell Microsoft Access you want to change data. After you've finished setting values of one or more fields in the recordset, as you do here in the second statement, you complete the change by using the Update method.

■ The Next statement tells Microsoft Access to repeat the For Each block of code for the next item in the list. After the block of code has run for each selected item, the procedure will continue running from this point.

■ The final line of code you entered uses the CommitTrans method of the DBEngine object. This method tells the database engine to save all the changes you made since the beginning of the transaction in this procedure.

7   Click the Compile Loaded Modules button on the toolbar.

Compile Loaded Modules button

If the procedure has any typographical errors, compiling will bring them to light so you can fix them before trying to run the code.

Save button

8 Click the Save button on the toolbar.

9 Close the Module window.

Try out the ReassignSelected_Click procedure

Now you're ready to test the procedure by selecting issues and reassigning them.

Form View button

1 Click the Form View button on the toolbar.

2 In the Show Issues Assigned To combo box, select Bonnie Christensen.

3 In the Reassign Issues To combo box, select Charles Willmes.

4 Click issue number 4 in the list (the second item), and then click issue number 8 (the third item).

5 Click the Reassign Selected button, and then click OK when the procedure asks you to confirm that you want to reassign the selected issues.

Your code runs, opening the Issues recordset, and then cycling through the two records you selected and changing their AssignedTo values in the Issues table. When the procedure finishes, the list box displays the issues that changed hands, but now they belong to a different employee, Charles Willmes.

6 Click the Close button.

295

> ## Handling Errors in DAO Code
>
> For the sake of simplicity, the procedure you worked with in this lesson doesn't contain error-handling code. However, any time *you* use DAO to change records, you should definitely include error-handling code in the procedure. Errors can occur for many reasons when your code changes records, and without error-handling code, your application could end abruptly with a run-time error. For example, suppose another user is changing data at the same time your code is running. The records you're trying to update might be locked, causing an error.
>
> To handle these types of errors, you would add an On Error GoTo statement at the top of the procedure, and then include error-handling code at the end of the procedure; it's similar to the technique you used in Lesson 7. In the error-handling code, you might want to check which error occurred, and if records are locked, give the user the option to resave them. In any case, if you aren't able to update records as expected, your procedure should exit gracefully, displaying a message telling the user about the problem. If you do decide to exit the procedure, you may want to include the Rollback method of the DBEngine object, which undoes any changes made since you started the transaction using the BeginTrans method—this way, records won't be partially updated, which could confuse the user.

Creating and Running an Action Query

The first command button on the Reassigner dialog box is now complete. The second one, however, still needs some work. This button, labeled Reassign All, is there so that users can reassign all issues, rather than selected issues, from one employee to another. In this section, you'll add the code to do this.

The technique you used to reassign selected issues—opening a recordset, and then locating and changing each record—is perfect for reassigning a few individual issues. On the other hand, when you want to change values in a whole group of records, changing each record individually isn't the most efficient way. To modify a group of records most efficiently, you use an *action query*. With an action query, you can update, add, or delete many records in a single step.

Normally, you use the Microsoft Access query window to create an action query. However, you can also create and run queries in your code by using the DAO QueryDef object. To make the Reassign All button do its work, you'll write code that creates and runs a query. The query you create will change the values in the AssignedTo field for all records in the Issues table from one employee's ID to another.

Using Structured Query Language (SQL)

When defining the action query in this section, you'll use the Microsoft Access query language, called *Structured Query Language*, or SQL. You've probably already noticed examples of SQL statements in the property sheet—SQL is commonly used in the RecordSource and RowSource settings of your forms, combo boxes, and list boxes. When you use wizards to create objects, they frequently set these properties to an appropriate SQL statement. On the Reassigner form, for example, the AssignedTo combo box was created using the Combo Box Wizard. The wizard set the RowSource property for the combo box to the following SQL statement:

```
SELECT DISTINCTROW Employees.EmployeeID, Employees.EmployeeName
FROM Employees
ORDER BY Employees.EmployeeName;
```

This statement tells Microsoft Access to retrieve ("select") the values of two fields—EmployeeID and EmployeeName—from every record in the Employees table, sorting the records by name. In your Microsoft Access applications, you can substitute an SQL statement just about anywhere that the name of a table or query is called for. Additionally, as you'll see in this section, you can build queries in your code using SQL.

To learn SQL, you might want to browse the many SQL topics in online Help. Additionally, there's a handy technique you can use to help you learn SQL. Queries you create using the Query Design window—including action queries—have an SQL view maintained automatically by Microsoft Access. To see the SQL statement corresponding to any query in Design view, just click SQL on the View menu. You can even copy this SQL text into your DAO code.

Edit the Click event procedure for the Reassign All button

Just like the Reassign Selected button, the Reassign All button already has an event procedure—it's just missing the code that actually reassigns issues. You'll add code that creates and runs an action query to update records.

1   In the Database window, click the Reassigner form, and then click the Design button.

2   With the right mouse button, click the Reassign All button, and then click Build Event on the shortcut menu.

The Module window appears and displays the ReassignAll_Click procedure. As you can see, the procedure already contains several lines of code. The code that's there is nearly the same as the code in the

ReassignSelected_Click procedure: it makes sure the user has selected employees to assign issues to and from, asks the user to confirm the reassignment, and then displays the hourglass cursor.

To complete the procedure, you'll add a line near the top to declare variables, and then you'll add the code that actually runs the query to change data.

3 Click underneath the Dim statement in the procedure, and then enter the following line of code:

```
Dim dbs As Database, qdfReassign As QueryDef
```

You'll use the *dbs* variable to represent the current database. You'll use the *qdfReassign* variable—an object variable with the QueryDef data type—to store the query object you define and run it in the procedure.

4 Click the blank area underneath the DoCmd.Hourglass True statement and enter the following code:

```
' Open a temporary query object in the current database.
Set dbs = CurrentDb()
Set qdfReassign = dbs.CreateQueryDef("")

' Define the SQL update query to reassign issues.
qdfReassign.SQL = "UPDATE Issues " & _
    "SET AssignedTo = " & NewAssignee & _
    " WHERE AssignedTo = " & AssignedTo

' Run the query.
qdfReassign.Execute
```

NOTE Be sure you put spaces before and after quotation marks, exactly as shown in this code. Otherwise, you may encounter an error when you try to run it.

Here's what this code does:

- The first line you added uses the CurrentDb function to store a reference to the current database.

- The second line uses the CreateQueryDef method of the database to open a new query object, storing it in the variable qdfReassign. The argument to the CreateQueryDef function allows you to specify a name for the query—using an empty string ("") as you have here creates a temporary query object. Because you're going to use the query in this procedure only, you don't need to give it a name.

- The next line sets the SQL property for the query object. Setting this property tells the query what data you want it to return—or, in the case of an action query, what changes you want it to make. For example, using the UPDATE statement tells Microsoft Access that you want it to change values in existing records. As you can see, this line of code concatenates several items together to produce the SQL statement. This code could be typed as one line, but here it's broken up using the underscore (_) character to make it easier to see in the Module window.

The string you create for the SQL property setting combines the SQL text itself with the values of two fields on the Reassigner form: the AssignedTo field and the NewAssignee field. When the code runs, Microsoft Access will combine all this text to produce a single string that defines the action query. For example, the complete string might look like this:

```
UPDATE Issues SET AssignedTo = 14 WHERE AssignedTo = 20
```

If you ran this particular query, Microsoft Access would find all records in the Issues table that were assigned to employee 20 and reassign them to employee 14.

■ The final line you added uses the Execute method of the QueryDef object, which tells Microsoft Access to go ahead and run the query you've defined.

Compile Loaded Modules button

5 Click the Compile Loaded Modules button on the toolbar.

6 Click the Save button on the toolbar.

7 Close the Module window.

Save button

Try out the ReassignAll_Click procedure

Now you're ready to test the procedure. You just need to select two employees and click the button.

Form View button

1 Click the Form View button on the toolbar.

2 In the Show Issues Assigned To box, select Charles Willmes.

The two issues you reassigned previously show up in the list.

3 In the Reassign Issues To box, select Bonnie Christensen.

4 Click the Reassign All button, and then click OK when the procedure asks you to confirm the reassignment.

Your code runs, creating and running the action query for the employee values you selected. When it finishes, the list box displays Bonnie Christensen's issues—and as you can see, all four issues belong to her as they did at the beginning of the lesson, which is just what you want.

The Recordset and QueryDef objects you've learned to use in this lesson are perhaps the most common DAO objects for working directly with databases. However, they are just the tip of the iceberg. Fortunately, most of the techniques you've learned in this lesson will apply to any work you do with objects and collections. Just remember that by working directly with objects in your code, you can accomplish practically anything Microsoft Access does on its own— and even more.

Close the dialog box and exit Microsoft Access

1   Click the Close button.

2   On the File menu, click Exit.

Lesson Summary

To	Do this	Button
View the objects in an object library	In the Module window, click the Object Browser button. Select an object library or database, and then click object classes to view their members.	
Refer to an object in a collection	Follow the collection reference with the number or name of the object in parentheses, such as *Forms!Issues.Controls(0)* or *Forms!Issues.Controls("IssueID")*. Or, if the item is the default member of the collection, use the exclamation point operator, as in *Forms!Issues!IssueID*.	
Run a block of code for each item in a collection, such as every control on a form	Use a For Each...Next block, specifying a variable for storing each object as your code loops through the collection.	
Create a list box that allows multiple selections	Set the MultiSelect property of the list box to Simple or Extended. Get the position of each selection in the ItemsSelected collection, and then access the selected data using the ItemData method.	

To	Do this	Button
Find a record in a table-type recordset	Use the Index method of the recordset to specify the field you want to search, and then use the Seek method to move to a record in the table.	
Change data in the current record of a recordset	Use the Edit method of the recordset, assign values to fields, and then use the Update method to save the changes.	
Group several changes to data so that they all occur at once	Open a transaction using the BeginTrans method, and then use the CommitTrans method to commit changes when you're finished. If you don't want to save changes, use the Rollback method to discard all changes made since the beginning of the transaction.	
Run an action query in code	Using the CreateQueryDef method, create a temporary query object in the database. Set its SQL property to the SQL statement you want to run, and then use the Execute method to run the query.	
Keep the Debug window on top of other windows	Using the Options command (Tools menu), select the Debug Window On Top option.	

For online information about	On the Help menu, click Contents and Index, click the Index tab, and then
Using the Object Browser	Search for "Object Browser"
Referring to objects and collections	Search for "referencing, object variables"
Using DAO to work directly with databases	Search for "DAO collections"
Handling run-time errors	Search for "error handling"
Writing applications for multiple users on a network	Search for "multiuser environment"
Using Structured Query Language (SQL)	Search for "SQL statements"

For more information on	In *Building Applications with Microsoft Access 97*, see
Using the Object Browser, or referring to objects and collections	Chapter 5, "Working with Objects and Collections"
Using DAO to work directly with databases	Chapter 9, "Working with Records and Fields," and Chapter 18, "Accessing External Data"
Handling run-time errors	Chapter 8, "Handling Run-Time Errors"
Writing applications for multiple users on a network	Chapter 10, "Creating Multiuser Applications"
Using Structured Query Language (SQL)	Chapter 9, "Working with Records and Fields"

Preview of the Next Lesson

In this lesson, you learned general rules for referring to objects and collections, and you discovered a few new types of objects. You'll continue working with new objects throughout Part 4. In the next lesson, for example, you'll learn more about using report objects in your code. Although most of the code you've written so far in this book has applied to forms, you'll find that you can customize reports with code as well—providing more power and flexibility for your applications.

Customize Reports with Visual Basic

Estimated time
25 min.

In this lesson you will learn how to:

- Respond to events that occur in reports.
- Change the formatting of individual fields and records as a report prints.
- Calculate totals while a report is running.

When you're learning a whole new subject, such as database programming, it's easy to lose the forest for the trees: picking up lots of details but forgetting the main purpose your applications will serve. And as your experience increases, there's still a tendency to spend lots of time adding frills to an application while losing track of its primary goals. Let's face it—for all the complexities involved in working with databases, the whole endeavor comes down to two basic activities: getting data into the database, and getting data back out.

So far, you've spent lots of energy on ways to get data into forms and work with it easily. In this lesson, you'll turn your attention to one of the primary ways to get data *out* of a Microsoft Access database: by printing it in reports. You'll team up the built-in reporting tools with your own Visual Basic procedures to customize and enhance an application's reports—and you'll learn techniques for taking control of exactly what prints on the page.

Start the lesson

 Start Microsoft Access and open the 13Issues database in the practice files folder.

303

Using Standard Reporting Features

Microsoft Access reports are extremely powerful tools for presenting information, regardless of whether you write any Visual Basic code for them. The Report Wizard can help you create many complex types of reports for grouping or summarizing information—or, by designing your own custom reports, you can accomplish most anything you'll need in your applications. Before you write any code, be sure to explore the powerful features built into reports, such as grouping and totaling, automatic growing and shrinking of sections, and flexible page numbering, just to name a few. The Issues report included in the practice database shows off some of these features.

Preview the Issues report

Before you begin customizing the Issues report, let's take a look at what's already there. As you'll see, the report prints all the open issues in the database, grouped by the employee they're assigned to.

1 In the Database window, click the Reports tab.

2 Double-click the Issues report.

The Issues report appears in Print Preview.

The Issues report is based on a query called IssuesForReport, which combines information from several tables. The report was initially created using the Report Wizard, and then rearranged and polished a bit in Report Design view.

3 Using the vertical scroll bar on the report window (not the Microsoft Access scroll bar), scroll down a bit to view additional issues on the page.

The report groups all the issues assigned to each employee—in this case, the first group of issues belongs to Bonnie Christensen. The report also

304

displays the total number of issues for each group at the bottom of the employee's section.

The following illustration points out several features of the Issues report.

Issue records are grouped by employee, with headers repeated for each group of issues.

Microsoft Access automatically counts the number of issues in each group.

Each page shows the current date, page number, and total number of pages.

All the elements you see on the Issues report as it exists in the practice file—grouping of data, automatic totals, and a customized layout, for example—are standard features of reports that don't require any code. And this is just the beginning of what you can do in your reports.

In some cases, however, you won't be able to accomplish what you want using standard reporting features alone. For example, if you want to make changes to the formatting of certain fields depending on the data that appears in any given record, or if you want to change the layout of the report only in certain cases, no standard mechanism will get the job done—it will take some creative intervention on your part. In the following sections, you'll start adding features to this report that require a bit of Visual Basic code.

Responding to Report Events

When you want to accomplish something in your reports that isn't possible using standard reporting features, you'll be happy to know that you can control nearly everything about your reports by writing Visual Basic code. Programming reports is very similar to programming forms: reports have events you can respond to with Visual Basic event procedures. But the event model for reports is a bit trickier, because users don't actually interact with reports, as they do with forms. Instead, report events occur at certain points during the report printing process—the time between when you tell Microsoft Access to preview or print a report and when it arrives on the screen or at the printer—and you can write Visual Basic code to change the outcome of this process.

Here are the two types of report events you'll commonly respond to, along with typical reasons for using them:

General report events   There are several events that apply to a report as a whole. Some of these will be familiar to you from programming with forms, such as the Open event, which you can use to perform actions when the user first asks to preview or print the report. Two other useful report events are the NoData event, which allows you to intervene if the record source of the report turns out to have no records, and the Page event, which gives you a chance to run code once for each page—to draw a border around every page, for example.

Events for each report section   The most interesting events are those that occur one or more times for each section in the report, including the report header and footer, page header and footer, group headers and footers, and of course the Detail section, where individual records appear. The two most important section events are the Format event, which occurs just before Microsoft Access lays out each section of the report, and the Print event, which occurs after page layout is complete but before printing actually occurs. During these events, you have access to the data in the record being formatted or printed—and as you'll see, this gives you the opportunity to make changes based on what's about to print.

In this lesson, you'll write event procedures that respond to the Format and Print events, customizing the Issues report that's included in the practice database. Although you'll try only a few of the many techniques for controlling report output, you'll learn the fundamental concepts you need for customizing reports.

Customizing Reports by Setting Properties at Run Time

You can determine the look of the formatting on your reports to a great extent by setting properties for controls and sections. You might change the text of an important control on your report to a larger font size, or perhaps to a bold font style—and your change will be reflected throughout the report. But what if you want a control to print differently depending on the data contained in each record? For example, suppose you want the text of the Priority field on the Issues report to appear bold if the priority of the issue is high, while continuing to appear normal for other records. You need a way to change the font properties for the control while the report is printing.

This is where event procedures come in. By responding to the Print event for the report's Detail section, which occurs just before each record is printed, you can change the control to display the way you want it to. Your code will check whether the record that Microsoft Access is about to print is high priority, and set the FontWeight property of the Priority field accordingly.

Make the Priority field appear bold for high-priority records

When you work with an event procedure in a report, it's important to make sure you associate it with the appropriate section in the report. In this case, you'll select the Detail section of the Issues report, because you want your code to run for every detail record—every single issue printed in the report.

1 On the View menu, click Design View.

The report switches into Design view.

In order to create an event procedure for the Detail section, you'll first view event properties for that section in the property sheet.

2 Double-click the Detail section bar.

Microsoft Access displays the property sheet for the Detail section.

Double-click the Detail section bar to display the section's properties.

3 In the property sheet, click the Event tab, click the OnPrint property, and then click the Build button.

307

4 Double-click Code Builder.

Microsoft Access opens the Issues report's module and displays the Detail_Print event procedure.

5 Add the following code to the event procedure:

```
Private Sub Detail_Print(Cancel As Integer, PrintCount As Integer)
' Perform desired actions just before each issue record prints.

    Const conNormal = 400
    Const conHeavy = 900        ' Extra bold.

    ' If the priority of the issue is high, display the
    ' Priority field in bold.
    If Priority = "High" Then
        Priority.FontWeight = conHeavy
    Else
        Priority.FontWeight = conNormal
    End If

End Sub
```

Here's what this code does:

- At the beginning of the procedure, the two Const statements declare constants that set the FontWeight property. When setting the font style to light, bold, or extra bold, you use a number, such as 400, 700, or 900—these constants will make your code easier to read by providing names for these numbers.

- The If...Then statement checks to see if the Priority field contains the string High, which determines whether you want to display the field in bold or normal style. As this procedure illustrates, each time the Detail_Print procedure runs, it will have access to the fields of the current record—in other words, the Priority field expression will return the value of the issue record that's just about to print.

- Depending on whether the priority is high, one of two statements sets the FontWeight property for the priority field to the appropriate constant value.

This code will run every time Microsoft Access prepares to print data for an issue in the report. If you print the complete report, which currently contains 11 issues, the procedure will run 11 times.

Preview the report

Let's preview the report again and see how it works now.

1 Switch to the Issues report window, still in Design view.

Print Preview button

2 Click the Print Preview button on the toolbar.

Although it happens so quickly you'll doubt it happens at all, Microsoft Access runs your event procedure once for every single issue record on the page, allowing your code to set the Priority control's property separately for each one.

3 Scroll down in the window to display the fourth issue on the page.

The priority field for this issue—which contains the value High—stands out because it's displayed in bold.

	with our latest promotional campaign.			
4	Need to expand phone service	Open	Low	
Description:	We will need two more lines in the main office sooner or later.			
8	Computer equipment	Open	Medium	
Description:	It's time to put together recommendations for this year's computer upgrades. The admin staff can collect this data.			
11	Standard Products account	Open	**High**	
Description:	These guys are considering jumping ship to the competitor. Let's meet with them to discuss their needs -- it's a big account.			

Your event procedure changed the text to bold in this record.

Changing Report Layout Programmatically

The Print event procedure is a good place to perform most types of actions on a report section, because it occurs for every record in the section. Beware, however: when the Print event occurs, Microsoft Access has already laid out all the elements of the section to be printed, so it's too late to make any changes to the layout of the section. For example, if your code performs actions that affect the current section by changing how many records fit on a page, the Print event won't work. If you want to perform actions that affect the layout of a section, you should attach the code to the Format event instead.

In the Issues report, you probably noticed the three labels at the right side of each issue record. Although most issue records in the report don't have any values for these fields (because the issues themselves aren't resolved), these labels appear in every record of the Detail section. To cause them not to display except when the current issue is resolved, you can write an event procedure. And because the changes you'll make in your code *will* affect the layout of the section, you'll add this code to the Format event procedure of the Detail section, rather than to its Print event procedure.

309

Add code that hides the labels of unresolved fields

To show or hide controls, you set their Visible property. If you do this for the resolution fields in the Format event procedure, Microsoft Access will take into account whether the controls are to be shown when laying out the section.

1   On the toolbar, click the Close button.

   The report returns to Design view.

2   In the property sheet, click the OnFormat property, and then click the Build button.

3   Double-click Code Builder.

   Microsoft Access displays the Detail_Format event procedure.

4   Add the following code to the event procedure:

```
Private Sub Detail_Format(Cancel As Integer, FormatCount As Integer)
' When formatting each issue record, display the labels for
' the resolution fields only if the issue is resolved.

    Dim blnResolved As Boolean

    ' Determine whether the DateResolved field has a value.
    blnResolved = Not IsNull(DateResolved)

    ' Set the Visible property for the three labels.
    DateResolvedLabel.Visible = blnResolved
    ResolutionLabel.Visible = blnResolved
    ResolvedByLabel.Visible = blnResolved

End Sub
```

Here's what this code does:

■ The procedure uses a Boolean variable, called blnResolved, to record whether or not the current issue record is resolved. The second statement sets the variable to True or False based on the expression *Not IsNull(DateResolved)*, which refers to the DateResolved field in the Detail section of the report. If the DateResolved field contains a date—if it doesn't contain a null value—blnResolved gets set to True.

■ The next three lines of code use the blnResolved value—which is True if the resolution fields should appear, False if they shouldn't—to set the Visible property for the three labels.

This procedure will run each time Microsoft Access starts to lay out a record on the page—at least once and potentially several times for each record in the report. Because most issues aren't resolved, it will make these labels invisible in most cases.

Set properties to shrink
the Detail section as appropriate

By default, Microsoft Access leaves space for fields on a report—even if they're blank—so even when the resolution labels on the Issues report are invisible, there will be extra space for them in every record on the report. Fortunately, Microsoft Access provides the CanShrink property to correct this situation automatically. By setting this property to True for the three text boxes and for the Detail section itself, you'll tell Microsoft Access to "shrink" these fields whenever they're empty, effectively making sure they don't take any space at all.

1 Switch back to the Issues report window.

2 If the Detail section isn't still selected, double-click its section bar.

3 In the property sheet, click the Format tab, and then set the CanShrink property to Yes.

4 At the right side of the Detail section, select the three text boxes that display resolution information. (Click one of the text boxes, and then hold down the SHIFT key while clicking the other two. Be sure to select only the text box controls, not their labels.)

Select these three text boxes so you can set properties for all of them at once.

5 In the property sheet, set the CanShrink property to Yes.

Preview the report

It's time to see how the changes affect your report.

Print Preview button

1 Click the Print Preview button on the toolbar.

Again, Microsoft Access runs your code for every issue on the page—first the Detail_Format procedure runs several times as Microsoft Access lays out each record on the page, and then the Detail_Print procedure runs as it prints each record. Your newest event procedure makes the three labels invisible in most issue records, because only a few issues have been resolved.

You'll notice that the first page of the report now fits several more issues than before, because it no longer displays empty fields for issues that aren't resolved. By scrolling down in the report, you can verify that the three text boxes do still appear for any issue that is resolved.

2 Scroll down in the window to display the fifth record on the page—the first issue in the second group. (If necessary, scroll to the right a bit to display the resolution fields.)

The three resolution fields appear only once on the page, for the one issue that's currently resolved.

For unresolved issues, the Detail section shrinks to fit only fields that contain data.

These fields appear only for issues that are resolved.

Issues						
	Computer equipment	Open	Medium	9/12/96	Paul Vornund	
tion:	It's time to put together recommendations for this year's computer upgrades. The admin staff can collect this data.					
	Standard Products account	Open	**High**	9/12/96	Rob MacDougall	
tion:	These guys are considering jumping ship to the competitor. Let's meet with them to discuss their needs – it's a big account.					
4						

ned To: *Darren Demerais*

ID	Title	Status	Priority	Date	Entered By
	Trade show plans	Resolved	**High**	9/12/96	Darren Demerais
tion:	Our booth at the trade show will need rented equipment like last time.	*Date Resolved:* 9/12/96	*Resolution:* Fixed	*Resolved By:* Rob MacDougall	

Page: |◄ ◄ [1] ► ►| ◄

You've now seen how to make two types of changes while Microsoft Access prepares your report for printing: changes both before and after the section is formatted. But your changes so far have been limited to setting properties for controls in the section. Although these common types of changes can be very powerful, it's only the beginning—you can also perform calculations, set control values, and even combine various event procedures throughout the report to achieve the results you want. In the next section, you'll use a simple example of these techniques to improve on the Issues report.

Calculating Totals While a Report Is Printing

One standard feature of reports is the ability to calculate totals—the sum or average of values, for example—for all the records in a section or in the entire report. The Report Wizard often sets up such totaling fields for you. You can also add them yourself by placing a text box in a group footer or report footer section and setting its ControlSource property to the appropriate expression. The Issues report has just such a control in the group footer section for each employee: the TotalIssues control calculates the "count" or number of issues assigned to that employee.

Although standard totals can perform a wide variety of operations for your reports, you may also want to perform your own calculations using Visual Basic. A common reason for doing this is to include totals for a group of records other than the standard grouping in a report. For example, in addition to the total for each group, you might want to display a running total on the current page of the report. To accomplish this, you would have to keep track of the running total in code while Microsoft Access prints the report. At the appropriate points, you would put the running total into a text box control on the report.

Another similar reason for calculating totals yourself is to break down the values in a way that the default report grouping cannot. The Issues report, for example, groups issue records by the employee they're assigned to. But suppose you want to display the number of open issues or high-priority issues at the end of each employee's section. In other words, you want the report to summarize by saying, "This employee has four issues total, three of which are open and one of which is high priority." There's no simple way to ask for these values in an expression—you have to write Visual Basic code to count the issues yourself. In this section, you'll add code in event procedures that calculates these totals and displays them for each employee in two text boxes in the group footer.

Create text boxes to display section totals

To print the results of calculations you perform in a report's event procedures, you need to put unbound controls on the report to contain them. You'll create two text boxes for the group footer section of the Issues report, one to show the number of open issues each employee has, and another to show the number of high-priority issues.

1   On the toolbar, click the Close button.

The report returns to Design view.

2   If you can't see the AssignedTo Footer section of the report, scroll down in the window to display it.

In this group footer section, you'll notice the TotalIssues control, which demonstrates the standard method for showing section totals. The control source expression for the control, *=Count([IssueID])*, tells Microsoft Access to count the number of records in the section that contain an IssueID value.

313

Text Box tool

3 In the toolbox, click the Text Box tool.

4 Click the AssignedTo Footer section of the report, to the right of the TotalIssues field and near the center of the report.

```
Issues : Report                                                    _ □ ×
```

Click here to create the text box.

An unbound text box appears on the report. Its label shows a default name (something like Text55). To make it easier to refer to in code, you'll enter a new name for the control.

5 In the property sheet, click the Other tab, and then set the Name property to **OpenIssues**.

You also need to change the label to the left of the text box.

6 Click the label for the new text box to select it.

7 Change the control's label: double-click the text in the label, and then type **Open Issues** to replace the existing text.

This finishes the OpenIssues text box, which you'll use to display the number of open issues for each employee's section of the report. Next, you'll create a second unbound text box to the right of the one you just finished.

8 In the toolbox, click the Text Box tool, and then click the AssignedTo Footer section between the OpenIssues text box and the right edge of the report.

Another unbound text box appears in the footer section.

9 In the property sheet, set the Name property to **HighPriority**.

10 Change the control's label to **High Priority**.

314

11 If necessary, drag the two text boxes to position them evenly across the AssignedTo Footer section of the report.

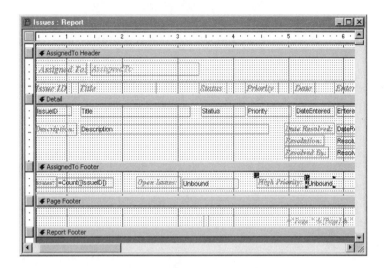

Add code that increments
the OpenIssues and HighPriority fields

As an employee's issue records print, you want your code to count the number of open and high-priority issues. You could keep track of the count in either of two ways: by storing the totals in variables you declare, or by placing them in the two unbound text boxes themselves. Here you'll use the latter method (the simpler of the two). Each time the report prints an open or high-priority issue, you'll increment the value of one or both of the text boxes you created. You can do this in response to the Print event, which occurs just before each issue is printed.

Additionally, you'll need to reset the values of these fields each time you begin a new employee's section—otherwise, the code would create a cumulative total, adding the new issues onto those of the previous employees. To reset these fields to 0, you'll add code to the AssignedTo Header section's Print event procedure, which occurs just before each employee's section begins printing.

1 Click the AssignedTo Header section bar.

2 In the property sheet, click the Event tab, click the OnPrint property, and then click the Build button.

3 Double-click Code Builder.

The report's GroupHeader0_Print procedure appears in the Module window. Microsoft Access will run this procedure each time it's about to print the AssignedTo header for another employee.

4 Add the following code to the procedure:

```
' Reset the totals boxes in the footer for each employee.

    OpenIssues = 0
    HighPriority = 0
```

This code sets the values of both of the unbound text boxes you created to 0, because at the beginning of each section an employee has no issues. As Microsoft Access progresses through the report, of course, these numbers may change. That will be up to the Detail_Print event procedure, your next stop. The Detail_Print event procedure already contains the code you added earlier in the lesson.

5 Scroll up in the Module window to show the Detail_Print event procedure, click just above the End Sub statement, and then enter the following code:

```
' Increment total fields if issue is open or high priority.
If PrintCount = 1 Then
    If Status = "Open" Then
        OpenIssues = OpenIssues + 1
    End If
    If Priority = "High" Then
        HighPriority = HighPriority + 1
    End If
End If
```

This code will keep track of the open and high priority issues while the report is printing. While the code is simple, it illustrates a couple of key concepts. Here's how it works:

■ The Print event usually occurs only once for each section printed in a report. In certain cases, however, it can occur more than once, such as when the Detail section spans two pages. For this reason, the Print event procedure has an argument called PrintCount, which can tell you whether the event is occurring for the first time. Because you wouldn't want to count any records twice, the code uses an If...Then statement, running the rest of the code in the procedure only if PrintCount is 1—in other words, only the first time the procedure runs for a given issue.

■ The rest of the code consists of two nearly identical If...Then blocks. The first block checks whether the current issue record is open— whether the Status field contains the value Open—and increments the value shown in the OpenIssues control by one if the issue is open. The second block does the same for high-priority issues, incrementing the value of the HighPriority control if the Priority field contains the value High.

As you see here, when you want to increment a value in Visual Basic, you follow the control or variable name with an equal sign, and then with the expression that calculates the new value. The first of these statements, for example, can be read as: "Set the value of the OpenIssues field to its existing value plus 1."

After this code runs for a given record, the OpenIssues field will contain the number of open issues printed so far, and the HighPriority field will contain the number of high-priority issues printed so far. By the time the group footer section prints, these fields will contain their final values, which are what will appear on the report.

Compile Loaded Modules button

6 Click the Compile Loaded Modules button on the toolbar.

7 Click the Save button on the toolbar.

8 Close the Module window.

Save button

Preview the report

You're ready to try the report and see how your totals work.

Print Preview button

1 Click the Print Preview button on the toolbar.

Now that you've added even more code, all sorts of things are happening when you preview or print the report! When Microsoft Access gets ready to print the header section for each employee that has open issues, the GroupHeader0_Print procedure runs, setting the unbound fields to 0. Then the Detail_Print procedure runs for every issue record. By the time the footer section for an employee prints, the text boxes should contain the correct values. Then, when Microsoft Access moves on to the next employee's section, your code again resets the text boxes to 0.

2 If necessary, scroll down in the window to display the footer section for Bonnie Christensen, and then the one for Darren Demarais.

As you can see, the text boxes you created now display the correct totals.

Your new
fields display
the totals for
each group.

The examples you've used in this lesson demonstrate how you can access the data in individual records of a report. Your own needs in customizing reports will vary greatly, and you'll probably need to experiment quite a bit to get your reports right. You'll have a head start, however, if you remember the different places you can attach code to—the Format and Print events for each section—and the ways you can affect the report, such as setting report and control properties, and setting the values of unbound controls.

Advanced Control of Section Printing and Placement

The report changes you made using code in this lesson had a very practical effect on the way the Issues report prints. But even though your code set a few properties and values, it didn't significantly change the course of the report—it more or less assumed that the report would print along to completion, including every record and section in its turn. Because you may want to change which sections print and where, Microsoft Access provides run-time report properties and event procedure arguments that allow your code to affect the printing process.

The simplest technique for controlling whether a section prints is setting the Cancel argument for the Print event procedure. If you determine in your code that you don't want to print a given section at all, you can set the Cancel argument in the procedure to True, and Microsoft Access won't print the section. For example, in the Issues report, you might want to exclude issues that belong to the employee who's currently logged in. To do this, you'd write code to cancel printing of sections in which the AssignedTo field contains that employee's ID number.

For finer control over which sections print and where, you can use three run-time properties: MoveLayout, NextRecord, and PrintSection. All three of these properties are normally set to True for every section and record. By setting them to False in your code, you can change how the report prints.

MoveLayout   tells Microsoft Access whether to move to the next position on the page after printing the current section. If you set this property to False, the following section will print in the same place on the page.

NextRecord   tells Microsoft Access whether to move to the next record in the recordset. If you set this property to False, you can cause the current record to be repeated on the page. You might want to do this in a mailing labels report, for example, to print more than one of each label for each address.

> **PrintSection** determines whether the current section prints on the page. You can set this property to False to leave a blank space on the page.
>
> By experimenting with these properties in various combinations, you'll be able to control printing in endless ways. Beware, however: some combinations of these properties can produce strange results, and you may have trouble diagnosing problems that arise.

Close the report and exit Microsoft Access

1 Close the report window.

2 On the File menu, click Exit.

Lesson Summary

To	Do this
Perform actions before each record gets laid out on the page of a report	Write a Format event procedure for the Detail section of the report.
Perform actions before each record (or header or footer section) of a report prints	Write a Print event procedure for the Detail section (or other section) of the report.
Cause controls not to print if they don't have values	Set the CanShrink property of the controls, and the section they belong in, to True. If the controls have labels in the Detail section that you don't want to show, set the Visible property to False for records that don't have values.
Calculate section totals while a report prints and display them on the report	Create unbound text box controls to store and display the totals in the appropriate footer section on the report. Write one event procedure that resets the total values to 0 at the beginning of each section, and another that updates the value as each record or section prints.

319

For online information about	On the Help menu, click Contents and Index, click the Index tab, and then
Creating and customizing reports	Search for "reports"
Grouping data in reports	Search for "grouping records in reports"
Responding to report events using event procedures	Search for "Format event" or "Print event"
Changing the layout of data and blank space on a report	Search for "CanShrink property" and "MoveLayout property"

For more information on	In *Building Applications with Microsoft Access 97*, see
Opening and filtering reports in your applications	Chapter 3, "Using Forms to Collect, Filter, and Display Information"
Using events in reports	Chapter 6, "Responding to Events"

Preview of the Next Lesson

The techniques you're learning in the final lessons of this book are more specialized, teaching you about new Microsoft Access objects, and pointing you in the direction of new areas of programming you may want to explore as you create more advanced applications on your own. In the next lesson, you'll delve into yet another heap of concepts known as Automation, which allows you to work directly with other Windows applications from within your Visual Basic code in Microsoft Access. In particular, you'll combine the capabilities of Microsoft Access with those of Microsoft Word, learning how to send commands from Microsoft Access to Word in Word's own programming language.

14

Share Data with Other Applications

Estimated time
25 min.

In this lesson you will learn how to:

- Use Automation objects to work with other Windows applications.
- Send commands and data to Microsoft Word.
- Gather data from another application, such as Microsoft Excel.

When traveling far from home, communicating with strangers can be both challenging and rewarding. Although differing cultures and languages can present obstacles, it seems we humans can usually find a way to communicate our messages to one another, whether by body language, hand signals, or perhaps a broken approximation of a foreign tongue. And as anyone who has traveled much will attest, exposure to other cultures can be very broadening—we seem to absorb a bit of the experience and wisdom of others out of such encounters.

As a Microsoft Access programmer, working with other Windows applications is a little like communicating with people of different cultures—it's a challenge, but there's a lot to gain in sharing the capabilities of other systems. Fortunately, Visual Basic provides a mechanism for talking between two different applications, such as Microsoft Access and Microsoft Excel, or Microsoft Access and Word. It's called *Automation*. Automation gives you a framework for using objects that belong to another application as if those objects were an extension of the application you're working within. But just as with human communication, you'll find that it helps to know a bit about the other party's language. With Automation, you combine the objects, properties, and

321

methods of the other application with the Visual Basic code you write in Microsoft Access.

In this lesson, you'll learn the general techniques of communicating using Automation. Working with Microsoft Word, you'll find out how to combine the capabilities of two systems to accomplish more in your database applications.

NOTE You must have Microsoft Word 97 installed on your computer in order to complete the steps in this lesson.

Start the lesson

➤ Start Microsoft Access and open the 14Issues database in the practice files folder.

Using Automation Objects

Microsoft Access isn't a very good word processor. Sure, you could create a Microsoft Access report that would look a lot like a professional letter—but it would take a great deal of work, and would lack the flexibility you take for granted in any word processing application. By the same token, Microsoft Access isn't a statistical calculator, a project manager, or a presentation graphics program. But it's a great place to store your data!

One way to extend the capabilities of your Microsoft Access applications is by teaming them up with the capabilities of other applications. Automation is the mechanism that Visual Basic provides for doing this. If the databases you're creating need the capabilities of other Windows applications—and if those other applications use Visual Basic for Applications—you can use Visual Basic code to combine the power of Microsoft Access with the strengths of other systems.

In previous lessons, you've learned about several types of objects you can control in Microsoft Access, such as the Form, Report, Database, and Recordset objects. Other applications have objects as well, and your code running in Microsoft Access can work with them behind the scenes. Microsoft Excel, for example, has the Worksheet and Chart objects, which you could incorporate seamlessly into a Microsoft Access application using techniques similar to those you've learned for working with Microsoft Access objects. And many other Windows applications expose their objects for use through Automation.

Although the possible ways you could combine applications are endless, here are some common ways to use Automation with Microsoft Access:

Create or edit documents. From your Visual Basic code in Microsoft Access, you can create or open a document in Microsoft Word or a worksheet in Microsoft Excel, for example, and control it using the other application's commands. Without any interaction by the user, you can send data from your database to the document or worksheet, and even use the other application's commands to print it. You'll use these techniques in this lesson to work with a document in Microsoft Word.

Gather data from another application.   Although you'll usually store your application's data in Microsoft Access tables (or another format that Microsoft Access can link to), you might occasionally want to bring in data from another application's files. For example, you might want to incorporate a list of project milestones and dates stored in Microsoft Project. Using Automation in Visual Basic, you can use the properties and methods of Microsoft Project to access this information.

Provide data to other applications.   All the techniques discussed to this point involve writing code in Microsoft Access to control other applications—alternatively, you can write Automation code in another application to work with data or other objects in Microsoft Access databases. This strategy makes most sense if your application is primarily suited for another programming system. For example, if you create a financial system using VBA in Microsoft Excel, you might want to store some of the data in Microsoft Access tables, and perhaps even print Microsoft Access reports from the Microsoft Excel application.

Although you won't get a chance to try all these techniques in this lesson, you'll discover many Automation concepts that apply to all of them.

More Ways to Share Data

Although you won't try them out in this book, there are two additional Windows technologies that, like Automation, help you use other applications with Microsoft Access. The first is Object Linking and Embedding (OLE). Through OLE, you can insert one application's objects or documents into another. For example, you can place an *object frame control* on a Microsoft Access form or report, and then insert a worksheet from Microsoft Excel or a chart from Microsoft Graph into the new frame. Although this strategy doesn't usually involve any programming—OLE objects work automatically based on properties you set—you can use Visual Basic code in Microsoft Access to control when the object gets updated or to change OLE property settings.

For applications that don't support Automation or OLE, you may be able to write code that uses Dynamic Data Exchange (DDE). With DDE, you can send data and commands from one application to another behind the scenes. For example, some Windows communications applications support DDE, and you could use DDE commands in Visual Basic to gather data via modem and store it in a Microsoft Access database.

For information on these techniques, search the Microsoft Access Help index for "OLE objects" or "DDE."

Sending Commands to Microsoft Word

Suppose you want your application to create and print a memo, merge names into a mailing list, or print envelopes—tasks you want to perform in Microsoft Word. Fortunately, Microsoft Word uses Visual Basic as its programming language, and supports Automation, so you can perform virtually any task from Microsoft Access that you could perform in Word itself.

One strategy for Automation is to open a document object directly, and then use its methods and properties to control it in Visual Basic. Alternatively, every application that supports Automation has a special object, the *Application* object, through which you can send commands to Word, just as if you were programming in Word itself. You can open documents, insert text, and control Microsoft Word in any way you please—all from within a procedure in your Microsoft Access application. Either way, you declare one or more object variables, use special statements to make the variables refer to objects in Word, and then use Word methods and properties.

In this lesson, you'll write Visual Basic code to perform actions in Word: creating a memo and inserting text into it. The memo your application creates will be a reminder to employees who have open issues stored in the database—and your code will automatically determine which employees to include on the "To" line of the memo.

Open the Microsoft Word template that your application will use

Before you write the Automation code in the Issues application, you'll first open a Microsoft Word document template, from which you'll create the memo. Using a template is a great way to get a head start on a document you send regularly, such as a form letter. If your template is nearly complete, all your code has to do is fill in any missing information, such as names or addresses stored in your database.

1 Start Microsoft Word 97. (Click the Windows Start menu, point to Programs, and then click Microsoft Word.)

2 On the File menu, click Open.

3 In the Files Of Type box, select Document Templates.

4 Move to the practice files folder on your hard disk and open the 14Memo template.

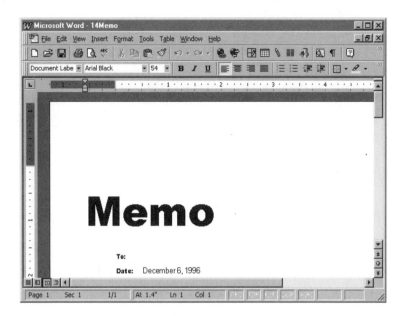

Add a bookmark to the template

When your code creates the memo, you'll want to insert employee names into it. The first step is to mark the spot where you'll enter text in the document, so your code can locate it easily. A simple way to do this is to use a *bookmark*, a named Word place marker, because you can jump to any bookmark in a document by using the GoTo method in Word.

1 Click the second line of the memo document to the right of the string *To:* to position the insertion point.

   This is where you'll enter employee names from Microsoft Access.

2 On the Insert menu, click Bookmark.

   Word displays the Bookmark dialog box.

3 Type **MemoToLine** in the Bookmark Name box and then click Add.

   Although you can't actually see the bookmark in the document, it will provide a quick way to jump to this spot from code in Microsoft Access.

4 Close the 14Memo document, clicking Yes when Microsoft Access asks if you want to save changes.

5 On the File menu, click Exit.

   Word closes, and Microsoft Access returns to the front.

Open the CreateWordMemo function in the Miscellaneous module

The Tools menu on the Issues form includes the command Create Word Memo, placed there so users can run the Automation code you'll write. The menu item runs a function called CreateWordMemo, which already exists in the Miscellaneous module. You just need to open this function and then add the Automation code to make it work.

➤ In the Database window, click the Modules tab, and then double-click the Miscellaneous module.

Microsoft Access displays the Miscellaneous module. The first procedure in the module is the CreateWordMemo function.

The function already contains some important code—but it's also code you're familiar with from earlier lessons. Here's what it does:

■ The Dim statement declares variables used to open a recordset.

■ The next two lines of DAO code open a recordset based on a query called EmployeesWithOpenIssues. As its name declares, this query returns a record for each employee who has at least one issue open in the Issues table—exactly the list of people you want to send the memo to. The code assigns this recordset to the rstEmployees variable.

■ The If...Then...End If block makes sure there is at least one employee in the recordset—otherwise, there would be no point in sending the memo. The condition that the If...Then statement tests refers to a property of the Recordset object that you haven't seen yet: the RecordCount property. This property returns the number of records in the recordset that

Microsoft Access has read from disk so far. (Note that this isn't necessarily the total number of records in the recordset, unless you've already moved to the end of the recordset.) If the RecordCount property returns 0, it means that the recordset is empty; in this case the code would display a message and exit the procedure.

Set a reference to Word's object library

Microsoft Word has its own object library, similar to the Access, VBA, and DAO object libraries you explored in Lesson 12. Before you can use Word's objects in your code, you need to tell Microsoft Access that you intend to do so by setting a *reference* to the Microsoft Word object library.

1   On the Tools menu, click References.

The References dialog box appears and displays all the object libraries that are registered on your system.

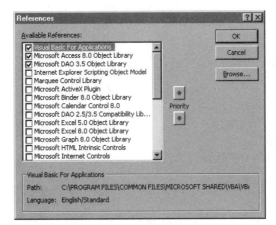

2   Locate Microsoft Word 8.0 Object Library in the list of available references, and then click the check box next to the entry to select it.

3   Click OK.

TIP   In addition to preparing to work with a new object library, you can use the References command to make Visual Basic code in another database available—in order to call procedures from a database, you need only establish a reference to it. In the same way, a reference is often required in order to use add-in products for Microsoft Access, such as ActiveX controls. To establish a reference to a file that isn't listed in the References dialog box, just click the Browse button and locate the file.

Write code that creates a Word document and inserts text

It's time to get your feet wet. First, you'll add a line of code to declare a variable for the Word Application object; this variable will provide your gateway from Microsoft Access to Word. Then, you'll add a block of Automation code that switches to Word and stores an actual reference to its Application object using the GetObject function. Your Automation code will "talk" to the Word Application object, telling it to create the memo document and sending various other commands, and then inserting the employee names from the rstEmployees recordset into the document. As you'll see, Automation programming is just like ordinary programming with Microsoft Access and DAO objects—except that in order to send commands to the other application, you need to learn about a whole new object library, complete with properties, methods, and constants.

1 Add the following code underneath the existing Dim statement:

```
Dim appWord As Word.Application
```

You'll use the object variable *appWord* throughout the procedure to refer to Word and run its commands. Note that the statement declares the variable with the special data type *Word.Application*—this data type is available only because you established a reference to Microsoft Word.

2 Add code at the end of the procedure, just above the End Function statement (if Microsoft Word or the Step by Step practice files are not in their default folders on your hard disk, be sure to substitute the correct path names in the code):

```
' Switch to Microsoft Word so it won't go away when you finish.
On Error Resume Next
AppActivate "Microsoft Word"

' If Word isn't running, start and activate it.
If Err Then
    Shell "c:\Program Files\Microsoft Office\Office\" _
        & "WinWord /Automation", vbMaximizedFocus
    AppActivate "Microsoft Word"
End If
On Error GoTo 0

' Get an Application object so you can automate Word.
Set appWord = GetObject(, "Word.Application")

' Open a document based on the memo template, turn off the
' automatic spell check, and move to the MemoToLine bookmark.
With appWord
    .Documents.Add "C:\Access VBA Practice\14Memo.dot"
    .ActiveDocument.ShowSpellingErrors = False
```

```
        .Selection.Goto wdGoToBookmark, Name:="MemoToLine"
End With

' Loop through the recordset returned by the query, inserting
' the name of each employee into the document.
Do Until rstEmployees.EOF
    appWord.Selection.TypeText rstEmployees!EmployeeName & "   "
    rstEmployees.MoveNext
Loop
```

Here's how this code does its work:

- The first block of code uses the AppActivate statement to switch to Microsoft Word if a copy of it is already running. Switching to Word from the start ensures that when the procedure finishes, the memo document it creates won't disappear. Although not the most common way to use Automation—you don't usually want the other application to appear at all, but just to do its thing—this strategy allows users to do as they please with the memo in Word after you create it.

- The On Error Resume Next statement is included before the AppActivate statement to tell Microsoft Access to ignore any errors that may occur in trying to switch to Word. If Word isn't running, the AppActivate statement would cause a run-time error. This strategy allows code to continue, so that you can check whether or not an error occurred.

- To determine whether AppActivate caused an error, the If...Then statement checks the value of the Err object. If Err is 0 (or False), it means that the code successfully switched to Word. If Err is non-zero (or True), you assume that the code couldn't start Word, and the line of code underneath the If...Then statement runs. This line uses the Shell statement to start a copy of Microsoft Word. Like AppActivate, Shell ensures that Word—and the memo you create—will stick around after the procedure ends. The second argument to the Shell statement tells Word how to start; the constant vbMaximizedFocus tells it to use the whole screen and to become the active window. After the Shell statement, another AppActivate statement ensures that code doesn't begin running again until after Word is completely started and ready.

- On Error GoTo 0 tells Microsoft Access not to ignore subsequent errors in the procedure—it cancels out the earlier On Error Resume Next statement so as to avoid overlooking unexpected problems. (Note, however, that a more complete version of this procedure would also have its own error-handling code, because working with other applications can often cause errors. To keep things simpler, we've left it out here.)

- The next line uses the GetObject function to store a reference to the Word Application object in the appWord variable. Since your code already made sure that Word is open and active, this object will simply refer to the copy of Word that's already running.

  Note that the first argument to the GetObject function is left out. You use this argument if you want a reference to a specific document, rather than to the Application object. If Word weren't running, this statement would cause an error to occur. Alternatively, you could use one of several methods (such as the CreateObject function) to cause a new copy of Word to start up automatically in the background—but when your code finished, the copy of Word would automatically shut down.

  Now that you have a Word Application object, you can use it to send commands to Word—as you do in the next block of code.

- The next block of code uses something new: a With...End With block. The With statement simply provides a shortcut in your code for performing several actions using the same object. Microsoft Access interprets this code as if you'd put the name of the object before each period in the subsequent lines. For example, the first line below the With statement is equivalent to *appWord.Documents.Add*, even though the appWord variable isn't specified. Note that you can use a With...End With block in any object manipulation code—but it's especially useful for Automation, because you often want to perform several commands at a time concerning one object.

- The first statement inside the With...End With block uses the Add method of Word's *Documents* collection. The Documents collection in Word contains one Document object for each Word document that's currently open, in much the same way that the Microsoft Access Forms collection contains one Form object for each form that's open. Using the Add method creates a new Document object—just as if the user clicked the New command on the File menu. The argument provided for the Add method specifies a Word template on which to base the new document, in this case the 14Memo template you just viewed. (Leaving this argument out would create a blank Word document.)

- The next statement in the block sets a property of the Word document you've just created: the ShowSpellingErrors property. Setting this property to False prevents Word from displaying wavy red lines under words it doesn't recognize, such as the employee names your code will enter in the document.

- The final statement in the block moves the insertion point in Word to the MemoToLine bookmark you created. To do this, it refers to an important Word object, the *Selection* object, which represents the insertion point (or currently selected text) in a Word document. The

GoTo method of the Selection object moves the insertion point to a new location. Used with the wdGoToBookmark constant as its first argument, the GoTo method moves to the bookmark you specify using the Name argument.

■ Now that the memo is ready and you're in the right spot, the code can go ahead and insert the names from the recordset. To insert every name in the recordset, this code introduces a new method for repeating code, a Do...Loop block. The Do statement is followed by an Until condition: as long as the condition returns False, the block of code runs. The Loop statement tells it to run again—assuming the condition still isn't True—and the loop continues until the condition returns True.

The condition for the Do Until statement refers to the EOF property (EOF stands for End Of File) of the Recordset object. The value of a recordset's EOF property is False so long as there is a "current" record in the recordset. If you move past the last record in the recordset (or if there aren't any records to begin with), the value of the EOF property will be True.

■ The next line uses the TypeText method of the Word Selection object to actually type a name into the Word document. You can follow the TypeText method with any string expression that you want to put into the document—in this case, it's the value of the EmployeeName field in the recordset, followed by three spaces (to separate each name from the next).

■ The next statement uses the MoveNext method of the Recordset object to move to the next record in the rstEmployees recordset. Then it's time to loop: if there is another employee, the TypeText code runs again; if not, the expression *Not rstEmployees.EOF* returns False, and the loop is complete. As is the memo!

3 Click the Compile Loaded Modules button on the toolbar.

4 Click the Save button on the toolbar.

Compile Loaded Modules button

Save button

Note that when your procedure finishes, the appWord variable goes away. If you hadn't used the AppActivate and Shell statements to ensure that a copy of Word was open and active, Word would go away as well—but as it stands, Word should stay open and display the memo for users to edit as they please.

Try out your OLE automation procedure

Let's create a memo! To run the event procedure, you can use the custom menu command on the Tools menu of the Issues form's menu bar.

1 Click the Database Window button on the toolbar.

2 In the Database window, click the Forms tab, and then double-click the Issues form.

Database Window button

331

3 On the Tools menu, click Create Word Memo.

Your code runs—it opens a recordset, activates Word and grabs hold of its Application object, creates the new memo, and then inserts names from the recordset. In fact, you can even see it happening. When it finishes, you're left in Microsoft Word looking at the completed memo.

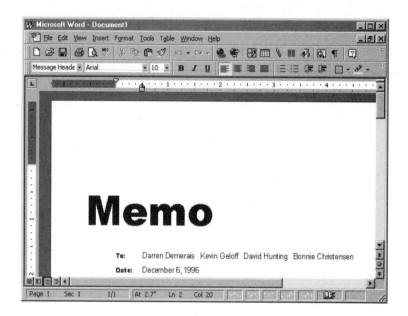

4 Close the memo document, clicking No when Word asks if you want to save changes.

5 Minimize Microsoft Word.

The Issues Tracking Application returns to the front.

Although this memo involves transferring only a small amount of data, you can easily imagine more powerful uses for this type of Automation. With Word, for example, you could use the same techniques to do easy printing of envelopes, merge data into documents and save them, or even create and print an entire mailing to clients stored in your database. And if you don't want users to have to work in Word themselves, you can do all this work behind the scenes.

Getting Information from Another Application

So far, you've sent commands and data from Microsoft Access—even set a property in Word—but you haven't gotten anything back from Word. Using Automation, you can also request information from an application's objects, such as the value of a function or property. This allows you to interact with its objects in more powerful ways. For example, suppose you want to run a Microsoft

Excel financial function that doesn't exist in Microsoft Access. You can create an Automation object, and then use it to run the Microsoft Excel function, assigning the answer to a variable in your Microsoft Access code.

Now, you'll add a final section to the CreateWordMemo procedure that will run the Word Information function and use its return value, in this case, the number of pages in the memo. In this code, you'll display a message box that announces the number of pages in the finished memo and asks the user whether to print it.

Display a message box in Word that responds to the user's choice

Before you add code to the end of the procedure, you'll need to declare a couple of variables at the beginning.

1   On the Window menu, click Miscellaneous : Module.

    The Miscellaneous module still shows the CreateWordMemo function.

2   Add code below the two existing Dim statements:

```
Dim intPages As Integer, strMessage As String
```

This line declares two variables you'll use with the Word function: intPages to store the number of pages that Word tells you are in the memo, and strMessage to store the message you'll display.

3   Add code just before the End Function statement, beneath the Do...Loop block:

```
' Return to Access.
AppActivate "Issue Tracking Application"

' Get the number of pages in the memo, ask the user whether
' to print it, and then tell Word to print it.
intPages = appWord.Selection.Information(wdNumberOfPagesInDocument)
strMessage = "The memo is complete, and has " & CStr(intPages) & _
    " pages. Send it to the printer?"
If Confirm(strMessage) Then
    appWord.ActiveDocument.PrintOut
End If
```

Here's what the code does:

- The first statement reactivates Microsoft Access using the AppActivate statement. It specifies the title of the Issues application rather than Microsoft Access, because AppActivate always looks in the title bar to locate the application you want.

- The next line uses the Information function, which is a property of the Word Selection object you used earlier. This function can return many different bits of information about a document; what information you get back depends on the constant you provide. By specifying the wdNumberOfPagesInDocument constant, this statement retrieves the number of pages in the Word document and assigns that number to the intPages variable.

- The next line assigns the text of your message to the strMessage variable. It uses the CStr function to convert the page count value to a string, and then concatenates the text with this number to create a message. The code then uses this string to ask the user a question, calling the Confirm function you wrote way back in Lesson 5.

- If the user clicks OK in the message box, the statement in the If...Then block runs. The statement sends one final command to Word: it runs the PrintOut method of the Document object. The document it tells Word to print is the one referred to by the ActiveDocument property—which is, of course, the memo.

4 Click the Compile Loaded Modules button on the toolbar.

Compile Loaded Modules button

5 Close the Module window, clicking Yes when Microsoft Access asks if you want to save changes.

The Issues form becomes active again.

Create the memo again

Let's try out the procedure with these changes.

1 On the Tools menu, click Create Word Memo.

This time, when the memo finishes, the focus switches back to the Issues application and a message box appears on top of the document.

As you can see, your code discovered from Word the number of pages in the document. If you were to click OK, your code would tell Word to print it—but you don't need to test it unless you actually want to print the memo.

2 Click Cancel.

3 Close the memo document, clicking No when Word asks if you want to save changes.

4 Close Microsoft Word.

Using Microsoft Access Objects from Microsoft Excel

Programming with Automation is a two-way street: just as the procedure you wrote in Microsoft Access controlled Word, you can write code in another application to control Microsoft Access. For example, if you write Visual Basic code in Microsoft Excel, you can open and work directly with Microsoft Access and DAO objects.

Here's a Visual Basic procedure that works in Microsoft Excel. It creates a Microsoft Access Application object, and then uses it to open the Issues database and print a report:

```
Sub PrintIssuesReport()

    ' Declare and create an Access application object.
    Dim appAccess As New Access.Application

    ' Open the Issues application with Access.
    appAccess.OpenCurrentDatabase_
        "c:\Access VBA Practice\14Issues.mdb"

    ' Print the Issues report.
    appAccess.DoCmd.OpenReport "Issues"

End Sub
```

In declaring the appAccess variable used to send commands to Microsoft Access, the first line of code uses an important keyword you haven't yet seen: the *New* keyword. Using New in a Dim statement for an object variable, you can create an object variable *and* create an instance of that object all in one step. When this line runs, Microsoft Access starts in the background.

The next line in the procedure uses the OpenCurrentDatabase method of the Application object, which exists specifically to facilitate Automation in Microsoft Access when it's used from other applications. The last line uses a technique very familiar to you by now—a method of the DoCmd object—to open and print the Issues report.

Although this example performs only the simplest task, it demonstrates how powerful Automation can be between applications that support Visual Basic for Applications, such as Microsoft Word, Microsoft Excel, and Microsoft Project. If you write code in these applications, you can control everything from their programming languages in nearly the same way you can from Microsoft Access.

Exit Microsoft Access

➤ On the File menu, click Exit.

Lesson Summary

To	Do this
Tell Microsoft Access that you want to use another application's objects	With the Module window open, click References (Tools menu), and then select the object library you want to use.
Use Automation to send commands to another application	Declare an Application object variable for the other application, and then use the GetObject function, CreateObject function, or New keyword to assign an instance of the Application object to the variable. Then, use the variable to run statements and methods or access objects and properties in the other application's object model.
Carry out multiple statements pertaining to the same object without retyping the object name	Use a With...End With block, specifying the object variable on the With line and starting each line of code in the block with a period.
Activate another Windows application	Use the Shell statement, or if the application is already running, use the AppActivate statement.
Loop through all the records in a recordset	Use the Do Until statement, specifying a condition that checks the EOF property of the recordset. Just before the Loop statement, use the MoveNext method to move to the next record in the recordset.

For online information about	On the Help menu, click Contents and Index, click the Index tab, and then
Working with Automation objects	Search for "Automation"
Creating an instance of another application's object	Search for "GetObject function," "CreateObject function," and "New keyword"
Repeating code with the Do...Loop statement and control-flow statements	Search for "loops"

For more information on	In *Building Applications with Microsoft Access 97*, see
Working with Automation objects	Chapter 11, "Communicating with Other Applications"
Using the With statement, or referring to Microsoft Access objects	Chapter 5, "Working with Objects and Collections"
Using DAO objects, the MoveNext method, or the EOF property	Chapter 9, "Working with Records and Fields"

Preview of the Next Lesson

In the last three lessons, you've been working with specific areas of Access programming, discovering powerful possibilities. In the final lesson, you'll explore one of the hottest areas in Microsoft Access, its support for sharing data on the Internet or on an intranet. You'll learn to control hyperlinks from within Visual Basic, and you'll try out the WebBrowser control, which lets you display Web pages in a Microsoft Access form.

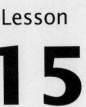

Lesson

15

Connect to the Internet

Estimated time

45 min.

In this lesson you will learn how to:

- Create and update hyperlinks to Internet data on your Microsoft Access forms.
- Create a simple Web browser in Microsoft Access.

With the increasing popularity of the Internet, the world of information is getting more accessible by the day. Companies large and small have sites on the World Wide Web, making new sources of data available to anyone who's connected. Many workplaces also have an *intranet*, an internal networked "web" containing information for employees to use in their work. If you are connected to the Internet or an intranet, your Microsoft Access applications can help users work with data on the network more effectively.

Some of the most exciting innovations in Microsoft Access are designed to take advantage of the Internet. In this lesson, you'll explore two of the features that are likely candidates for your applications. First, you'll learn to enhance your Microsoft Access forms with *hyperlinks*, clickable images and text that are used to navigate through pages in a Web browser. Second, you'll learn to incorporate the Web browsing features of Microsoft Internet Explorer into your Microsoft Access applications.

339

NOTE In order to complete the steps in this lesson, you must have Microsoft Internet Explorer 3.01 installed on your computer and be connected to the Internet via a modem or network. Microsoft Internet Explorer is included on the Microsoft Office 97 CD-ROM; you can also download it for free from the Microsoft corporate Web site (http://www.microsoft.com/ie3/).

Depending on your system configuration for connecting with the Internet, the steps in this lesson may not work exactly as written. If you can't complete the lesson, you may still be able to learn from your reading and use some of the Internet features it covers. Additionally, note that the content of the Web sites may have changed and may no longer match the content shown.

Start the lesson

 Start Microsoft Access and open the 15Issues database in the practice files folder.

Using Hyperlinks

NEW for 97

If you've used any Web browser, or even viewed online Help files, you're familiar with hyperlinks. They're often indicated by blue underlined text, but they can also appear with other formatting and in other text colors. (Buttons and images can also be hyperlinks.) Clicking a hyperlink tells the software to jump to another place, either in a file on your computer or network, or to a location on the Internet. If you want to provide this ease of navigation to users of your applications, you can include hyperlinks on your forms. As you'll see, hyperlinks make navigation easier for the application developer as well—while the buttons you've created in previous lessons require Visual Basic code to make them work, hyperlinks are automatic. They need only an *address*, the location that they jump to.

Two ways of using hyperlinks are especially suited for forms in your applications. You can create controls on a form, and then set properties for the controls to define hyperlinks to Web sites. The addresses associated with the controls are saved with the form and don't change as you move among records. You can also add a field to a table in your database, give the field the Hyperlink data type, and then store hyperlinks there. If you then create a text box on a form that's bound to your Hyperlink field, the hyperlinks appear in the text box. As users navigate among records in the form, the text box displays a hyperlink that changes with every record. With either method, users can simply click any hyperlink to jump to the address it contains.

In this lesson, you'll use both methods of creating hyperlinks to enhance the Issues application. First, you'll add a hyperlink label control to the Issues form. The hyperlink will allow users to jump to a Web site that offers help with

Microsoft Access. Next, you'll add a new field to the Issues form that displays hyperlinks stored in the Issues table. These hyperlinks will let users jump to Web sites related to each issue in the database. Finally, you'll discover how to work with each type of hyperlink in Visual Basic, writing code that opens hyperlinks automatically and modifies them behind the scenes.

You'll add hyperlinks to the Issues form to make it easy for users to jump to Web sites.

Creating Hyperlink Controls on a Form

To define a hyperlink to a Web site, all you need to do is create a control—a command button, a label, or an image control—and then set properties that tell the hyperlink where to jump. When users click the control, Microsoft Access jumps directly to the location defined by the hyperlink. If the hyperlink's address points to a Web site, the user's Web browser will open automatically to display the site.

Create a label with a hyperlink

To give users an easy way to find help on the World Wide Web, you'll add a new label to the Issues form and define the Web address that its hyperlink will jump to. You'll use the Insert Hyperlink command, a shortcut for creating a hyperlink label and setting some of its properties.

Insert Hyperlink button

1 In the Database window, click the Forms tab.

2 Click the Issues form, and then click the Design button.

3 Click the Insert Hyperlink button on the toolbar.

   The Insert Hyperlink dialog box appears, asking for the hyperlink address.

4 In the Link To File Or URL box, type **http://www.microsoft.com/ MSAccessSupport**, and then click OK.

341

Microsoft Access creates a label that displays your hyperlink address, and inserts it at the top left corner of the form. Next, you'll move the label to the bottom of the Issues form, a blank area you'll use to display this and other Web-related controls.

5 Drag the label down to the bottom of the form, placing it in the blank area just to the right of the existing label that says "Need More Help?" (If the bottom of the form is not visible, you may need to drag the label down below the form window until Microsoft Access scrolls down in the window for you.)

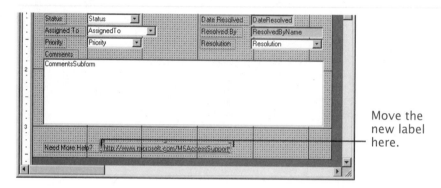

Move the new label here.

Now that the label is where it belongs, you'll set a couple of properties.

Properties button

6 If the property sheet isn't displayed, click the Properties button.

7 Click the All tab in the property sheet.

8 Set the Name property to **HelpLinkLabel**.

You'll refer to this name in code later in the lesson. Next, you'll set the Caption property, which determines the text that's displayed for the hyperlink.

9 Set the Caption property to **Microsoft Access Product Support**.

As you may have noticed, the HyperlinkAddress property for the label is set to the Web address you entered when creating the label. That's really all there is to a hyperlink—a control with an address.

10 Close the property sheet.

The text in the label appears in blue and with an underline, showing that it's a hyperlink. Soon, you'll use it to jump to the World Wide Web.

Storing Hyperlinks in a Table

If users of your application are frequently accessing Web sites, you may want to let them store hyperlinks for these sites within records in a Microsoft Access database. The Hyperlink data type can store all the information that might be needed for a hyperlink, including the text the hyperlink displays and the address it jumps to. Using the Hyperlink data type, you can create a table just for the purpose of storing and managing hyperlinks—in a Web site management database, for example. You can also allow users to associate Web sites with other types of records in the database.

The Issues table in the practice database contains a new field called WebSite, which already has several useful hyperlinks stored in it. If you open that table, you'll see a new column containing hyperlinks, with their familiar blue clickable text.

This new field in the Issues table uses the Hyperlink data type to store Web-site information related to each record.

Add the WebSite field to the Issues form

Your next step is to create a text box control to display the hyperlink that's stored with each issue.

Field List button

1   If the field list isn't displayed, click the Field List button on the toolbar.

    The field list displays all the fields in the Issues table. As you'll see, the new WebSite field is there, ready to display a hyperlink for each issue.

2   Scroll down in the field list to display the WebSite field, and then click the WebSite field and drag it to the blank area of the form, just above the hyperlink label you created earlier.

343

The text box and its label appear on the form.

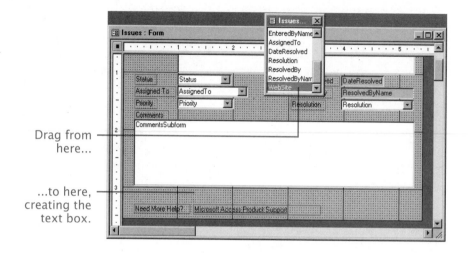

Drag from here...

...to here, creating the text box.

Because the field it's bound to has the Hyperlink data type, the text box displays its contents as a blue underlined hyperlink, ready to be clicked.

3 Close the field list.

4 Close the Issues form, clicking Yes when Microsoft Access asks if you want to save changes to the form.

Try out hyperlinks in the Issues form

1 In the Database window, double-click the Issues form.

The form opens and shows the two hyperlinks at the bottom.

2 Press the PAGE DOWN key twice to move between records in the form.

As you can see, the Related Web Site field displays a different hyperlink for each issue record. By contrast, the hyperlink label underneath it remains the same; unless you change its properties in Design view, it will always provide a link to the same Web site.

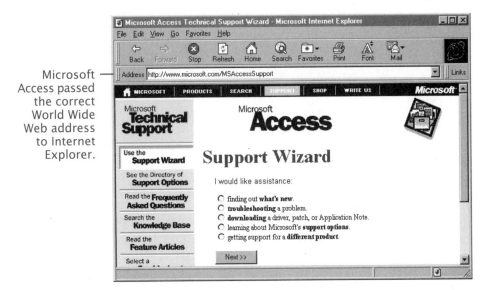

The text box displays a different hyperlink for each record.

The hyperlink for the label is always the same.

NOTE Although the Web sites included in the practice database aren't actually related to the sample issues in the Issues table, they may be of general interest to you. In a real-world situation, users would set these hyperlinks to point to Web sites that other employees could refer to.

3 Click the Microsoft Access Product Support hyperlink.

Microsoft Internet Explorer opens (asking you to establish an Internet connection if necessary) and displays the site on the World Wide Web. (If a message appears asking whether you want to disconnect from the Internet, click No.)

Microsoft Access passed the correct World Wide Web address to Internet Explorer.

345

If you like, you can browse this Web site or add it to your list of favorite sites by clicking Add To Favorites (Favorites menu).

4 Close Internet Explorer and switch back to Microsoft Access. (If a message appears asking whether you want to disconnect from the Internet, click No.)

Microsoft Access returns to the front.

5 Click the blue underlined hyperlink in the Related Web Site field. (If another message appears asking whether you want to disconnect from the Internet, click No.)

The second Web site opens.

6 Close Internet Explorer and switch back to Microsoft Access. (If you like, you can disconnect from the Internet for the time being.)

As you can see, it's a snap to provide jumps to the Internet on your forms. In your own applications, you'll need to decide which strategy is appropriate: creating hyperlinks directly on forms, or storing hyperlinks in a table. Although the former strategy is most straightforward, the latter is more flexible, especially if you have many sites to track or want to associate other information with them.

Connecting Hyperlinks to Files or Database Objects

The hyperlinks you'll use in this lesson all point to the World Wide Web. However, your hyperlinks don't all have to jump to Web sites, or even to the Internet. In fact, they can jump to various types of documents, either on the Internet, on your network, or on your own computer.

Access database objects   A hyperlink can open any database object, such as a form or report—a task you're accustomed to accomplishing with a command button. Here's how it works: In addition to its address, each hyperlink has a *subaddress* which points to a specific object or location within a file. To define a hyperlink that opens a database object, you set the hyperlink's subaddress to the object's type followed by its name, separated by a space. For example, to create a hyperlink to the Issues report, you'd just create a label and set its HyperlinkSubaddress property to Report Issues. When you click the hyperlink, the report opens in Print Preview, just as if you'd used the OpenReport method to open it.

Microsoft Office documents   A hyperlink can also open any Office document. To create a hyperlink that opens an Office file, just set its address to the path and file name of the document. For example, you could create a label and set its HyperlinkAddress property to c:\My Documents\Letter.doc. To move to a specific location in the file, such as a

Connecting Hyperlinks to Files or Database Objects, *continued*

bookmark in a Word document, set the hyperlink's subaddress to the name of the location. Click the hyperlink to open and display the document.

HTML documents   Web browsers such as Internet Explorer display documents that are formatted using Hypertext Markup Language (HTML). An HTML document doesn't have to be on the Internet—it can be at an intranet address on your company's network, or even sitting right there on your computer. For example, if you have the Microsoft Office 97 CD-ROM, you could create a hyperlink that opens the Building Applications manual on the disc by setting its address to \valupack\access\bldapps\default.htm on your CD-ROM drive. When you click that hyperlink, your Web browser opens and displays the document.

Other Internet addresses   While the addresses you've used with hyperlinks so far have all been for World Wide Web sites (they begin with http://www), there are several other types of Internet addresses that Microsoft Access recognizes. For example, you can set a hyperlink address to transfer a file from an FTP server or to send electronic mail (these types of Internet addresses begin with ftp: or mailto:).

As you can see, hyperlinks are extremely flexible. And although you need to set the Address and Subaddress properties appropriately for each type, the hyperlink display text is independent of the address, so users don't necessarily need to be aware of the differences between types. Only you need to know where the documents are located—on the user's computer, a company intranet, or the Internet. Users can just click them.

Following Hyperlinks from Visual Basic

The Issues form menu bar has two custom menu commands included as alternate ways to jump to Web sites. As you saw in Lesson 10, custom menu commands can run Visual Basic functions; at this point, however, these two menu commands don't have any functions to run. You'll create two functions that jump to the Web sites defined by these hyperlinks.

You'll create functions to make these menu commands work.

Create a procedure that follows a hyperlink

To open, or *follow*, the hyperlink defined for a control, you use the Follow method of the Hyperlink object.

*Database
Window button*

1   Click the Database Window button on the toolbar.

2   Click the Modules tab, and then double-click the Miscellaneous module.

3   On the Insert menu, click Procedure.

4   In the Name box, type **OpenHelpSite**, and then press ENTER.

Microsoft Access creates the OpenHelpSite function.

5   Add the following code to the procedure:

```
' Follow the hyperlink in the HelpLinkLabel control.

    On Error Resume Next
    Forms!Issues!HelpLinkLabel.Hyperlink.Follow
```

The first line of code uses the On Error statement to tell Microsoft Access to suspend error handling. This is important because if there's a problem connecting with the Internet, your system (or Internet Explorer) will display an error message automatically, and you don't want your program to stop running and display an error.

The second line of code specifies a control on the Issues form—the HelpLinkLabel control—using the expression *Forms!Issues!HyperlinkLabel*. To refer to the hyperlink that this control contains, rather than to the control itself, it uses the Hyperlink property. Finally, it runs the Follow method of the hyperlink. If you find it easier, you can read the line from right to left: it tells Microsoft Access to follow the hyperlink defined in the HelpLinkLabel control on the Issues form. When a user clicks the Open Help Site menu command to run this line of code, it will have the same effect as clicking the hyperlink.

Create a procedure that follows a hyperlink stored in a field

With a hyperlink stored in a field, you can't use the Hyperlink property. Instead, you use a more general method, the FollowHyperlink method, specifying the address that you want to jump to.

1   On the Insert menu, click Procedure.

2   In the Name box, type **OpenRelatedSite**, and then press ENTER.

Microsoft Access creates the OpenRelatedSite function.

3   Add the following code to the procedure:

```
' Follow the hyperlink stored in the WebSite field.
   Dim Address As String, Subaddress As String

   Address = HyperlinkPart(Forms!Issues!WebSite, acAddress)
   Subaddress = HyperlinkPart(Forms!Issues!WebSite, _
      acSubAddress)

   On Error Resume Next
   FollowHyperlink Address, Subaddress
```

Here's what this code does:

- The function begins by defining two string variables, Address and Subaddress, to store the address information for a hyperlink.

- A hyperlink has several components: an address, a subaddress, and the text that's displayed for the hyperlink. The next two lines of code use a new function, the HyperlinkPart function, to extract the address and subaddress parts of the hyperlink and store them in the two string variables. The first argument for the HyperlinkPart function is the hyperlink value itself, in this case the value of the WebSite control on the Issues form. The second argument to the function is a constant that specifies which part of the hyperlink you want it to return.

- The next line suspends error handling, so that your application won't stop running when there's a problem connecting with the Internet.

- The final line uses the FollowHyperlink method, specifying the string values you just put into the Address and Subaddress variables.

When a user clicks the menu item and runs this function, it will have the same effect as clicking the hyperlink in the WebSite text box.

Compile Loaded Modules button

4 Click the Compile Loaded Modules button on the toolbar.

Microsoft Access makes sure your code is correct.

5 Close the module window, clicking Yes when Microsoft Access asks if you want to save changes to the Miscellaneous module.

Try out your code

The custom menu items are now ready to follow some hyperlinks.

1 On the Window menu, click Issues.

The Issues form, still in Form view, returns to the front.

2 On the Tools menu, click Open Help Web Site.

349

Your code runs the Follow method for the HelpLinkLabel, which causes Microsoft Access to open the Web site in Internet Explorer.

3 Close Internet Explorer and switch back to Microsoft Access. (If a message appears asking whether you want to disconnect from the Internet, click No.)

4 On the Tools menu, click Open Related Web Site.

This time, your code gets the address information from the WebSite field and then runs the FollowHyperlink method to open the Web site.

5 Close Internet Explorer and switch back to Microsoft Access. (If you like, you can disconnect from the Internet.)

Modifying Hyperlinks Using Visual Basic

When you store hyperlinks in a table, you'll not only want to jump to them, you'll want to work with them, changing the text they display and the address they jump to. The practice application contains a simple dialog box form, called EditLink, which is designed to allow users to modify the related Web site hyperlink stored with each record in the Issues form. In this section, you'll create the button and add code to open the dialog box and make it work.

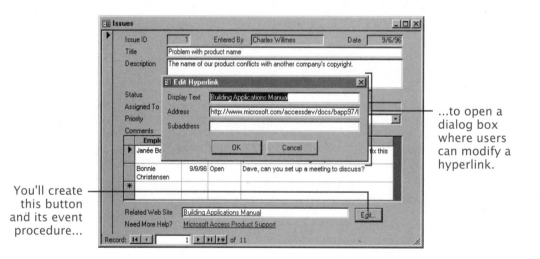

...to open a dialog box where users can modify a hyperlink.

You'll create this button and its event procedure...

Create a button that opens the EditLink form

Your first step is to create a button on the Issues form that opens the dialog box. You'll place the button right next to the WebSite field you created, so that users will know what it's for.

Design View button

1 Click the Design View button on the toolbar.

2 Scroll down in the form to display the area below the Comments subform.

Toolbox button

Control Wizards tool

Command Button tool

3 If the toolbox isn't displayed, click the Toolbox button on the toolbar.

4 In the toolbox, make sure the Control Wizards tool is deselected, and then click the Command Button tool.

5 Click on the form just to the right of WebSite text box.

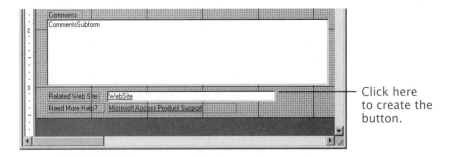

Click here to create the button.

The command button, with a default name such as Command26, appears next to the text box.

Properties button

6 Click the Properties button on the toolbar.

7 Set the Name property to **EditHyperlink**.

8 Set the Caption property to **E&dit....**

9 Close the property sheet.

10 With the right mouse button, click the EditHyperlink button, and then click Build Event.

11 Double-click Code Builder.

The Module window displays the EditHyperlink_Click event procedure.

12 Add the following code to the procedure (except the Sub and End Sub lines, which are already there):

```
Private Sub EditHyperlink_Click()
' Open the EditLink form.

    DoCmd.OpenForm "EditLink"

    ' If there is a hyperlink, copy its components
    ' to the text box controls on the form.
    If Len(WebSite) Then
        Forms!EditLink!DisplayText = _
            HyperlinkPart(WebSite, acDisplayText)
        Forms!EditLink!Address = _
            HyperlinkPart(WebSite, acAddress)
        Forms!EditLink!SubAddress = _
            HyperlinkPart(WebSite, acSubAddress)
    End If
End Sub
```

351

This code opens the EditLink form, using the OpenForm method of the DoCmd object. It then checks to see if the WebSite field for the current record on the form contains a hyperlink. If it does, you want to copy the components of this hyperlink to the dialog box so users can work with them.

Compile Loaded Modules button

13 Click the Compile Loaded Modules button on the toolbar.

14 Close the Module window.

15 Close the Issues form, clicking Yes when Microsoft Access asks if you want to save changes to the form.

Add code to change the hyperlink

Next, it's about time you take a look at the dialog box form we've been talking about. Before you try it out, however, you need to open the form in Design view and add an event procedure—the one that actually modifies the hyperlink stored in the WebSite field.

1 In the Database window, click the Forms tab.

2 Click the EditLink form, and then click the Design button.

The form has three text boxes where users enter the information for a hyperlink, as well as two command buttons. The Cancel button already contains code that closes the dialog box without doing anything; you'll add code for the OK button.

3 With the right mouse button, click the OK button, and then click Build Event.

4 Double-click Code Builder.

The Module window displays the OK_Click event procedure.

5 Add the following code to the procedure:

```
Private Sub OK_Click()
' Set the WebSite field on the Issues form.

    Forms!Issues!WebSite = DisplayText & "#" & _
        Address & "#" & Subaddress

    Forms!Issues!WebSite.SetFocus
    DoCmd.Close

End Sub
```

Here's what the code does:

- The first line sets the WebSite field on the Issues form. To create the new value, it concatenates the values the user enters in the three text boxes on the form, including the pound sign (#) character between each of the values.

- The next line uses the SetFocus method to move back to the WebSite field on the form.

- The final line in the procedure closes the dialog box using the Close method of the DoCmd object.

Compile Loaded Modules button

6 Click the Compile Loaded Modules button on the toolbar.

7 Close the Module window.

8 Close the EditLink form, clicking Yes when Microsoft Access asks if you want to save changes to the form.

Try out the EditLink form

Let's try out the code you've written by changing one of the hyperlinks stored in the Issues form.

1 In the Database window, double-click the Issues form.

The first record, currently displayed in the form, has a Web site stored with it. Suppose you want to change the hyperlink to a different site.

2 Click the Edit button next to the Related Web Site field.

The EditHyperlink_Click event procedure runs, opening the EditLink form and filling in the text boxes with the components of the existing hyperlink.

3 Select the existing text in the Display Text box, and then type **The Tax Man**.

4 Select the existing text in the Address box, and then type **http:// www.irs.ustreas.gov/**.

353

5 Click OK.

The OK_Click event procedure runs, setting the hyperlink value in the WebSite field. Back on the Issues form, you can see that the hyperlink in the field has changed. (If you like, you can click the hyperlink to try it out, but be sure to close Internet Explorer and return to Microsoft Access when you're finished browsing.)

TIP In this section, you modified a hyperlink stored in a field. Modifying a hyperlink control—such as the Microsoft Access Product Support label you created earlier in the lesson—is even easier. To modify the hyperlink defined for a control, all you need to do is set the control's properties, and the hyperlink automatically changes. For example, you could change the hyperlink label on the Issues form with the following code:

```
HelpLinkLabel.Caption = "Computer Books Galore"
HelpLinkLabel.HyperlinkAddress = _
    "http://www.microsoft.com/mspress"
```

Creating a Custom Web Browser

So far, you've seen how hyperlinks can put an external Web browser to work in conjunction with your applications. But what if you want to allow users to view Web sites or HTML documents from within Microsoft Access? If users will need to view Web sites frequently while using your Microsoft Access application, you'll want to incorporate Web browsing into your applications' forms, rather than sending users off to a separate Web browser application. In effect, you want to create your own custom Web browser on a form.

Microsoft Internet Explorer provides this capability through an *ActiveX control*, a special type of control that is separate from Microsoft Access but works much like a built-in control. The ActiveX control you'll use is called the WebBrowser control. It was automatically installed on your system when you installed Internet Explorer.

In this section, you'll add the WebBrowser control to a form, and then create event procedures to make it display Web documents within your application. In the code, you'll use objects, methods, and events that are unique to the WebBrowser control. In return, the WebBrowser control will automatically connect to the Internet and interpret the HTML language of the Web sites you specify, merging the power of Internet Explorer seamlessly into your application.

Using Other ActiveX Controls

The WebBrowser control is just one example of an ActiveX control. Microsoft Access comes with one additional ActiveX control, the Calendar control, which you can use to display a calendar on your forms. Because ActiveX is a standard interface for adding new capabilities to applications, there are many additional controls available from Microsoft and other vendors.

Beware, however, that although the names of all ActiveX controls registered on your system are displayed when you try to insert a control, they may not all be compatible with Microsoft Access. To find out whether a control is compatible, consult the documentation or online Help for that control. For general information on using ActiveX controls, search online Help for "ActiveX controls."

Open the Browser form

The Issues application already contains the form you'll use to create your Web browser. The custom menu bar for the Issues form includes a menu command to open the form.

➤   On the Tools menu, click View Web Browser Form.

The Browser form already has a Web Address combo box and an Add command button at the top. The combo box contains several Internet addresses, which are stored in a table in the Issues database called WebAddresses. The Add button allows users to include additional addresses in the table, so they will show up in the combo box list. But the form doesn't yet include the ActiveX control it needs to display Web documents.

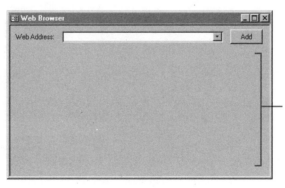

The Browser form has some of the controls it needs, but you'll add the WebBrowser control here.

355

Using the WebBrowser Control

To create a simple HTML browser using the WebBrowser control, all you have to do is place the control on a form, and then use the Navigate method of the control to tell it what to display. Web pages will appear automatically with all their graphical elements, and users will be able to click hyperlinks to navigate. However, there are many other features of a Web browser that require Visual Basic code in order to be included. For example, you can write event procedures that allow users to save Web sites they've followed, and you must write code if you want to give users feedback or let them control the browser beyond clicking hyperlinks. In this section, you'll add a few of these features and learn the basic concepts necessary for creating a complete custom browser in your Microsoft Access applications.

Add the WebBrowser control

The first thing you'll do is add the WebBrowser ActiveX control itself—the area of the form in which HTML documents will be displayed. When you do this, Microsoft Access will automatically load the object libraries that come with the control, so that it will understand all the objects, properties, and methods you'll use in your code.

Design View button

1 Click the Design View button on the toolbar.

2 On the Insert menu, click ActiveX Control.

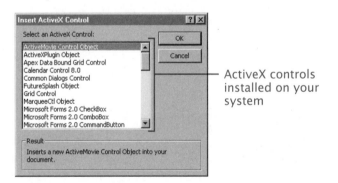

ActiveX controls installed on your system

As you can see, there are many ActiveX controls available to you, depending on which software development packages you've installed.

3 Select Microsoft Web Browser Control, and then click OK.

The WebBrowser control appears in the upper left corner of the form.

4 Move the WebBrowser control down a bit on the form, so it doesn't obscure the combo box (but keep it at the far left side of the form).

5   Drag the bottom right corner of the WebBrowser control to make it large enough to entirely fill the rest of the form window.

The form should look like this:

6   Click the Properties button on the toolbar.

Properties button

The property sheet displays properties for the ActiveX control. As you can see in the Name property box, the control has a default name, such as ActiveXCtl3; you should give it a friendlier name.

7   Change the Name property to **BrowserControl**.

Your WebBrowser control is ready to go. Next, you'll write event procedures to make it work.

Navigating to Web Sites

Before the WebBrowser control can display a Web site, you have to tell it what to open. You do this in Visual Basic using the Navigate method. In the Browser form, you want to display a Web site when the user first opens the form, and then change Web sites whenever the user enters an address in the combo box or selects one from the list. To do this, you'll add code to respond to two events: the form's Load event, and the AfterUpdate event for the WebAddress combo box.

Add code to navigate to Web sites

1   With the right mouse button, click the form selection box at the upper left corner of the form (it's at the intersection of the rulers), and then click Build Event on the shortcut menu.

2   Double-click Code Builder.

The Module windows opens and displays the Form_Load event procedure.

357

3   Add the following code to the procedure:

```
Private Sub Form_Load()
' When the form loads, open the Microsoft Press Web site.

    BrowserControl.Navigate "http://www.microsoft.com/mspress"

End Sub
```

This simple line of code uses the Navigate method of the WebBrowser control to tell the control what to display. The argument that follows the method provides a Web address (or the path to any HTML document). In this case, you've specified the address for the Microsoft Press Web site. Your code will open this site when the user first opens the Browser form.

4   On the Window menu, click Browser : Form.

The form returns to the front. Next, you'll add an event procedure to respond whenever the user selects a new address in the WebAddress combo box.

5   Click the WebAddress combo box.

6   Click the Event tab in the property sheet.

7   Click the AfterUpdate property, and then click the Build button.

8   Double-click Code Builder.

The Module window displays the WebAddress_AfterUpdate event procedure.

9   Add the following code to the procedure:

```
Private Sub WebAddress_AfterUpdate()
' Open the selected Web site.

    BrowserControl.Navigate WebAddress

End Sub
```

Like the previous procedure you wrote, this code uses the Navigate method of the WebBrowser control to tell the control what to display. This time, your code passes the value that's found in the WebAddress combo box—the address the user entered.

Responding to WebBrowser Events

With the event procedures you just created, the WebBrowser control will know where to start. This is really all that's required to make the control work; after a Web site is displayed, the WebBrowser control navigates automatically as users click. However, you may want to perform actions in response to what users do in the browser. For example, you might want to respond in some way each time the user jumps to a new Web site. Or, you might want to display a status message while files are downloading.

To let you perform these tasks at the right times, the WebBrowser control provides several events, just like built-in controls. For example, to respond when the user attempts to navigate to a new document, you can write code for the BeforeNavigate event—and you can even prevent the navigation from taking place. To respond when the WebBrowser control has successfully navigated to a new location, you write code for the NavigateComplete event. In this section, you'll respond to this latter event in order to provide some feedback to the user.

Add code to update the WebAddress combo box

When a user navigates using the WebAddress combo box, the Web site displayed in the WebBrowser control will of course correspond to the address in the combo box. However, when a user clicks a hyperlink in the WebBrowser control and changes Web sites, the combo box won't automatically change—it will continue to display the initial Web address. To fix this problem, you'll write code that responds to the NavigateComplete event, using Visual Basic code to update the combo box with the address of the currently displayed site.

1   In the Object box near the upper left corner of the Module window (the box that now shows WebAddress), select BrowserControl.

The Module window creates a procedure called BrowserControl_Updated (the default event procedure for the WebBrowser control). Since this isn't the event procedure you want, you'll just ignore it.

2   In the Procedure box near the upper right corner, select NavigateComplete.

The module window creates the BrowserControl_NavigateComplete event procedure. Take a look at the function's header line. The NavigateComplete event passes a very convenient argument to your event procedure: the URL argument. When the event occurs, this string variable will contain the address that the user has just navigated to—exactly the value you want to display. (URL, the name of this argument, is an abbreviation for Uniform Resource Locator, the general term for any type of Internet address.)

3   Add the following code to the procedure:

```
Private Sub BrowserControl_NavigateComplete(ByVal URL As String)
' Update the combo box with the current URL.

    WebAddress = URL

End Sub
```

This simple line of code sets the combo box to the value of the URL variable, effectively entering the address of the Web site into the combo box. Now, regardless of how the user navigates to a Web site, the combo box will always display the correct text.

Putting Final Touches on Your Custom Browser

There's one more important thing you need to do before the Browser form will be ready to roll. Users can resize this type of form when it's in Form view; this is a very useful feature, since they'll want to take advantage of their screen space when browsing Web sites. However, if you want the form's controls to appear correctly no matter what the user does, you'll need to write code that resizes them—if you don't, the Form window may become larger, but the area that displays Web documents will remain the same size.

Add code to resize the Browser control automatically

Whenever the user changes the size of a form, the form's Resize event occurs; this provides you with a chance to resize the corresponding controls. In fact, the Browser form already has a Resize event procedure, which contains code to set the size and position of the combo box and command button at the top of the form. You just need to add two lines of code to resize the WebBrowser control, expanding it to use the entire available form area.

1   Scroll down in the Module window to display the Form_Resize procedure.

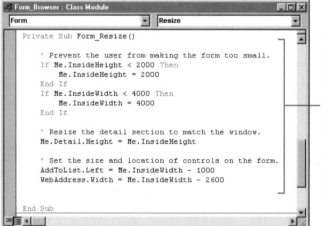

The event procedure already contains code that resizes the Detail section of the form, repositions the AddToList command button, and resizes the WebAddress combo box.

The code that's already here does a few things:

- The two If...Then blocks at the beginning check to see whether the user has made the form too small. These lines refer to the InsideHeight and InsideWidth properties of the form, which contain the interior dimensions of the Form window. The dimensions are measured in strange small units called *twips* (there are 1440 of these to an inch). Their minimum values are 2000 twips and 4000 twips, respectively.

- The next line sets the Height property for the Detail section of the form to the same height as the window (found in the window's InsideHeight property). Because the size of a form's sections is independent of the window they're displayed in, you'll always need to be aware of this distinction when setting the locations and sizes of controls. In this case, changing the height of the section prevents Microsoft Access from thinking that the window is too small to display the whole section, or that the section is too small for the controls.

- The last two lines set the size and position of the AddToList command button and the WebAddress combo box. The first sets the Left property of the command button, moving it near the right side of the form (1000 twips short of the right side, to be exact). This leaves room for the combo box to expand.

- The second line sets the Width property of the combo box. Because you always want the combo box to stay near the left edge of the form, you don't need to reposition it when the size of the form changes. But to make it expand on its right side to fill the space on the form, it's necessary to set its Width property. With experimentation, you'll find that 2600 twips narrower than the form window's width is just right.

To resize the WebBrowser control, you'll now add two more lines to the procedure.

2 Add the following lines of code at the end of the procedure, just above the End Sub line:

```
BrowserControl.Width = Me.InsideWidth
BrowserControl.Height = Me.InsideHeight - 600
```

This code resizes the ActiveX control to match the available room on the Form window. The first line ensures that the control will completely fill the window from right to left by setting the Width property to the entire width of the form. The second line sets the Height property to a bit shorter than the form, leaving room for the combo box and button at the top of the form.

Now, each time the Browser form is adjusted, everything on the form will match the new size.

3 Click the Compile Loaded Modules button on the toolbar.

4 Close the Module window.

5 Click the Save button on the toolbar.

Compile Loaded Modules button

Save button

361

Try out your custom Web browser

You're ready to browse the Web from within the Issues application.

**Form View
button**

1   Click the Form View button on the toolbar.

The Form_Load event procedure runs, sending the Navigate method to the WebBrowser control and setting it on its way to the World Wide Web. If necessary, the WebBrowser control connects to the Internet; it then displays the Microsoft Press Web site in the Browser form.

The Load
event for the
form sends a
Web site
address...

...to the WebBrowser control, which takes over from there, connecting to the Internet automatically.

2   Select an address from the Web Address combo box.

Your AfterUpdate event procedure runs the Navigate method a second time, passing it the address you selected. The Browser form displays the new Web site.

3   Drag the lower right corner of the Form window to make the Browser form larger.

The form's Resize event occurs, running the code that resizes all the controls to match the size of the form.

4   Locate a hyperlink somewhere in the Web site you're viewing and click it.

The WebBrowser control automatically searches for the new address on the Internet. When it finds the new site, the NavigateComplete event occurs, and your code sets the combo box to the new address.

5   Select the existing text in the Web Address combo box, type **www.usps.gov**, and then press ENTER.

As you can see, you can type an address in the list as well as select an existing one. You'll also notice that when your NavigateComplete code updates the combo box, the string returned from the WebBrowser control is the complete address (including the http: prefix), which may be slightly different from what you typed.

6 Click the Add button.

The code behind this button copies the address from the combo box into the WebAddresses table. (You can find this code in the form's module in the AddToList_Click procedure.)

7 Close the Browser form, and then close the Issues form.

As you can see, with the WebBrowser control, creating a Web browser within your applications is a simple matter. Of course, you can greatly enhance such a browser in your own applications. For example, there are methods of the WebBrowser object that let you provide Back and Forward buttons for your own browser, and the StatusTextChange event makes it easy to display the same text to your users that Internet Explorer provides as it connects to servers and downloads data. Moreover, you can provide any additional controls you like on the same form that includes the WebBrowser control—so that you can combine database functions and HTML document capabilities in the same form.

Exit Microsoft Access

➤ On the File menu, click Exit.

More Internet Features in Microsoft Access

In addition to hyperlinks and the WebBrowser control, Microsoft Access includes many other Internet-related features. Most of these features don't involve any Visual Basic programming, however, and therefore aren't covered in this book. Here are some features you may want to explore using online Help:

Getting data from the Internet To incorporate data from the Internet (or an intranet) into your databases, you can import it from HTML format, the language of Web browser software. Alternatively, you can create links to HTML tables or lists, so that the most current Internet data is always displayed in your application. To import or link data, use the Get External Data command (File menu). Then, in the Import Or Link Tables dialog box, select HTML Documents in the Files Of Type box.

Putting data onto the Internet To make data from your databases available on a Web site, you can export your tables, queries, forms, or reports to HTML format. To export an object, use the Save To HTML command (File menu). When you save an object using this command, the Publish To The Web Wizard helps you choose where the HTML document should go.

None of these features requires Visual Basic programming—they're all available through standard Microsoft Access commands. If you want to

continued next page

Additional Internet Features in Microsoft Access, *continued*

perform these tasks in Visual Basic, however, use the TransferDatabase method of the DoCmd object. For more information on these and other Internet features, search the online Help index for "Internet, what's new in Microsoft Access."

Lesson Summary

To	Do this	Button
Insert a hyperlink on a form	Click the Insert Hyperlink button, and then specify the hyperlink address (or create a label, command button, or image control and set its HyperlinkAddress property). To change the text that the hyperlink displays, set the control's Caption property.	
Store hyperlinks in a table	Create a field with the Hyperlink data type in the table and add information for each hyperlink there. To display these hyperlinks on a form, create a text box that's bound to the Hyperlink field.	
Follow a hyperlink using Visual Basic	To simulate clicking a hyperlink on a label, command button, or image control, use the Follow method on the Hyperlink object (*control*.Hyperlink.Follow). To simulate clicking a hyperlink stored in a field, use the FollowHyperlink method, specifying the address you want to jump to.	
Modify a hyperlink using Visual Basic	Change the hyperlink control's HyperlinkAddress and HyperlinkSubaddress properties. For a hyperlink stored in a field, set the field's value to a concatenated string containing the text you want to display in the hyperlink, its address, and its subaddress, separated by pound signs (#).	

To	Do this	Button
Create a form that can browse Web sites and display other HTML documents	On the Insert menu (in Form Design view), click ActiveX Control, and then select Microsoft Web Browser Control. In Visual Basic code, use the Navigate method of the WebBrowser control to tell the control what address to display.	
Resize controls on a form when a user changes the size of the window	In the form's Resize event procedure, set the Top, Left, Height, and Width properties of the sections and controls on the form based on the form's InsideHeight and InsideWidth property values.	

For online information about	On the Help menu, click Contents and Index, click the Index tab, and then
Working with hyperlinks	Search for "hyperlinks"
Using the WebBrowser control	Search for "WebBrowser control"
Moving data to and from the Internet	Search for "Internet, importing and linking files" and "Internet, creating HTML documents"
Resizing sections and controls of a form	Search for "InsideHeight property" and "Resize event"

For more information on	In *Building Applications with Microsoft Access 97*, see
Working with hyperlinks, the WebBrowser control, and other Internet features	Chapter 21, "Developing Applications for the Internet and the World Wide Web"
Using objects, methods, and properties	Chapter 5, "Working with Objects and Collections"
Working with ActiveX controls	Chapter 16, "Using ActiveX Controls"

365

Where Do I Go Next?

Congratulations—you've covered a great deal of ground concerning Microsoft Access and VBA in these lessons. Microsoft Access application development is an enormous subject, and as you continue working with Microsoft Access, you'll find many new frontiers to explore. Here are a few places where you may want to start:

Building Applications with Microsoft Access 97   In addition to the material referred to at the end of each lesson, this Microsoft Access manual includes chapters on advanced topics not covered here, such as using DLLs, creating your own wizards, and developing applications for a client-server environment. A printed version of this book is included with Microsoft Access 97 and with Microsoft Office 97, Developer's Edition. If you have Microsoft Office 97 Professional, you don't have the printed version of this book, but your Microsoft Office 97 CD-ROM includes an HTML version of the book (in the ValuPack folder on the disc), which you can view using a Web browser such as Microsoft Internet Explorer. Alternatively, you can find the book on the World Wide Web at

> http://www.microsoft.com/accessdev/docs/bapp97/bapp97.htm

Orders and Solutions sample applications   Microsoft Access includes two sample applications that you can take a look at to gather ideas for your own projects. The Orders application is a custom order-entry system. The Solutions database is a learning tool that shows you examples of many form, report, and Visual Basic strategies and includes instructions on how to create each sample object yourself.

Microsoft Office 97, Developer Edition   This add-on product allows you to distribute your applications to users who don't have Microsoft Access— and it includes additional programming information about Microsoft Office, VBA, and data access objects (DAO).

Your own applications   Your database needs are different from anyone else's—for this reason, you'll probably learn more by creating your own Microsoft Access applications than you'll ever pick up in a book. So jump right in! Just as you did in the first lessons of this book, start by automating tasks on forms in an existing database. After you're comfortable writing and debugging Visual Basic code, try creating a custom application of your own. Then, as you discover complex tasks that you want to accomplish in your procedures, delve into new areas of the Microsoft Access and DAO object models.

Index

errors, *continued*
    displaying your own message for specific
        errors, 155–57
    introduced, 152
    responding to error events, 152–55
  responding to combo box errors, 158–62
  run-time, 142, 164–65
  syntax, 141
  types of, 141–42
event procedures. *See also* **general procedures**
  adding
    to act when the user filters, 70–72
    error-handling code, 165–68
    KeyDown event procedure to set control
        values, 85–87
    to run option groups, 68–69
    to set the Dear control's value, 82–83
  BeforeUpdate, 88, 91–94, 131–37
  changing the background color of combo
      boxes, 78–81
  Click
    Add Record button, 25–29
    Edit Record button, 36–39
    Reassign All button, 297–300
    Reassign Selected button, 290–95
  Close, 258
  compiling and resolving errors in, 142–49
  creating, for form events, 41–43
  focus and, 30–32
  introduced, 20
  stepping through, 131–37
  that fill in values, 138–41, 143–49
  validating data using, 91–94
events, 20
Excel, using Access objects from, 335
exclamation point (!), 280
exiting Access, applications, and databases, 21
Explicit option, 104–5

F

F1 (Help) key, 45
Field List button, 343
Fill/Back Color button, 52
Filter By Form button, 59, 61
Filter By Form command, 58, 59, 60, 61–62
Filter By Selection button, 70, 72
Filter By Selection command, 58
Filter event, 59, 60

filtering data
  Advanced Filter/Sort command, 58
  Debug window and (*see* Debug window)
  Filter By Form command, 58, 59, 60, 61–62
  Filter By Selection command, 58
  introduced, 58
  option groups and (*see* option groups)
  in reports (*see* mailing label dialog boxes)
  responding to filtering events, 59–60
  understanding filtering properties, 62
  using the If...Then statement, 61–62
FilterOn property, 62, 63–65, 205
Filter property, 62, 63–65, 205
Find Record combo box
  adding code to synchronize, 55–57
  changing the appearance, 52
  changing the background color, 78–81
  creating, 51–52
  modifying the combo box list, 53–55
  trying, 52–53, 55
focus, 30–32
For Each statement, 283–85
ForeColor property
  running the procedure from the Debug
      window, 285
  writing a procedure that changes, 283–85
form modules
  defined, 25
  functions in, 115–20
forms. *See also* **Contacts form; Issues form;**
    Subscribers form
  adding command buttons, 16–21
  based on queries, 205
  creating event procedures for form events, 41–43
  creating hyperlink controls on, 341–42
  dialog boxes as (*see* dialog boxes)
  editing a form's module while in Form View, 33
  general procedure use on, 112–15
  main, 177
  making forms read-only by default, 33–35
  making forms work together, 210–11
  opening to add related records
    adding a button to open, 220–21
    adding code to set subscribers automatically,
      223–24
    adding code to update other open forms,
      225–26
    introduced, 220
    trying new features, 226–28

Index

Index

objects, *continued*
  introduced, 27–28
  local, 134
  parent, 282
  referring to, 280–83
  understanding, 274–79
object-specific procedures, 120
object variables, 161, 187
Office 97, Developer Edition, 266–67, 366
OLE (Object Linking and Embedding), 323
On Error GoTo Next statement, 170
On Error GoTo statement, 28, 165–67, 170
one-to-many relationships, 177
online Help, 45, 278–79
OpenReport WhereCondition argument, 205
option groups
  adding event procedures
    to act when the user filters, 70–72
    to run, 68–69
  creating, 66–67
  introduced, 65–66
  trying, 69–70
Option Group tool, 66
Option Group Wizard, 66–67
Option keyword, 104–5
OrderByOn property, 205
OrderBy property, 205

P

parent objects, 282
passwords for applications, 262
PaymentHistory form
  adding buttons
    to the Subscribers form to open, 213–14
    a toolbar button that runs the Visual Basic function, 249–50
  adding code
    to close automatically, 217
    to keep the form synchronized, 215–16
  changing records in the Subscribers form, 215
  displaying as a pop-up form, 212
  opening, 212
  testing, 217–18
  testing the Visual Basic function, 250
  writing a Visual Basic function to open, 248–49

pop-up forms
  adding a button to open, 213–14
  adding code
    to close automatically, 217
    to synchronize, 215–16
  changing records, 215
  displaying, 212
  introduced, 211
  testing, 217–18
postal codes
  creating an event procedure that checks for a postal code, 91–94
  letting the user leave the postal code field blank, 94–97
PreviewLabels button, 202–3
PrintLabels button, 200–202
Print Preview button, 309, 312, 317
PrintSection property, 319
private procedures, 120
Private Sub line, 28
private variables, 121
procedure-level variables, 121
procedures. *See also* event procedures; general procedures
  compiling and resolving errors, 142–49
  defined, 25
  guidelines for, 120
  introduced, 102
  object-specific, 120
  private, 120
  public, 120
properties
  CurrentView, 219
  Filter, 205
  FilterOn, 62, 63–65, 205
  InputMask, 88
  list of, 31
  MoveLayout, 318
  NextRecord, 318
  OrderBy, 205
  OrderByOn, 205
  PrintSection, 319
  RecordsetClone, 187
  RecordSource, 205
  Required, 88, 89
  ValidationRule, 88, 89–90
  ValidationText, 88, 90

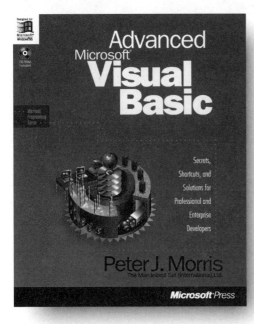

Take productivity in stride.

Microsoft Press® *Step by Step* books provide quick and easy self-paced training that will help you learn to use the powerful word processor, spreadsheet, database, desktop information manager, and presentation applications of Microsoft Office 97, both individually and together. Prepared by the professional trainers at Catapult, Inc., and Perspection, Inc., these books present easy-to-follow lessons with clear objectives, real-world business examples, and numerous screen shots and illustrations. Each book contains approximately eight hours of instruction. Put Microsoft's Office 97 applications to work today, *Step by Step*.

Microsoft® Excel 97 Step by Step
U.S.A. $29.95 ($39.95 Canada)
ISBN 1-57231-314-5

Microsoft® Word 97 Step by Step
U.S.A. $29.95 ($39.95 Canada)
ISBN 1-57231-313-7

Microsoft® PowerPoint® 97
 Step by Step
U.S.A. $29.95 ($39.95 Canada)
ISBN 1-57231-315-3

Microsoft® Outlook™ 97 Step by Step
U.S.A. $29.99 ($39.99 Canada)
ISBN 1-57231-382-X

Microsoft® Access 97 Step by Step
U.S.A. $29.95 ($39.95 Canada)
ISBN 1-57231-316-1

Microsoft® Office 97 Integration
 Step by Step
U.S.A. $29.95 ($39.95 Canada)
ISBN 1-57231-317-X

Microsoft Press® products are available worldwide wherever quality computer books are sold. For more information, contact your book retailer, computer reseller, or local Microsoft Sales Office.

To locate your nearest source for Microsoft Press products, reach us at www.microsoft.com/mspress/, or call 1-800-MSPRESS in the U.S. (in Canada: 1-800-667-1115 or 416-293-8464).

To order Microsoft Press products, call 1-800-MSPRESS in the U.S. (in Canada: 1-800-667-1115 or 416-293-8464).

Prices and availability dates are subject to change.

Get hardcore!

HARDCORE VISUAL BASIC, Second Edition, shows you techniques for expanding the capabilities of Visual Basic and exploiting its object-oriented code to achieve behavior that once seemed the sole province of C or C/C++. Like the first edition, this one tackles tough issues with smart coding, practical tools and analysis, and an unblinking style. As Visual Basic continues to evolve, it delivers more power and complexity to its audience. This book is a valuable way for you to keep up with that evolution.

U.S.A. **$39.99**
U.K.   £37.49 [V.A.T. included]
Canada $54.99
ISBN 1-57231-422-2

Get active!

ACTIVE VISUAL BASIC® introduces the features and capabilities of Visual Basic that allow for the creation of Internet-enabled applications and interactive Web content. After a technical overview of the Internet and the Internet-related capabilities of Visual Basic, the book covers the Internet Control Pack, ActiveX™ control creation, and creating Doc Objects. Advanced topics in the final section include overviews of developing Internet servers and accessing the Windows® Internet API. If you're entering this exciting growth area for Visual Basic development, you'll want this book.

U.S.A. **$39.99**
U.K.   £37.49 [V.A.T. included]
Canada $54.99
ISBN 1-57231-512-1

IMPORTANT—READ CAREFULLY BEFORE OPENING SOFTWARE PACKET(S). By opening the sealed packet(s) containing the software, you indicate your acceptance of the following Microsoft License Agreement.

MICROSOFT LICENSE AGREEMENT

(Book Companion CD)

This is a legal agreement between you (either an individual or an entity) and Microsoft Corporation. By opening the sealed software packet(s) you are agreeing to be bound by the terms of this agreement. If you do not agree to the terms of this agreement, promptly return the unopened software packet(s) and any accompanying written materials to the place you obtained them for a full refund.

MICROSOFT SOFTWARE LICENSE

1. GRANT OF LICENSE. Microsoft grants to you the right to use one copy of the Microsoft software program included with this book (the "SOFTWARE") on a single terminal connected to a single computer. The SOFTWARE is in "use" on a computer when it is loaded into the temporary memory (i.e., RAM) or installed into the permanent memory (e.g., hard disk, CD-ROM, or other storage device) of that computer. You may not network the SOFTWARE or otherwise use it on more than one computer or computer terminal at the same time.

2. COPYRIGHT. The SOFTWARE is owned by Microsoft or its suppliers and is protected by United States copyright laws and international treaty provisions. Therefore, you must treat the SOFTWARE like any other copyrighted material (e.g., a book or musical recording) except that you may either (a) make one copy of the SOFTWARE solely for backup or archival purposes, or (b) transfer the SOFTWARE to a single hard disk provided you keep the original solely for backup or archival purposes. You may not copy the written materials accompanying the SOFTWARE.

3. OTHER RESTRICTIONS. You may not rent or lease the SOFTWARE, but you may transfer the SOFTWARE and accompanying written materials on a permanent basis provided you retain no copies and the recipient agrees to the terms of this Agreement. You may not reverse engineer, decompile, or disassemble the SOFTWARE. If the SOFTWARE is an update or has been updated, any transfer must include the most recent update and all prior versions.

4. DUAL MEDIA SOFTWARE. If the SOFTWARE package contains more than one kind of disk (3.5", 5.25", and CD-ROM), then you may use only the disks appropriate for your single-user computer. You may not use the other disks on another computer or loan, rent, lease, or transfer them to another user except as part of the permanent transfer (as provided above) of all SOFTWARE and written materials.

5. SAMPLE CODE. If the SOFTWARE includes Sample Code, then Microsoft grants you a royalty-free right to reproduce and distribute the sample code of the SOFTWARE provided that you: (a) distribute the sample code only in conjunction with and as a part of your software product; (b) do not use Microsoft's or its authors' names, logos, or trademarks to market your software product; (c) include the copyright notice that appears on the SOFTWARE on your product label and as a part of the sign-on message for your software product; and (d) agree to indemnify, hold harmless, and defend Microsoft and its authors from and against any claims or lawsuits, including attorneys' fees, that arise or result from the use or distribution of your software product.

DISCLAIMER OF WARRANTY

The SOFTWARE (including instructions for its use) is provided "AS IS" WITHOUT WARRANTY OF ANY KIND. MICROSOFT FURTHER DISCLAIMS ALL IMPLIED WARRANTIES INCLUDING WITHOUT LIMITATION ANY IMPLIED WARRANTIES OF MERCHANTABILITY OR OF FITNESS FOR A PARTICULAR PURPOSE. THE ENTIRE RISK ARISING OUT OF THE USE OR PERFORMANCE OF THE SOFTWARE AND DOCUMENTATION REMAINS WITH YOU.

IN NO EVENT SHALL MICROSOFT, ITS AUTHORS, OR ANYONE ELSE INVOLVED IN THE CREATION, PRODUCTION, OR DELIVERY OF THE SOFTWARE BE LIABLE FOR ANY DAMAGES WHATSOEVER (INCLUDING, WITHOUT LIMITATION, DAMAGES FOR LOSS OF BUSINESS PROFITS, BUSINESS INTERRUPTION, LOSS OF BUSINESS INFORMATION, OR OTHER PECUNIARY LOSS) ARISING OUT OF THE USE OF OR INABILITY TO USE THE SOFTWARE OR DOCUMENTATION, EVEN IF MICROSOFT HAS BEEN ADVISED OF THE POSSIBILITY OF SUCH DAMAGES. BECAUSE SOME STATES/COUNTRIES DO NOT ALLOW THE EXCLUSION OR LIMITATION OF LIABILITY FOR CONSEQUENTIAL OR INCIDENTAL DAMAGES, THE ABOVE LIMITATION MAY NOT APPLY TO YOU.

U.S. GOVERNMENT RESTRICTED RIGHTS

The SOFTWARE and documentation are provided with RESTRICTED RIGHTS. Use, duplication, or disclosure by the Government is subject to restrictions as set forth in subparagraph (c)(1)(ii) of The Rights in Technical Data and Computer Software clause at DFARS 252.227-7013 or subparagraphs (c)(1) and (2) of the Commercial Computer Software — Restricted Rights 48 CFR 52.227-19, as applicable. Manufacturer is Microsoft Corporation, One Microsoft Way, Redmond, WA 98052-6399.

If you acquired this product in the United States, this Agreement is governed by the laws of the State of Washington. Should you have any questions concerning this Agreement, or if you desire to contact Microsoft Press for any reason, please write: Microsoft Press, One Microsoft Way, Redmond, WA 98052-6399.

The
Step by Step
Practice Files CD-ROM

The enclosed CD-ROM contains time-saving, ready-to-use practice files that complement the lessons in this book. To use the practice files, you'll need Microsoft Access 97 (version 8) or Microsoft Office 97 and either the Microsoft Windows 95 operating system or version 3.51 Service Pack 5 or later of the Microsoft Windows NT operating system.

Most of the *Step by Step* lessons use practice files from the disk. Before you begin the *Step by Step* lessons, read the "Installing the Practice Files and Additional Microsoft Access Tools" section of the book. There you'll find a description of each practice file and easy instructions for installing the files on your computer's hard disk.

Please take a few moments to read the license agreement on the previous page before using the enclosed disk.

Register Today!

Return this
Microsoft® Access 97/Visual Basic® Step by Step
registration card today

mspress.microsoft.com

OWNER REGISTRATION CARD   1-57231-319-6

Microsoft® Access 97/Visual Basic® Step by Step

_____   _____   _____
FIRST NAME   MIDDLE INITIAL   LAST NAME

_____
INSTITUTION OR COMPANY NAME

_____
ADDRESS

_____

_____

_____   _____   _____
CITY   STATE   ZIP

                                              (   )
_____   _____
E-MAIL ADDRESS   PHONE NUMBER

U.S. and Canada addresses only. Fill in information above and mail postage-free.
Please mail only the bottom half of this page.

**For information about Microsoft Press®
products, visit our Web site at
mspress.microsoft.com**